THE SHAPE AND SHAPING
OF THE BOOK OF PSALMS

Society of Biblical Literature

Ancient Israel and Its Literature

Thomas C. Römer, General Editor

Number 20

THE SHAPE AND SHAPING
OF THE BOOK OF PSALMS

THE CURRENT STATE OF SCHOLARSHIP

Edited by

Nancy L. deClaissé-Walford

SBL Press

Atlanta

Copyright © 2014 by SBL Press

Library of Congress Cataloging-in-Publication Data

The shape and shaping of the book of Psalms : the current state of scholarship / edited by Nancy L. deClaissé-Walford.
　　　　p. cm. — (Society of Biblical Literature ancient Israel and its literature ; number 20)
　　Includes bibliographical references and index.
　　Summary: "This volume explores questions of communities of faith, of collections of psalms, of theological viewpoints, of sovereignty, and, most of all, of the shape and shaping of, arguably, the most beloved book of the Old Testament"— Provided by publisher.
　　ISBN 978-1-62837-001-0 (paper binding : alk. paper) — ISBN 978-1-62837-002-7 (electronic format) — ISBN 978-1-62837-003-4 (hardcover binding : alk. paper)
　　1. Bible. Psalms—Criticism, interpretation, etc. I. deClaissé-Walford, Nancy L., 1954–.
　　BS1430.2.S477 2014
　　223'.206—dc23　　　　　　　　　　　　　　　　　　　　　　　　　2014013643

Printed on acid-free, recycled paper conforming to
ANSI/NISO Z39.48-1992 (R1997) and ISO 9706:1994
standards for paper permanence.

This volume is dedicated to the memory of Gerald H. Wilson and his seminal work on the Psalter, *The Editing of the Hebrew Psalter*. In addition, it is dedicated to those gifted scholars who have studied, and will continue the work of studying, the Psalter's shape and shaping.

Contents

PREFACE

Nancy L. deClaissé-Walford

The publication of *The Editing of the Hebrew Psalter* in 1985 inaugurated a new era in the study of the book of Psalms.[1] A biblical book, the study of which had been driven by form and cult-functional criticism for many years, was about to be subject to a very different kind of scrutiny—an examination of its shape and shaping. Within a few years, a Book of Psalms Consultation was formed in the Society of Biblical Literature, and Ph.D. students in many institutions were writing dissertations on both the macro- and micro-structuring of the Psalter.

In 2010, the twenty-fifth anniversary of the publication of *The Editing of the Hebrew Psalter*, the Book of Psalms Section determined that it would be appropriate to dedicate two of its 2011 Society of Biblical Literature sessions to the topic of the shape and shaping of the Psalter. Many of the essays in this volume were presentations in those sessions, including Nancy L. deClaissé-Walford's "The Canonical Approach to Scripture and *The Editing of the Hebrew Psalter*, Harry P. Nasuti's "The Editing of the Psalter and the Ongoing Use of the Psalms," J. Clinton McCann's "Changing Our Way of Being Wrong," Derek Wittman's "Let Us Cast Off Their Ropes from Us," Christine Brown Jones's "The Message of the Asaphite Collection and Its Role in the Psalter," Catherine Petrany's "Instruction, Performance, and Prayer: The Didactic Function of Psalmic Wisdom," Karl N. Jacobson's "Perhaps YHWH (Baal) is Sleeping: 'Awake' and 'Contend' in the Book of Psalms," W. Dennis Tucker's "The Role of the Foe in Book 5," Robert E. Wallace's "Gerald Wilson and the Characterization of David in Book 5," and Rolf A. Jacobson's "Imagining the Future of Psalm Studies."

---

1. Gerald H. Wilson, *The Editing of the Hebrew Psalter* (SBLDS 76: Chico, Calif.: Scholars Press, 1985).

The authors listed above represent a fairly diverse group of American scholars—in terms of denomination, gender, and points in their careers. The study of the shape and shaping of the Psalter, however, is not confined to American scholars. Therefore the editor of this volume invited scholars from other parts of the world—Germany, South Africa, Canada, and England—to contribute essays in order to provide a broader perspective on the subject. Their responses were gracious and enthusiastic and their contributions add a rich depth to the volume: Erhard Gerstenberger's "The Dynamics of Praise in the Ancient Near East, or Poetry and Politics," Jaco Gericke's "Philosophical Perspectives on Religious Diversity as Emergent Property in the Redaction/Composition of the Psalter," Phil J. Botha's "Wealth and Riches Are in His House: Acrostic Wisdom Psalms the Development of Antimaterialism," Sampson S. Ndoga's "Revisiting the Theocratic Agenda of Book 4 of the Psalter for Interpretive Premise," Jonathan Magonet's, "On Reading Psalms as Liturgy—Psalms 96–99," and Peter W. Flint's "The Contribution of Gerald Wilson toward Understanding the 'Book of Psalms' in Light of the Dead Sea Scrolls."

The reader will find the name of Gerald Wilson, the author of *The Editing of the Hebrew Psalter*, invoked many times in the essays in this volume. Gerald Wilson, who was Professor of Biblical Studies at Azusa Pacific University in California, died unexpectedly in November 2005. This volume is not intended to be a Festschrift for Gerald Wilson, but its "shape and shaping" aptly reflects the tremendous impact that a single work can have on a discipline. Gerald Wilson embraced the canonical approaches to biblical criticism being advocated in the 1980s by scholars such as Brevard Childs and James Sanders and applied them to his study of the Hebrew Psalter.[2]

The canonical study of the book of Psalms is an interesting discipline. It calls itself "canonical criticism," but it actually employs a number of historically traditional and nontraditional approaches to reading the text. Hermann Gunkel's form-critical categorization of the psalms is a mainstay of psalm scholarship, although the designation of and assignment to various categories remains an open question. The historical-critical under-

---

2. Brevard S. Childs, "Reflections on the Modern Study of the Psalms," in *Magnalia Dei: The Mighty Acts of God* (ed. Frank M. Cross, Werner E. Lemke, and Patrick D. Miller Jr., Garden City, N.Y.: Doubleday, 1976), 377–88; Childs, *Introduction to the Old Testament as Scripture* (Philadelphia: Fortress, 1979); James A. Sanders, *From Sacred Story to Sacred Text* (Philadephia: Fortress, 1987).

standing of individual psalms as well as of the whole Psalter is a major area of examination for canonical critics. They are concerned with questions about the origins and uses of individual as well as collections of psalms. And, finally, redaction questions interest canonical critics. How were collections of psalms and various individual psalms incorporated into the Psalter? When? By whom? For what reason?

For all of its likeness to traditional critical approaches to the study of the Psalter, the canonical approach is a new and innovative way to approach the Psalter (and other books of the Bible). In 1976, Brevard Childs wrote that, because of the vagaries of culture and time, the authors and the editors of the biblical text simply cannot be known, and therefore the main focus of research should not be to pursue what he calls the editors' "motivations and biases."[3] The canonical critic, rather, can only study the "final form" of the text—the form provided to us in the Hebrew Psalter. James Sanders, as he outlines in "Canonical Context and Canonical Criticism," agrees with Childs, but he maintains that the scholarly community has been looking in the wrong place for the "motivations and biases" behind the shape and shaping of texts such as the Psalter. The final shape of biblical texts should not be attributed to individual redactions, but to communities of faith—those who found value in various texts and preserved and transmitted them over the millennia. Sanders writes, "There has been a relationship between tradition, written and oral, and community, a constant, ongoing dialogue, a historical memory passed on from generation to generation, in which the special relationship between canon and community resided."[4]

This volume explores questions of communities of faith, of collections of psalms, of theological viewpoints, of sovereignty, and, most of all, of the shape and shaping of what is arguably the most beloved book of the Old Testament.

Many thanks are due. To the authors of the essays, no words are adequate. This volume would not have been possible without your generous contributions. To the Society of Biblical Literature Press, many thanks for working with the editor to craft a volume that would be reader-worthy. To my dean, Alan Culpepper, my heartfelt gratitude for believing wholeheartedly in the contributions that his faculty members make to

---

3. Childs, *Introduction to the Old Testament as Scripture*, 79.
4. Sanders, *From Sacred Story to Sacred Text*, 166.

their own distinct disciplines in this somewhat crazy world we call theological education.

McAfee School of Theology
Atlanta, Georgia
December 2013

Abbreviations

AB	Anchor Bible
ABD	*Anchor Bible Dictionary.* Edited by D. N. Freedman. 6 vols. New York: Doubleday, 1992.
ANESSupS	Ancient Near Eastern Studies Supplement Series
AS	Assyriological Studies
AThANT	Abhandlungen zur Theologie des Alten und NeuenTestaments
BBB	Bonner biblische Beiträge
BCOTWP	Baker Commentary on the Old Testament Wisdom and Psalms
BDB	Brown, F., S. R. Driver, and C. A. Briggs. *A Hebrew and English Lexicon of the Old Testament.* Oxford: Clarendon, 1907.
BETL	Bibliotheca ephemeridum theologicarum lovaniensium
BEvT	Beiträge zur evangelischen Theologie
Bib	*Biblica*
BJS	Brown Judaic Studies
BTB	*Biblical Theology Bulletin*
BWANT	Beiträge zur Wissenschaft vom Alten und Neuen Testament
BZAW	Beihefte zur Zeitschrift für die alttestamentliche Wissenschaft
CBQ	*Catholic Biblical Quarterly*
CC	Continental Commentaries
CM	Cuneiform Monographs
CurBS	*Currents in Research: Biblical Studies*
DJD	Discoveries in the Judaean Desert
DJDJ	Discoveries in the Judaean Desert of Jordan
DNEB	Die Neue Echter Bibel
ETCSL	Electronic Text Corpus of Sumerian Literature

FAOS	Freiburger Altorientalische Studien
FAT	Forschungen zum Alten Testament
FOTL	Forms of the Old Testament Literature
HBS	Herders Biblische Studien
HBT	Horizons in Biblical Theology
HTKAT	Herders theologischer Kommentar zum Alten Testament
HTR	Harvard Theological Review
HTS	Hervormde Teologiese Studies
IBC	Interpretation: A Bible Commentary for Teaching and Preaching
IBT	Interpreting Biblical Texts
IEJ	Israel Exploration Journal
Int	Interpretation
JAJSup	Supplements to the Journal of Ancient Judaism
JAOS	Journal of the American Oriental Society
JBL	Journal of Biblical Literature
JBTh	Jahrbuch für Biblische Theologie
JBQ	Jewish Bible Quarterly
JHS	Journal of Hebrew Scripture
JSOT	Journal for the Study of the Old Testament
JSOTSup	Journal for the Study of the Old Testament Supplement Series
JSJSup	Supplements to the Journal for the Study of Judaism
LHBOTS	Library of the Hebrew Bible and Old Testament Studies
McCQ	McCormick Quarterly
NIDOTTE	New International Dictionary of Old Testament Theology and Exegesis. Edited by W. A. VanGemeren. 5 vols. Grand Rapids: Zondervan, 1997.
NIVAC	New International Version Application Commentary
OBO	Orbis biblicus et orientalis
OTE	Old Testament Essays
OTL	Old Testament Library
PTMS	Pittsburgh Theological Monograph Series
RB	Revue biblique
RevQ	Revue de Qumran
SBLAcBib	Academia Biblica
SBLDS	Society of Biblical Literature Dissertation Series
SBLMS	Society of Biblical Literature Monograph Series
SBS	Stuttgarter Bibelstudien

SBT	Studies in Biblical Theology
StBL	Studies in Biblical Literature
STDJ	Studies on the Texts of the Desert of Judah
SubBi	Subsidia Biblica
SVTQ	*St. Vladimir's Theological Quarterly*
THAT	*Theologisches Handwörterbuch zum Alten Testament.* Edited by E. Jenni, with assistance from C. Westermann. 2 vols. Munich: Kaiser, 1971–1976.
ThSt	Theologische Studiën
ThWAT	*Theologisches Wörterbuch zum Alten Testament.* Edited by G. J. Botterweck and H. Ringgren. Stuttgart: Kohlhammer, 1970–2006.
TWOT	*Theological Wordbook of the Old Testament.* Edited by R. L. Harris and G. L. Archer Jr. 2 vols. Chicago: Moody Press, 1980.
VE	*Verbum et Ecclesia*
VT	*Vetus Testamentum*
VTSup	Supplements to Vetus Testamentum
WBC	Word Biblical Commentary
WTJ	*Westminster Theological Journal*
WW	*Word and World*
ZAW	*Zeitschrift für die Alttestamentliche Wissenschaft*
ZTK	*Zeitschrift für Theologie und Kirche*

The Canonical Approach to Scripture and *The Editing of the Hebrew Psalter**

Nancy L. deClaissé-Walford

Introduction

Early in my Ph.D. studies, I came across an article by Robert Polzin in the journal *Semeia* entitled "'The Ancestress of Israel in Danger' in Danger."[1] The article examines the three stories in the book of Genesis about Abraham and Isaac passing their wives off as their sisters. Polzin addresses the work of source and form critics who were attempting to, according to Polzin, "resurrect the original story behind the three versions," with little "concern for how stories fit into their present literary context."[2]

One sentence in the article seized my attention and has stuck with me over the years. Polzin writes, "Traditional biblical scholarship has spent most of its efforts in disassembling the works of a complicated watch before our amazed eyes without apparently realizing that similar efforts by and large have not succeeded in putting the parts back together again in a significant or meaningful way."[3] Polzin invites us to picture a magnificent timepiece made up of cogs and wheels, springs and tiny mechanisms, delicate hands and precious stones, each with its own place in the dance of the whole. We dissect it, lay it out before us, piece by piece, study it, and marvel at the beauty, the intricacy, and the craftsmanship.

---

* This paper was originally presented as part of a session of the Psalms Section of the Society of Biblical Literature on November 20, 2011 in San Francisco.
1. Robert E. Polzin, "'The Ancestress of Israel in Danger' in Danger," *Semeia* 3 (1975): 81–98.
2. Ibid., 82.
3. Ibid.

Then a passerby stops to watch our work and finally asks, "What is it?" "A watch," we reply. "Oh! Well, what does it do?" the observer asks. "It keeps time," we respond. "Really? Wonderful! Show me how it works," says the passerby. And we try, we try our best, but we are unable to reassemble the watch, to restore it to the form in which we found it so that once again it can perform the task for which it was created—to keep time. The disassembled watch—the biblical text. A wonderful metaphor. Much of the work of biblical scholars in the nineteenth and early twentieth centuries was focused on "dissecting" the text, searching for "strands of tradition," "original oral settings," and "redactional connections."

A New Approach

Gerald Henry Wilson's work entitled *The Editing of the Hebrew Psalter* was published in 1985 in the SBL Dissertation Series. Wilson gives particular attention to the closing psalms of each of Psalter's five books, maintaining that the psalms at the "seams" of the Psalter hold significant clues to its overall shaping.[4] Wilson argues that the Psalter's five books evince purposeful editing and that they tell a "story" to the ancient Israelites—a story about their past history, their present situation, and their hope for the future. That story, he maintains, narrates the rise of ancient Israel under the leadership of Kings David and Solomon in books 1 and 2; the demise of the northern kingdom of Israel, the destruction of Jerusalem by the Babylonians in book 3; the exile in Babylon in book 4; and the return from exile, the rebuilding of the temple, and the restoration of worship in book 5.

In a 1987 review of Wilson's book, James A. Sanders writes, "The result is well worth careful study, for it advances the field of Psalter study precisely to *that* extent. The methods applied in the dissertation are carefully described and followed, and represent a good amalgam of those worked out by both Childs and myself. In fact, Wilson's work is not only illuminat-

---

4. See Gerald H. Wilson, *The Editing of the Hebrew Psalter* (SBLDS 76; Chico, Calif.: Scholars Press, 1985), 139–97; Wilson, "The Use of Royal Psalms at the 'Seams' of the Hebrew Psalter," *JSOT* 35 (1986): 85–94; and Wilson, "Shaping the Psalter: A Consideration of Editorial Linkage in the Book of Psalms," in *The Shape and Shaping of the Psalter* (ed. J. Clinton McCann Jr.; JSOTSup 159; Sheffield: JSOT Press, 1993), 72–82.

ing but also very gratifying in many ways."[5] "Sanders states that Wilson's work is "an amalgam" of Childs's and Sanders's works"; let us briefly examine that statement.

BREVARD CHILDS

In the mid-twentieth century, Brevard Childs championed an approach to the biblical text called "canonical criticism." His 1976 essay entitled "Reflections on the Modern Study of the Psalms" and his 1979 book, *Introduction to the Old Testament as Scripture*, encouraged scholars to move away from dissecting the biblical text into its most minute components and to move toward examining the text in the form in which it was preserved for communities of faith, as a whole.[6] Childs maintained, in fact, that it was useless to attempt to understand the underlying layers of traditions that make up the biblical text because the editors who compiled and transmitted the texts deliberately obscured those layers in a process Childs calls "actualization." What he meant is that the editors of the biblical texts did not just update and transmit the texts, but they did so in such a way as to prevent their "being moored in the past."[7] In addition, Childs states that the scribes and editors usually obscured their own identities, so who they were and how their particular histories influenced them, while perhaps interesting, simply cannot be known. Therefore, the main focus of critical research should *not* be to pursue the editors' "motivations and biases."[8] It is not the process that is to function as the norm for interpretation, but the product of the process.[9]

In the case of the Psalter, Childs maintains that the canonical form of the text looses the psalms from their cultic settings and makes them testify to the common troubles and joys of ordinary human life in which all per-

---

5. James A. Sanders, "Review of *The Editing of the Hebrew Psalter*," *JBL* 106 (1987): 321.

6. Brevard S. Childs, "Reflections on the Modern Study of the Psalms," in *Magnalia Dei: The Mighty Acts of God* (ed. Frank M. Cross, Werner E. Lemke, and Patrick D. Miller Jr., Garden City, N.Y.: Doubleday, 1976), 377–88; and Childs, *Introduction to the Old Testament as Scripture* (Philadelphia: Fortress, 1979).

7. Childs, *Introduction to the Old Testament as Scripture*, 79.

8. Brevard S. Childs, "Response to Reviews of *Introduction to the Old Testament as Scripture*," *JSOT* 16 (1980): 54.

9. Childs, *Introduction to the Old Testament as Scripture*, 75–76.

sons participate.[10] Regardless of the intent of the editors of the Psalter, the end product has a universalized shape.

JAMES A. SANDERS

James A. Sanders shared Brevard Childs's interest in studying the final form of the biblical text. In 1977, he voiced his own call for a reevaluation of the way scholars approach biblical texts. He wrote, "The biblical story has become eclipsed by the work of the very professionals in seminaries and departments of religion who seem to know most about the Bible.... The 'experts' have lost perspective on the very object of their expertise [and have] reduced the Bible to grist for the historian's mill, the province of the professor's study."[11] But Sanders disagreed with Childs's assertion that it was useless to try to understand the underlying layers of tradition that constitute a text. According to Sanders, biblical texts are grounded in historical settings. Those settings can be discovered, and they are important for understanding the shapes of texts. He believed, however, that scholars had been looking in the wrong places for those historical settings. The underpinnings of the biblical texts are located in communities of faith, not in individual scribal settings. Sanders states, "There has been a relationship between tradition, written and oral, and community, a constant, ongoing dialogue, a historical memory passed on from generation to generation, in which the special relationship between canon and community resided."[12]

Community is thus the foundation of canon. Discovering the hermeneutics of the communities that shaped the traditions into canon is the foundation of canonical criticism. Sanders maintains that those hermeneutics cannot be discovered without as much knowledge as possible of the ancient historical contexts.[13]

---

10. Ibid., 521.
11. James A. Sanders, *From Sacred Story to Sacred Text* (Philadelphia: Fortress, 1987), 78–79.
12. Ibid., 166.
13. Ibid., 83.

OTHER VOICES

I would be remiss if I did not point out that Childs and Sanders were not the first or the only ones to call for a holistic reading of the book of Psalms. David M. Howard, in a 1989 article in the journal *Word and World* entitled "Editorial Activity in the Psalter: A State-of-the-Field Survey," provides information that is sometimes forgotten about those whose examination of the Psalter included an interest in its inner connectedness, in addition to the traditional form-critical and cult-functional approaches.[14] In 1846, Franz Delitzsch of Leipzig University wrote *Symbolae ad Psalmos illustrado isogogica*, in which he paid attention to connections between consecutive psalms, and concluded that the arrangement of the Davidic psalms—reflective of the Davidic covenant—provided the key, the unifying motif, of the book.[15] Delitzsch incorporated these ideas into his 1881 commentary on the Psalms, reprinted by Eerdmans in 1975.[16]

Joseph A. Alexander of Princeton University devoted a major section of his 1865 introduction to the Psalms to a treatment of the coherence of the psalms within the book.[17] Like Delitzsch, he determined that the Davidic covenant was a unifying theme of the book, and he attributed the juxtaposition of various psalms, one with another, to "resemblance or identity of subject or historical occasion, or in some remarkable coincidence of general form or of particular expressions."[18]

In more recent scholarship, just subsequent to the clarion cries of Childs and Sanders, but preceding the work of Wilson, Gerald Sheppard observed in a 1980 work entitled *Wisdom as a Hermeneutical Construct: A Study in the Sapientializing of the Old Testament*, first, that Pss 1 and 2 act as prefaces to the Psalter; second, that close lexical ties exist between the two psalms; and third, that David's identification with Ps 2 demonstrates his full embrace of the ideals of Ps 1. Sheppard writes, "The Psalter has gained,

---

14. David M. Howard, "Editorial Activity in the Psalter: A State-of-the-Field Survey," *WW* 9 (1989): 274–85.

15. Franz Delitzsch, *Symbolae ad Psalmos illustrados isogogicae* (Leipzig, 1846).

16. Franz Delitzsch, *Biblical Commentary on the Psalms* (3 vols.; Grand Rapids: Eerdmans, 1881; repr. 1975), 15–23.

17. Joseph A. Alexander, *The Psalms* (6th ed.; 3 vols.; New York: Scribner, 1865), 1:vii–xiv.

18. Ibid., 1:ix.

among its other functions, the use as a source for wisdom reflection and a model of prayers based on such pious interpretation of the Torah."[19]

Claus Westermann, in his 1981 work *Praise and Lament in the Psalms*, observes a movement in the Psalter from lament (at its beginning) to praise (at its end), and identifies royal psalms as an important aspect of the Psalter's framework.[20] And Michael Goulder, in his 1982 *Psalms and the Sons of Korah*, writes, "It is entirely proper to begin the study of the Psalter with the expectation that it will be an ordered and not an assorted collection; or, at the very least, that it will contain elements that were rationally ordered."[21] These voices, along with Childs and Sanders, called for a different approach to the book of Psalms; they are voices we should heed and appropriate.

CHILDS AND SANDERS ON *THE EDITING OF THE HEBREW PSALTER*

Returning to the discussion of the divergence between Childs and Sanders, recall that Childs states that the text is all we have and we need not concern ourselves with trying to understand the underlying layers of tradition behind it because such is a futile undertaking. Sanders maintains, on the other hand, that understanding the underlying layers of tradition—the hermeneutical dialogue—is crucial to a full understanding of the meaning of the text. According to Sanders's review of Wilson's 1985 work, Wilson applied methods that represented an amalgam of Childs—text without an understanding of the layers of tradition—and Sanders—text with an understanding of the hermeneutical dialogue.

In the introductory chapter of *The Editing of the Hebrew Psalter*, Wilson contends two things: first, that "there is evidence within the Hebrew Psalter itself of an editorial movement to bind the whole together"; and second, "that the unity achieved by this process is not merely a convenient combination of disparate items into an 'accidental' formal arrangement,

---

19. Gerald T. Sheppard, *Wisdom as a Hermeneutical Construct: A Study in the Sapientializing of the Old Testament* (New York: de Gruyter, 1980), 142.

20. Claus Westermann, *Praise and Lament in the Psalms* (Atlanta: John Knox, 1981), 250–58; trans. of "Zur Sammlung des Psalters," *Theologia Viatorum* 8 (1962): 278–84.

21. Michael Goulder, *The Psalms of the Sons of Korah* (JSOTSup 20; Sheffield: JSOT Press, 1982), 8.

but represents the end result of purposeful, editorial organization."[22] He therefore contends that the Psalter is a unified whole (à la Childs), and is the end result of purposeful activity (à la Sanders).

Wilson organizes his study into two large undertaking: first, to isolate and describe what evidence exists of editorial activity within the Psalter and to evaluate the extent of its unifying influence (what we now call the "shape" of the Psalter); and second, to determine the editorial purpose that governs the organizational process (what we now call the "shaping" of the Psalter).[23] He concludes that the psalms and psalm collections of the Hebrew Psalter were arranged to tell the story of the rise and fall of the Davidic kingship in Israel (books 1, 2, and 3) and the story of new hope for existence with YHWH as king in the exilic and postexilic eras (books 4 and 5). The closing words of Wilson's book are, "YHWH is *eternal* king, only *he* is ultimately worthy of trust. Human 'princes' will wither and fade like the grass, but the steadfast love of YHWH endures for ever."[24]

The Past Twenty-Five Years

How, then, has the study of the book of Psalms fared in the past twenty-five years? David Howard concludes his 1989 article with, "The current focus on unitary, literary, or 'canonical' reading of all portions of the Bible is bringing much new information to light about the messages and intents of the ancient authors. Studies in the Psalter are no exception."[25] Brevard Childs claims, in a 2005 article in *Pro Ecclesia*, that the period from the late 1960s to the end of the twentieth century was one in which large sections of the biblical discipline focused on issues related either directly or indirectly to the subject of canon.[26] Let me begin with some general observations.

In 1985 Gerald Wilson wrote the following about what he called the "energy expended on the question of the arrangement of the Psalter and its significance" in a survey of commentaries:

---

22. Wilson, *Editing of the Hebrew Psalter*, 4.
23. Ibid., 5.
24. Ibid., 228.
25. Howard, "Editorial Activity in the Psalter," 285.
26. Brevard S. Childs, "The Canon in Recent Biblical Studies: Reflections on an Era," *Pro Ecclesia* 14 (2005): 26.

H. J. Kraus [*Die Psalmen*, 1960] includes a section of about five pages while Mitchell Dahood [*Psalm I*, 1965/1966] disposes of all aspects of the subject in approximately two and a half. Most authors are content to allude to the earlier collections underlying the canonical Psalter as evidence of the complexity of the issue and then move quickly on to the consideration of individual psalms *a la* Gunkel and Mowinckel.[27]

In 1989, a full session of the Book of Psalms section of SBL was devoted to questions of the book's shape and shaping. Out of that session came a JSOT publication edited by J. Clinton McCann. Its contributors included James Mays, Roland Murphy, Walter Brueggemann, Gerald Wilson, David Howell, Patrick Miller, and J. Clinton McCann. In 1992, the entire April issue of the journal *Interpretation* was devoted to the shape and shaping of the Psalter. In addition, numerous books and articles have been published in the last twenty-five years, and many doctoral dissertations have been written, that address issues of the shape and shaping of the Psalter, both the overall story (the metanarrative), and the connectedness between psalms (the micro or local narrative). Publications include, but are not limited to, Klaus Seybold and Erich Zenger's edited volume *Neue Wege der Psalmenforschung*; M. Millard's *Die Komposition des Psalters*; Norman Whybray's *Reading the Psalms as a Book*; Dirk J. Human and Cas J. A. Vos's edited volume *Psalms and Liturgy*; Peter W. Flint and Patrick D. Miller's edited volume *The Book of Psalms: Composition and Reception*; Erich Zenger's edited volume *The Composition of the Book of Psalms*.[28]

The attention commentaries give to canonical questions has changed significantly. McCann's 1996 *New Interpreter's* commentary certainly takes into account the canonical shape of the book of Psalms; James Crenshaw's 2001 *The Psalms: An Introduction* provides an extensive treatment of the shape of the Psalter, as do Hossfeld's and Zenger's Hermenaia commentaries (*Psalms 51–100*, 2005; *Psalms 101–150*, 2011). Finally, forthcoming commentaries, including Rolf Jacobson, Beth Tanner, and

---

27. Wilson, *Editing*, 3.

28. Klaus Seybold and Erich Zenger, eds., *Neue Wege der Psalmenforschung* (Freiburg: Herder, 1994); M. Millard, *Die Komposition des Psalters* (FAT 9; Tübingen: Mohr, 1994); Norman Whybray, *Reading the Psalms as a Book* (JSOTSup 222; Sheffield: Sheffield Academic, 1996); Dirk J. Human and Cas J. A. Vos, eds., *Psalms and Liturgy* (London: T&T Clark, 2004); Peter W. Flint and Patrick D. Miller Jr., eds., *The Book of Psalms: Composition and Reception* (Leiden: Brill, 2005); and Erich Zenger, ed., *The Composition of the Book of Psalms* (BETL 238; Leuven: Peeters, 2010).

Nancy L. deClaissé-Walford's in Eerdman's New International Commentary on the Old Testament series, will pay close attention to questions of shape and shaping.

But not all Psalms scholars wholeheartedly agree with the findings of the study of the shape and shaping of the Psalter. Erhard Gerstenberger, for example, offers a different view. In his 2001 work *Psalms, Part 2, and Lamentations*, in The Forms of the Old Testament Literature series, he is skeptical about canonical interpreters' understanding of the role of Ps 107 as a response to the closing words of Ps 106, and, in the words of Erich Zenger, "a running commentary to the preceding four books of psalms, which want to be understood as a unit." Gerstenberger writes, "Modern 'holistic' readers of the Psalter pay much (in my opinion, too much) attention to this very late redactional division of the canonical collection of Psalms. Redactional activities, by and large, were not able to thoroughly mold transmitted texts to interconnect them and give them new meanings."[29] Erich Zenger, in an article entitled "Psalmenexegesis und Psalterexegese: Eine Forschungsskizze," relates a conversation with Gerstenberger, in which Gerstenberger claimed that "die Psalterexegese würde die Individualität der Psalmen missachten und sie … mache aus den wunderschönen Einzelfrüchten der Psalmen ein 'Früchtemus.'"[30]

So how have those of us who study the book of Psalms fared? Well, with a few asides and room for scholarly idiosyncrasies, the big "story"— the metanarrative—of the Psalter seems agreed upon and students of the shape of the book are now spending more time focusing on the smaller units of shape, the so-called "local narratives." And we are moving on to other questions about the book. Some are old questions, some are new, but all are now informed by the results of the study of the Psalter's shape and shaping as much as they are informed by Gunkel's form-critical and Mowinckel's cult-functional work on the text. The test of time will determine whether we have provided new insight into the book of Psalms or whether we have made, in the words of Erhard Gerstenberger, "marmalade out of wonderful pieces of fruit."

---

29. Erhard Gerstenberger, *Psalms, Part 2, and Lamentations* (FOTL 15; Grand Rapids: Eerdmans, 2001), 252.

30. Erich Zenger, "Psalmenexegese und Psalterexegese: Eine Forschungsskizze," in *The Composition of the Book of Psalms* (ed. Erich Zenger; Leuven: Peeters, 2010), 24–25.

Bibliography

Alexander, Joseph A. *The Psalms.* 6th ed. 3 vols. New York: Scribner, 1865.

Childs, Brevard S. "Reflections on the Modern Study of the Psalms." Pages 377–88 in *Magnalia Dei: The Mighty Acts of God.* Edited by Frank M. Cross, Werner E. Lemke, and Patrick D. Miller Jr. Garden City, N.Y.: Doubleday, 1976.

———. *Introduction to the Old Testament as Scripture.* Philadelphia: Fortress, 1979.

———. "Response to Reviews of Introduction to the Old Testament as Scripture." *JSOT* 16 (1980): 52–60.

———. "The Canon in Recent Biblical Studies: Reflections on an Era." *Pro Ecclesia* 14 (2005): 26–45.

Delitzsch, Franz. *Symbolae ad Psalmos illustrados isogogicae.* Leipzig, 1846.

———. *Biblical Commentary on the Psalms.* 3 vol. Grand Rapids: Eerdmans, 1881. Repr. 1975.

Flint, Peter W., and Patrick D. Miller Jr., eds. *The Book of Psalms: Composition and Reception.* Leiden: Brill, 2005.

Gerstenberger, Erhard. *Psalms, Part 2, and Lamentations.* FOTL 15. Grand Rapids: Eerdmans, 2001.

Goulder, Michael. *The Psalms of the Sons of Korah.* JSOTSup 20. Sheffield: JSOT, 1982.

Howard, David M. "Editorial Activity in the Psalter: A State-of-the-Field Survey." *WW* 9 (1989): 274–85.

Human, Dirk J., and Cas J. A. Vos, eds. *Psalms and Liturgy.* London: T&T Clark, 2004.

Millard, M. *Die Komposition des Psalters.* FAT 9. Tübingen: Mohr, 1994.

Polzin, Robert E. "'The Ancestress of Israel in Danger' in Danger." *Semeia* 3 (1975): 81–98.

Sanders, James A. "Review of *The Editing of the Hebrew Psalter.*" *JBL* 106/2 (1987): 321.

———. *From Sacred Story to Sacred Text.* Philadelphia: Fortress, 1987.

Seybold, Klaus and Erich Zenger, eds. *Neue Wege der Psalmenforschung.* Freiburg: Herder, 1994.

Sheppard, Gerald T. *Wisdom as a Hermeneutical Construct: A Study in the Sapientializing of the Old Testament.* New York: de Gruyter, 1980.

Westermann, Claus. *Praise and Lament in the Psalms.* Atlanta: John Knox, 1981. Translation of "Zur Sammlung des Psalters," *Theologia Viatorum* 8 (1962): 278–84.

Whybray, Norman. *Reading the Psalms as a Book*. JSOTSup 222. Sheffield: Sheffield Academic, 1996.

Wilson, Gerald H. *The Editing of the Hebrew Psalter*. SBLDS 76. Chico, Calif.: Scholars Press, 1985.

———. "Shaping the Psalter: A Consideration of Editorial Linkage in the Book of Psalms." Pages 72–83 in *The Shape and Shaping of the Psalter*. Edited by J. Clinton McCann Jr. JSOTSup 159. Sheffield: JSOT, 1993.

———. "The Use of Royal Psalms at the 'Seams' of the Hebrew Psalter." *JSOT* 35 (1986): 85–94.

Zenger, Erich. "Psalmenexegese und Psalterexegese: Eine Forschungsskizze." Pages 17–65 in *The Composition of the Book of Psalms*. Edited by Erich Zenger. Leuven: Peeters, 2010.

———, ed. *The Composition of the Book of Psalms*. BETL 238. Leuven: Peeters, 2010.

The Editing of the Psalter and the Ongoing Use of the Psalms: Gerald Wilson and the Question of Canon

Harry P. Nasuti

The Editing of the Hebrew Psalter: Canonical Shape and Editorial Purpose

It is useful to begin this reflection on *The Editing of the Hebrew Psalter* with a reminder of its opening chapters on comparative material from the ancient Near East and Qumran. I suspect that contemporary scholars who are now used to research on the Psalter as a whole often bypass these chapters in favor of the two final chapters (and Wilson's later works) on the Psalms and the shape of the Psalter.[1] One should, however, note the importance of these earlier chapters both for the development of Wilson's thesis and for this later shift in Psalms scholarship. Especially significant in this respect is the way that Wilson's comparative research and his detailed work on the Psalms' superscriptions and doxologies lead directly to his insights on the structural reliability and theological importance of the five-book division and the seams of the Psalter.

The reason Wilson begins his study with such comparative work is precisely to "impart a measure of objective control to the study of the Psalter, and to avoid the pitfall of 'imposing' non-existent structure on the text."[2] As may be seen from this work's title, Wilson is primarily interested

---

1. See the comment of David Howard on these earlier chapters: "Unfortunately, this aspect of Wilson's work has not received the attention it deserves" ("Recent Trends in Psalms Study," in *The Face of Old Testament Studies: A Survey of Contemporary Approaches* [ed. D. W. Baker and B. T. Arnold; Grand Rapids: Baker, 1999], 332).

2. Gerald H. Wilson, *The Editing of the Hebrew Psalter* (SBLDS 76; Chico, Calif.: Scholars Press, 1985), 5.

in the "editing" of the Psalter. His "major concern" is to "observe editorial technique in action."[3] In keeping with this goal, Wilson speaks throughout of determining the "purpose" and "intentions" of this text's editors.

Such an attempt to isolate the intentions of the text's final editors is fundamentally an exercise in redaction criticism and, as such, a historical-critical endeavor.[4] Indicative of this historical orientation is the fact that Wilson later attempts to date these editors' work and to explain their theological intentions in terms of a specific situation in the first century C.E.[5] While such a concern is obviously legitimate and important, it should be noted that it does not entirely cohere with the canonical approach of Brevard Childs to which Wilson sees himself indebted.

Childs is not uninterested in what scholars have seen as the final redaction of biblical books. It is also clear, however, that he does not want the analysis of biblical books to be narrowly tied to scholarly theories about editorial intent. His focus is rather more on such texts' final literary shapes and their subsequent reception and interpretation.[6] Wilson obviously shares Childs's concern for the final form of the Psalter. Nevertheless, the two scholars differ in that Wilson looks back from that final form to the intentions of the (hypothetical) editors responsible for it, while Childs reads the text with an eye on how it has later been understood and used by the Jewish and Christian communities for whom it has functioned as canon.[7]

---

3. Ibid., 10.

4. See Harry P. Nasuti, *Defining the Sacred Songs: Genre, Tradition, and the Post-Critical Interpretation of the Psalms* (JSOTSup 218; Sheffield: Sheffield Academic, 1999), 173.

5. Gerald H. Wilson, "The Shape of the Book of Psalms," *Int* 46 (1992): 137–38; see also his "A First Century C.E. Date for the Closing of the Psalter?" in *Haim M. I. Gevaryahu Memorial Volume* (Jerusalem: World Jewish Bible Center, 1990), 136–43.

6. See, for example Childs's statement that "attention to the subsequent history of interpretation of the Bible is absolutely essential for its understanding." For Childs, the exegetical task is "constructive as well as descriptive," in that "the interpreter is forced to confront the authoritative text of scripture in a continuing theological reflection. By placing the canonical text within the context of the community of faith and practice a variety of different exegetical models are freed to engage the text, such as the liturgical or the dramatic" (Brevard S. Childs, *Introduction to the Old Testament as Scripture* [Philadelphia: Fortress, 1979], 82–83).

7. Along these lines, it is perhaps significant that James Sanders's review of *Editing* in the *Journal of Biblical Literature* spoke of Wilson's methods as "a good amalgam of those worked out by both Childs and myself" ("Review of *The Editing of the Hebrew*

Occasionally, the tension between Wilson's historical concerns and the influence of Childs surfaces in *Editing* itself. So, for example, one of Wilson's most fundamental and far-reaching arguments is that "in its 'final form' the Psalter is a book to be *read* rather than to be *performed*; to be *meditated over* rather than to be *recited from*."[8] Yet in his analysis of the Davidic psalms, Wilson's appreciation of Childs's work on the "historical" superscriptions leads him to argue that David is a model whose prayer is to be imitated by those who encounter it in the book of Psalms.[9] Indeed, Wilson sees the Psalter as ending with a call for continuing praise of God, a call that he repeats in the final words of his own book.[10] All of this would seem to imply a view of the Psalms at odds with (or at least in addition to) the above statement on the priority of meditation over performance.[11]

The Canonical Psalter and the Ongoing Use of the Psalms

Through over two thousand years of Jewish and Christian history, the psalms have been recited and performed in a variety of ways and settings. If, as Wilson claims, the Psalter's final editors meant to rule out such recitation and performance in favor of reading and meditation, those who came after them seem to have been almost flagrant in their disregard for these editors' intentions. Rather, as Childs already noted in the Psalms chapter of his *Introduction*,

> The most characteristic feature of the canonical shaping of the Psalter is the variety of different hermeneutical moves which were incorporated within the final form of the collection. Although the psalms were often

---

Psalter," *JBL* 106 [1987]: 321). Wilson's more historical orientation may well reflect the Sanders part of that amalgam. It is perhaps worth noting that Childs considered at least part of Sanders's approach to be a "highly speculative enterprise" (*Introduction*, 57).

8. Wilson, *The Editing of the Hebrew Psalter*, 207 (emphasis original).

9. For Wilson (ibid., 173), the final effect of these historical superscriptions "has been to provide a hermeneutical approach to the use of the psalms by the *individual*. As David, so every man!" (emphasis original).

10. Ibid., 225–28.

11. More recently, William P. Brown has argued in a related, though slightly different, vein that one should not set the ritual and "meditative" usage of the psalms in opposition to each other, since both involve "performing" the psalms in an active and transformative way. See his *Psalms* (IBT; Nashville: Abingdon, 2010), x, 82–83.

greatly refashioned for use by the later generations, no one doctrinaire position received a normative role. The material was far too rich and its established use far too diverse ever to allow a single function to subordinate all others. The psalms were collected to be used for liturgy and for study, both by a corporate body and by individuals, to remind of the great redemptive acts of the past as well as to anticipate the hopes of the future.[12]

Such a view seems much more in keeping with the Psalms' subsequent history of interpretation and use than Wilson's attempt to define the Psalter's meaning on the basis of the redactional activity and intentions of its final editors.

Other scholars have followed Wilson's lead and sought to isolate the Psalter's last redactional level in order to discern the intentions of its final editors. It is, however, noteworthy that such scholars do not necessarily agree with Wilson, first of all as to these editors' identity and historical circumstances and, secondly, as to the nature of their redactional activity and editorial intent.[13] While such conjectures are legitimate and informative, their diversity once again highlights the difference between these efforts and Childs's approach to the text's canonical shape, which ultimately does not depend on the resolution of such historical questions.

In contrast to that of Wilson (and these other scholars), my own work has tended to approach the psalms from the perspective of their later interpretation and use in Jewish and Christian traditions. In doing so, I have been influenced by Childs's interest in the history of interpretation and his insistence that canon implies an ongoing relationship between these communities and their normative text. This has led me to appreciate both traditional authors and modern scholars whose approach to the canonical shape of the Psalter is less historical and more literary and theological.[14] It has also led me to recognize and appreciate the way that

---

12. Childs, *Introduction to the Old Testament as Scripture*, 522.

13. So, for example Frank-Lothar Hossfeld and Erich Zenger have argued for a second-century B.C.E. date for the Psalter's final redaction (*Die Psalmen I* [Würzburg: Echter, 1993], 14–16), while Susan Gillingham has argued for an even earlier date ("The Zion Tradition and the Editing of the Hebrew Psalter," in *Temple and Worship in Biblical Israel* [ed. J. Day; London: T&T Clark, 2005], 308–41).

14. For an example of a modern approach along these lines, see James Luther Mays, *The Lord Reigns: A Theological Handbook to the Psalms* (Louisville: Westminster

the Psalms' present canonical order has affected their appropriation in the spiritual and liturgical usage of both Judaism and Christianity.

At the same time, however, this interest in the history of the Psalms' interpretation and use has made me aware that this book has been appropriated not only as an ordered literary whole with a particular theological orientation but also as a collection of individual texts that have been used in a variety of settings.[15] Wilson may or may not be historically correct to deny the book of Psalms its once common title, "the Hymn Book of the Second Temple."[16] Nevertheless, it would certainly be incorrect to say that the Psalter has never functioned as a "hymn book" (or other type of collection) from which individual texts have been excerpted for a variety of purposes.

In my view, the history of the interpretation and use of the Psalms works against narrowly restricting the meaning of either this book or its component texts to that which they may have had in any one historical situation of the past. Both the Psalter as a whole and the individual psalms have informed and inspired Jews and Christians throughout history, just they continue to inform and inspire modern scholarship. Given this book's dual status as both a coherent whole and a collection of individual texts, perhaps the question that needs further examination is how the ongoing usage of the individual psalms in the lives of believing communities has interacted (and continues to interact) with the way that such communities have viewed the Psalter's overall literary shape and theological purpose. Such a question is explicitly canonical in that it is grounded in the ongoing relationship between these communities and the present form of the book of Psalms.

John Knox, 1994), 119–27. See especially his statement that "a literary reading requires one to hold historical questions and perspectives in abeyance," 127.

15. On the interplay between these two approaches, see Nasuti, "The Interpretive Significance of Sequence and Selection in the Book of Psalms," in *The Book of Psalms: Composition and Reception* (ed. Peter W. Flint and Patrick D. Miller Jr.; Leiden: Brill, 2005), 311–39.

16. Wilson, *The Editing of the Hebrew Psalter*, 206–7; cf. also his "Shaping the Psalter: A Consideration of Editorial Linkage in the Book of Psalms," in *The Shape and Shaping of the Psalter* (ed. J. Clinton McCann Jr. ; JSOTSup 159; Sheffield: Sheffield Academic, 1993), 72, 81–82.

CONCLUSIONS

Wilson's focus on the literary shape and theological purpose of the Psalter as a whole was an important corrective to a field that had almost ignored the final form of the text in favor of the life settings of the individual psalms in ancient Israel. Similarly, there is no denying that Wilson and those who, like him, have attempted to determine the intentions of this book's final redactors have produced a wealth of close readings and perceptive insights into this larger work. Many of these continue to influence my own understanding of the book of Psalms, even though I am inclined to reserve judgment about their more specific historical claims.

BIBLIOGRAPHY

Brown, William P. *Psalms*. IBT. Nashville: Abingdon, 2010.

Childs, Brevard S. *Introduction to the Old Testament as Scripture*. Philadelphia: Fortress, 1979.

Gillingham, Susan. "The Zion Tradition and the Editing of the Hebrew Psalter." Pages 308–41 in *Temple and Worship in Biblical Israel*. Edited by J. Day. London: T&T Clark, 2005.

Hossfeld, Frank-Lothar, and Erich Zenger, *Die Psalmen I*. Würzburg: Echter, 1993.

Howard, David M. "Recent Trends in Psalms Study." Pages 329–68 in *The Faces of Old Testament Studies: A Survey of Contemporary Approaches*. Edited by D. W. Baker and B. T. Arnold. Grand Rapids: Baker, 1999.

Mays, James Luther. *The Lord Reigns: A Theological Handbook to the Psalms*. Louisville: Westminster John Knox, 1994.

Nasuti, Harry P. *Defining the Sacral Songs: Genre, Tradition, and the Post-Critical Interpretation of the Psalms*. JSOTSup 218. Sheffield: Sheffield Academic, 1999.

———. "The Interpretive Significance of Sequence and Selection in the Book of Psalms. Pages 311–39 in *The Book of Psalms: Composition and Reception*. Edited by Peter W. Flint and Patrick D. Miller Jr. Leiden: Brill, 2005.

Sanders, James A. "Review of *The Editing of the Hebrew Psalter*." *JBL* 106 (1987): 321.

Wilson, Gerald H. *The Editing of the Hebrew Psalter*. SBLDS 76. Chico, Calif.: Scholars Press, 1985.

————. "A First Century Date for the Closing of the Psalter?" Pages 136–43 in *Haim M. I. Gevaryahu Memorial Volume*. Jerusalem: World Jewish Bible Center, 1990.

————. "The Shape of the Book of Psalms." *Int* 46 (1991): 129–42.

————. "Shaping the Psalter: A Consideration of Editorial Linkage in the Book of Psalms." Pages 72–82 in *The Shape and Shaping of the Psalter*. JSOTSup 159. Edited by J. Clinton McCann Jr. Sheffield: Sheffield Academic, 1993.

Changing Our Way of Being Wrong: The Impact of Gerald Wilson's *The Editing of the Hebrew Psalter*

J. Clinton McCann Jr.

I am going to keep it simple and use two words to describe my perception of the impact of Gerald Wilson's *The Editing of the Hebrew Psalter*—shock and awe. If this response seems a bit over the top, let me explain. Everything is contextual, of course, and my context is this: I am a teacher in a small, church-related school in a staid Midwestern suburb. Things are pretty routine—some might say "boring"—so it does not take much to create an atmosphere of excitement. In fact, one of the most exciting things I do every year is to attend the annual meeting of the Society of Biblical Literature, an event my family persists in calling "The Geek Convention." So, if I am shocked and awed by the impact of Wilson's work, do not begrudge me!

I am being a bit facetious, of course, but not completely, so let me say a bit less hyperbolically that I am very pleasantly and gratifyingly surprised by the direction of the field of Psalms studies since Wilson's work was published in 1985. I completed my dissertation in the spring of 1985. It focused on Ps 73, but included a forty-page section on the shape and shaping of the Psalter as a context for interpreting individual psalms, including Ps 73. Wilson's volume came out just as I was finishing my work, so I was not able to take it into account except in a footnote, where I said that *The Editing of the Hebrew Psalter* is "another attempt [that is, in addition to my own] to provide a new way of thinking about the Psalter by examining its canonical shape...."[1] No one has ever read my dissertation except

---

1. J. Clinton McCann Jr., "Psalm 73: An Interpretation Emphasizing Rhetorical and Canonical Criticism" (Ph.D. diss., Duke University, 1985), 144.

Roland Murphy, my supervisor, along with a few members of my committee, and no one really needs to. Wilson's work is far more detailed and comprehensive. My point is not that Gerald Wilson and I were thinking along the same lines, although we were, and I found that very encouraging at the time. Rather, my point here is that in 1985 I could find very few scholarly conversation partners when it came to thinking about the shape and shaping of the Psalter. There were a few—in English, Brevard Childs, with whom Wilson studied; and in German, Harmut Gese and Joachim Becker, particularly his volumes *Israel deutet seine Psalmen: Urform und Neuinterpretation in den Psalmen* and *Wege der Psalmenexegese*.[2]

When we compare the situation in 1985 with Psalms studies today, we find a major and marked contrast. Introducing the 2005 volume *The Book of Psalms: Composition and Reception*, which was planned in the late 1990s "with the objective of producing a new collection of studies on the Psalter in the early years of a century's turning," editors Pat Miller and Peter Flint say this: "Of special note is the lively interest in the Psalter as a collection or as a book comprised of various collections."[3] The more recent volume, *The Composition of the Book of Psalms*, edited by the late Erich Zenger, contains forty-four essays, over half of which have to do in some way with the shape and shaping of the Psalter.[4] To be sure, one might expect this, given Zenger's scholarly interests and influence; but the important point is that Professor Zenger could assemble a group of essays on the shape and shaping of the Psalter from twenty-five Psalm scholars representing twelve different countries.

When I collaborated with several Psalm colleagues in the late 1980s to help form a new program unit within the Society of Biblical Literature called The Book of Psalms Consultation, we identified the shape and shaping of the Psalter as an emphasis partly because several of us were inter-

---

2. See Brevard Childs, *Introduction to the Old Testament as Scripture* (Philadelphia: Fortress, 1979); Hartmut Gese, "Die Entstehung der Büchereinteilung des Psalters," in *Vom Sinai zum Zion: Alttestamentliche Beiträge zur biblischen Theologie* (BEvT 64; Munich: Chr. Kaiser, 1974), 159–67; Joachim Becker, *Israel deutet seine Psalmen: Urform und Neuinterpretation in den Psalmen* (SBS 18; Stuttgart: Katholisches Bibelwerk, 1966); Becker, *Wege der Psalmenexegese* (SBS 78; Stuttgart: Katholisches Bibelwerk, 1975).

3. Peter Flint and Patrick Miller Jr., eds., *The Book of Psalms: Composition and Reception* (VTSup 99; Leiden: Brill, 2005), 1.

4. Erich Zenger, ed., *The Composition of the Book of Psalms* (BETL 238; Leuven: Peeters, 2010).

ested in this approach, and partly to distinguish the new unit from the Biblical Hebrew Poetry Section. I thought that the Psalms Consultation might be renewed once beyond its initial two-year period of authorization. In fact, it has been renewed and reauthorized several times. And now, a generation later, what is now the Book of Psalms *Section* is going strong, bespeaking a "lively interest" and a seemingly still growing interest in the shape and shaping of the Psalter. I am pleasantly surprised—even somewhat shocked and awed, if you will.

The major and marked contrast in Psalms studies between 1985 and today is certainly due in part, perhaps in large part, to Gerald Wilson's *The Editing of the Hebrew Psalter*. Almost certainly, of course, the field eventually would have gone in the shape-and-shaping direction anyway. As mentioned above, Gerald had predecessors. Already in the mid-1970s, Joachim Becker was suggesting the importance of approaching the Psalms with what he called the "buchredaktionelle Geschichtspunkte,"[5] which included not only the consideration of redactional links between psalms, but also consideration of the importance of collections and the possible reasons for the five-book division of the Psalter. The European work on shape and shaping is probably rooted more directly in Becker's work than in Wilson's, although Wilson's work had an impact in Europe as well. As Erich Zenger says in an essay on Pss 90–106 (book 4), "The contrastive tension between Psalms Books 1–3 and 4–5 [that is, the 'theocratic' emphasis of 4–5 versus the 'messianic' emphasis of 1–3] was first seen with this degree of clarity, as far as I know, by Gerald H. Wilson, *The Editing of the Hebrew Psalter*."[6]

Numerous Psalms scholars in recent years have affirmed what they frequently call the "groundbreaking" character of Wilson's work, usually stating in addition that his work served as the foundation and point of departure for their own. In short, while the field of Psalms studies would have gone in the direction of shape and shaping without Wilson's volume, *The Editing of the Hebrew Psalter* certainly provided a major impetus in this direction and expedited the movement considerably.

It should be noted in conclusion that a great deal of good scholarly work on the Psalms is being done without any consideration of the shape and shaping of the Psalter. For example, Erhard Gerstenberger continues

---

5. Becker, *Wege der Psalmexegese*, 112; see 112–20.

6. Erich Zenger, "The God of Israel's Reign over the World (Psalms 90–106)," in *The God of Israel and the Nations: Studies in Isaiah and the Psalms* (ed. N. Lohfink and E. Zenger, trans. E. R. Kalin; Collegeville, Minn.: Liturgical Press, 2000), 161.

to offer fruitful and helpful insights from his thoroughgoing sociological perspective.[7] John Goldingay recently completed a very valuable three-volume commentary on the Psalms without mentioning shape and shaping, except to say that he was not going to pay any attention to it.[8] Norman Whybray, as far as I know, has been the most directly critical of the whole shape-and-shaping enterprise, suggesting that it is fundamentally misguided and too "purely speculative" to yield useful results.[9]

Whybray's criticism raises a very basic question: Aside from the obvious impact of *The Editing of the Hebrew Psalter*, was Gerald Wilson right, or has he led Psalms scholars astray? For my part, I think Wilson was essentially right. In his 1985 volume and in subsequent essays, his basic directions and conclusions are convincing. But in the larger scheme of things, I do not really claim to know whether he was right or not, and in a fundamental way I do not really care. If that sounds unscholarly, let me explain with one of my favorite quotations in all of Psalms literature. Joachim Becker wrote, "Von den Psalmen gilt, was T. S. Eliot über Shakespeare gesagt hat: 'About anyone so great, it is probable that we can never be right; and if we are never right, it is better from time to time that we change our way of being wrong.'"[10] At the very least, Wilson's *The Editing of the Hebrew Psalter* has had a profound impact on my way of being wrong about the Psalms; and I know that many other Psalms scholars can say the same.

Bibliography

Becker, Joachim. *Israel deutet seine Psalmen: Urform und Neuinterpretation in den Psalmen*. SBS 18. Stuttgart: Katholisches Bibelwerk, 1966.
———. *Wege der Psalmenexegese*. SBS 78. Stuttgart: Katholisches Bibelwerk, 1975.
Childs, Brevard. *Introduction to the Old Testament as Scripture*. Philadelphia: Fortress, 1979.

---

7. Erhard S. Gerstenberger, *Psalms, Part 1, with an Introduction to Cultic Poetry* (FOTL 14; Grand Rapids: Eerdmans, 1988); and Gerstenberger, *Psalms, Part 2, and Lamentations* (FOTL 15; Grand Rapids: Eerdmans, 2001).

8. John Goldingay, *Psalms 1–41* (BCOTWP; Grand Rapids: Baker, 2006), 37.

9. Roger Norman Whybray, *Reading the Psalms as a Book* (JSOTSup 222; Sheffield: Sheffield Academic, 1996), 119.

10. Becker, *Wege der Psalmenexegese*, 9.

Flint, Peter, and Patrick Miller Jr., eds. *The Book of Psalms: Composition and Reception*. VTSup 99; Leiden: Brill, 2005.

Gerstenberger, Erhard S. *Psalms, Part 1, with an Introduction to Cultic Poetry*. FOTL 14. Grand Rapids: Eerdmans, 1988.

———. *Psalms, Part 2, and Lamentations*. FOTL 15. Grand Rapids: Eerdmans, 2001.

Gese, Hartmut. "Die Entstehung der Büchereinteilung des Psalters." In *Vom Sinai zum Zion: Alttestamentliche Beiträge zur biblischen Theologie*. BEvT 64. Munich: Chr. Kaiser, 1974.

Goldingay, John. *Psalms 1–41*. BCOTWP. Grand Rapids: Baker, 2006.

McCann, J. Clinton Jr. "Psalm 73: An Interpretation Emphasizing Rhetorical and Canonical Criticism." Ph. D. diss., Duke University, 1985.

Whybray, Roger Norman. *Reading the Psalms as a Book*. JSOTSup 222. Sheffield: Sheffield Academic, 1996.

Zenger, Erich. "The God of Israel's Reign over the World (Psalms 90–106)." In *The God of Israel and the Nations: Studies in Isaiah and the Psalms*. Edited by N. Lohfink and E. Zenger. Translated by E. R. Kalin. Collegeville, Minn.: Liturgical, 2000.

———. ed. *The Composition of the Book of Psalms*. BETL 238. Leuven: Peeters, 2010.

The Dynamics of Praise in the Ancient Near East, or Poetry and Politics*

Erhard S. Gerstenberger

Language and Poetry, Linguistics and Poetics

Just as general anthropologists have a hard time intelligently defining the nature of human beings, various specialists in human speech have been challenged by an intrinsic exigency to understand and describe the essence of human vocal or verbal articulation and communication. Should we regard language as the unique divine gift that elevates humans above all other creatures? Can it be seen as the prime vehicle of interpersonal or intergroup communication? Is it perhaps only one type of countless systems of participation, be it in the physical, chemical, or organic world, a functional array of sounds, melodies, signifiers transporting information from sender to recipient, whatever they may be? The answers greatly depend on basic assumptions such as whether or not we consider human beings a supreme species *sui generis*, separated from the rest of being by power and glory. But are they really the "crown" or climax of creation? Does language *per se* belong to the metaphysical realm rather than to real and earthly existence?[1]

Poetic language certainly occupies a rank of its own among modes of verbal expression. Form, style, structure, and contents of cultivated

---

* This is a slightly revised version of a paper delivered at the Society of Biblical Literature annual meeting in Atlanta on November 21, 2010.

1. "What or who are human beings?" is a central question that has been agitating thinking minds from the very beginning of reasoning, probably some hundreds of thousands years ago. This innate quest for meaning also produced whole libraries in the past centuries; see only Herbert Wendt and Norbert Loacker, eds., *Kindlers Enzyklopädie: Der Mensch* (10 vols; Zürich: Kindler, 1981–1985).

verbal articulation do indicate "higher" levels of organization and meaning. Solemnity and emotion permeate pieces of poetry. Is the distinction of "low" day-to-day speech and "high" poetic articulation sufficient? Ought we to consider the contexts and functions of communication as well? Where are the dividing lines between those ways of expression, and how do we adequately define each of them?[2]

ARCHAIC UTTERANCES OF PRAISE

Just to remind ourselves of our prehistoric roots: Primitive exclamations in archaic guise, shouts of jubilation, outbreaks of joy and awe may be surmised to head the continuous tradition in all cultures of human praise expressions.[3] Short formulas, probably a heritage of preliterate epochs, abound even in much later literature; they appear like ancient rocks in the stream of eulogies directed to divine forces: Sumerian[4] *zà-mí* ᵈ*NN*, "praise [noun!] to the God NN," *zà-mí-zu dùg-ga*, "your praise is splendid" are the earliest extant examples. Hebrew[5] *halĕlûyāh*, "extol [imperative!] YHWH," *mĕhullāl yhwh*, "to be praised is YHWH," *bārûk yhwh*, "blessed be YHWH," follow at the end of the line. In between we may find similar formulas in Akkadian, Egyptian, Hittite, Ugaritic, and other ancient Near Eastern literature. Arabic "Allah is the greatest" (*allāhu akbar*) and other shouts are still used today in Islamic rituals. All these exclamations really are hymns in a nutshell, often condensed expressions of power. They already may tell us about the complex texture of praise in terms of its psy-

---

2. Poetic Hebrew language has always been a choice object of Old Testament scholars. See Adele Berlin, "Poetry, Hebrew Bible," in *Dictionary of Biblical Interpretation* (ed. John H. Hayes; 2 vols.; Nashville: Abingdon, 1999), 2:290–96. The express reference point of the SBL working-group session in which this paper was presented was Patrick D. Miller Jr.'s probe into "The Theological Significance of Poetry," in *Language, Theology, and the Bible* (ed. Samuel B. Balentine and John Barton; Oxford: Clarendon, 1994), 225–30.

3. See Hermann Gunkel and Joachim Begrich, *Einleitung in die Psalmen* (Göttingen: Vandenhoeck, 1933), 37–38; Maurice C. Bowra, *Primitive Song* (Cleveland: World, 1962), 57–64 ("emotive sounds" precede poetic songs).

4. Sumerian is the oldest written language known thus far. The largest collection of Sumerian literary texts is ETCSL (Electronic Text Corpus of Sumerian Literature), encompassing about four hundred individual texts. They are freely available in transliteration and English translation at http://etcsl.orinst.ox.ac.uk.

5. See Helmer Ringgren, "*hll* I und II," *ThWAT* 2:433–41.

chology, ritual fiber, and social setting. Furthermore, archaic shouts of praise, awe, glorification, enhancement, etc., still virulent in various contexts, may definitely alert us to the fact that praise is not only an aesthetic or stylistic speech form, with possible theological implications, but a real primordial force not to be tamed by modern interpretations.[6]

In historic times praise to the gods was couched in intricate oral and literary poetry (lyrical rhetoric). These artful compositions could appear and be handed down only after the invention of adequate writing systems (ca. 2600 B.C.E.). Cuneiform tablets found in Mesopotamia and other neighboring regions covering a period of more than two millennia constitute the first human written literature and demonstrate the level of literary achievement.[7] A special rhetoric of praise is already in full swing including a wide range of characteristics: terminology, metaphors, style, structure, and so on. We can probe only into very limited sections of this spectrum. And we have to keep in mind that verbal articulations are only vehicles of that internal or concomitant dynamic of theological rhetoric we are really looking for. The main questions are, why religious communication uses such special or "high" forms of linguistic expressions, and what makes poetic language suitable for dialogue with gods.

MOTIVATIONS, AFFECTS, LINGUISTIC FORM

Hymnic speech-forms in the Hebrew Scriptures first were investigated by Robert Lowth (1753) and Johann Gottfried Herder (1782), among others. Later, Hermann Gunkel and Sigmund Mowinckel took up their heritage.[8] Disciples of these scholars have enlarged and modified their research over the decades. Other literary and ritual experts have joined in and there have been harvested during the past century good amounts of insights.

---

6. See Bowra, *Primitive Song*; Dale E. Elliot, "Toward a Grammar of Exclamations," *Foundations of Language* 11 (1974): 231–46; Inger Rosengren, "Zur Grammatik und Pragmatik der Exklamation," in *Satz und Illokution* (ed. Inger Rosengren; Linguistische Arbeiten 278; Tübingen: Niemeyer, 1992), 1:263–306.

7. See Jeremy Black, *Reading Sumerian Poetry* (London: Athlone, 1998); Marianna E. Vogelzang and Herman L. J. Vanstiphout, eds., *Mesopotamian Poetic Language: Sumerian and Akkadian: Proceedings of the Groningen Group for the Study of Mesopotamian Literature*, vol. 2 (CM 6, Groningen: STYX, 1996).

8. Gunkel and Begrich, *Einleitung*; Sigmund Mowinckel, *Psalmenstudien* (Kristiania: SNVAO, 1921, 1922; repr. 1961); Mowinckel, *The Psalms in Israel's Worship* (2 vols.; Nashville: Abingdon, 1962).

There is a considerable range of verbal and nominal expressions connoting "praise" in all the ancient oriental languages. Starting with Sumerian, that millenary liturgical language, and moving to Akkadian and Hebrew (a glance at Hittite, Egyptian, and others, would be useful but is left aside at this point), we may marvel at the rich heritage of meaning. We list some main verbs and nouns: **Hebrew**—*hll* [*piel*]; *ydh*; *brk* [*qal*; *piel*]; *gdl* [*piel*]; *rûm* [*pil*]; *šbḥ* [*piel*]; *ydʿ* [*hiphil*]; *ngd* [*hiphil*]; *šyr*; *zmr* [*piel*]; *šlm* [*piel*]; *ʾdr* [*hiphil*]; *pʾr* [*hiphil*]; *rnn*; *pṣḥ*; *ṣhl*; **Sumerian**—*zà-mí* ("praise"), *ar* ("to praise"), *meteš* ("eulogy"), *šir* ("to sing; song"); **Akkadian**—*dalalu* ("venerate"); *nâdu* and *elû* D ("extol"); *karābu* ("greet reverently"); *alālu* ("sing joyfully"); *zakāru* ("mention with praise"); *šurbû* ("enlarge"); *šurruhu* ("praise"). Ugaritic, Syriac, and Arabic, to name only a few more Semitic languages, all show a similar vocabulary of praise. The examples adduced above betray a wide variety of connotations and emotive involvements. Noteworthy are ties to music, singing, instruments, to the tensions and grades of power between adorer and adored, and to the intention to lift up, enhance, and magnify the deities.

Attributions of power, majesty, and sovereignty to higher beings are so natural in praise language that we need not actually specify them.[9] But it is noteworthy that metaphors, similes, and comparisons abound in this rhetoric. The addressed ones are likened to, identified with, or brought into close contact with the animal kingdom (lions, bulls, dragons), weather phenomena (storms, floods, thunder), celestial potencies (light, radiance, beauty), war and battle insignias (weapons, prowess, revenge), universal order (justice, equity, castigation), and life-generative forces (fertility, wholesomeness, prosperity). Throughout the history of tradition there have occurred modulations of the praise attributes. What counts more, however, is the basic continuity of this "spiritual iconography," so that we

---

9. See Gunkel and Begrich, *Einleitung*, 42–71. Some basic forms of direct praise may have been: "God is great (majestic; powerful)," with the response "you are great" (e.g., Pss 24:8; 48:2; 62:12; 77:14; 104:1; 138:5–6), and "God has performed marvelous deeds" or, with direct address, "You have…": (Pss 40:6; 74:13–15; 77:15; 92:6; 126:2–3). As Gunkel and Begrich (*Einleitung*) prove, there is a rich variety of formulations in the Psalter. See also, e.g., Claus Westermann, *Praise and Lament in the Psalms* (Atlanta: John Knox, 1981); Patrick D. Miller Jr., *They Cried to the Lord: The Form and Theology of Biblical Prayer* (Minneapolis: Fortress, 1994), 178–232; and Walter Brueggemann, *Israel's Praise: Doxology against Idolatry and Ideology* (Philadelphia: Fortress, 1988).

may give examples from the Old Testament which is, in a sense, the last receiving link in the age-old Near Eastern chain of eulogy.

YHWH in particular is eulogized by images of glory, majesty, and power, which are "perhaps the essence of poetry," but also in very anthropomorphic ways.[10] Human occupations symbolically serve to describe God: He is "King," "Sovereign," "Warrior," "Craftsman," "Judge," "Avenger," "Shepherd," and "Farmer,"[11] and possibly "Midwife," "Spouse," "Mother," and "Wailing Woman." Animal metaphors for YHWH in the Bible include "Eagle," "Lion," "Bird," "Bear," and "Moth."[12] Gunkel paints a euphoric picture of Old Israel's praise in the Psalms.[13] He dares to affirm "that the hymns let transpire the objective side of religion, namely Yahweh himself, his qualities and actions."[14] Here we actually meet a deep theological appreciation of Old Testament praise rhetoric.

Structural and stylistic means constituting ancient poetic languages, especially praise rhetoric, are manifold and by no means translucent as yet.[15] The technical details of poetic language will not lead us much further individually, but in aggregate they reveal the possibilities of human mind and art to approach borderlines of existence in terms of space and time. Praise language in particular stretches out into the past, wrestles with reality by acknowledging accomplishments, grasping actuality and probing into the future, and in all these regards also tries to mold reality according to desired well-being, peace, and justice.

The specific problems, for example, of the oldest poetic literature in Mesopotamia, the "verbal art of these long lost civilizations"[16] are only

---

10. Luis Alonso Schökel, *A Manual of Hebrew Poetics* (SubBi 11; Rome: Pontificio Istituto Biblico, 1988), 95, 128–29: Human qualities are also named, such as faithfulness, justice, etc.

11. Ibid., 137–38.

12. Ibid., 138.

13. See Gunkel and Begrich, *Einleitung*, 71–83.

14. Ibid., 71.

15. Poetological studies in the different literatures of the Ancient Near East are not numerous. See Brigitte R. M. Groneberg, *Syntax, Morphologie, und Stil der jungbabylonischen "hymnischen" Literatur*, 2 vol. (FAOS 14; Stuttgart: Steiner, 1987); Schökel, *A Manual of Hebrew Poetics*.

16. Piotr Michalowski, "Ancient Poetics," in *Mesopotamian Poetic Language* (ed. Marianna E. Vogelzang and H. L. J. Vanstiphout; Groningen: STYX, 1996), 141. This is a clear warning not to overestimate the texts that were written down for "vocal expression." "The voice was an integral part of the text" (144). See also Jeremy Black,

beginning to be discussed by experts.[17] Some facts, however, are obvious: Poetic language, used in various settings, in its written form is linebound (i.e., is normally fixed in cuneiform lines). It possesses a wide range of vocabulary and structural forms, is highly figurative, and sometimes creates its own grammatical rules or even a complete (artificial?) language, like Emesal ("light/high [women's] language") in Sumerian.[18] Still, according to some Sumerologists and biblical exegetes, the borderline between prose and poetry is in constant flux. There is an "alternating movement of descent and ascent" in discourse, and "purism is a symptom of decadence" according to Luis Alonso Schökel.[19] Furthermore, many scholars stress the intimate yet little researched liaison of poetic literary speech forms with oral performance of the texts. "The rhythm and patterns of the poetry went hand in glove with musical expression," states Michalowski.[20] Language, as it were, is embedded in action, behavior, ritual, music. It is neither self-sustainable nor self-sustaining.

The Power of Praise

A close reading of any ancient Near Eastern hymnic text, including Old Testament praise poetry, will invariably reveal that our present day conceptions of "eulogy," "praise," "hymn," "laudation," and so on, do not completely coincide with the related ancient notions, a fact that should be considered normal in every crosscultural comparison. What is more significant is a possible basic divergence in theological ideas ancient and modern. Such a chasm would place the Bible into the realm of antique views in contrast to our present so-called "modern" perspectives. The other way around might indicate that "archaic" notions of power transfer

---

"Poesie/Poetry," *Reallexicon der Assyriologie* 10 (2003–2005): 196. According to him, all poetry "was performed aloud," some with musical accompaniment, some in ceremonial contexts.

17. See Black, *Reading Sumerian Poetry*; Black, "Poesie/Poetry"; Michalowski, "Ancient Poetics"; Groneberg, *Syntax, Morphologie*; Vogelzang and Vanstiphout, eds., *Mesopotamian Poetic Language*; Claus Wilcke, "Formale Gesichtspunkte in der sumerischen Literatur," in *Sumerological Studies in Honour of Thorkild Jacobsen on the Occasion of His Seventieth Birthday* (ed. Stephen J. Lieberman; AS 20; Chicago: University of Chicago Press, 1974).

18. See Black, "Poesie/Poetry"; Michalowski, "Ancient Poetics."

19. Schökel, *A Manual of Hebrew Poetics*, 19.

20. Michalowski, "Ancient Poetics," 144.

are still clandestinely present even today, against our dogmatic convictions, in real performances of collective praise.

Looking at Old Testament hymns, we sometimes are struck by a solidly "materialistic" and "dynamistic" understanding of praise. Psalm 29:1–2 summons the "divine beings" to "give, deliver"[21] "glory and power" to YHWH (just as "clans of the nations" are supposed to do in Ps 96:7), a phrase reminiscent also of Ps 19:2, where "the heavens tell the glory of God and the firmament announces his handiwork." The result of a laborsome attribution of "glory and power" is, among other aspects, the construction of a firm throne that YHWH needs for his universal government (Ps 22:4).[22] Enigmatic Ps 8:3, asserting something like the establishment of "power" by the "mouth of babes," may belong in this context.[23] Significantly, in a universal perspective, the supreme heavenly deity does insist on eulogies from the whole of creation (cf. Ps 148). Especially the primeval forces, overcome by the creator, have to extol the victorious God by clapping their hands (cf. Ps 93:3–4; 98:8; the empowering function of "applause" in contemporary societies comes to mind); thus they possibly lend their strength to him. Human praise in some texts apparently acquires an automatic dynamic when, for instance, the levitical singers defeat the enemies by their hymns alone (2 Chr 20:22) or faithful YHWH-believers are saved by their sacred songs (Dan 3 with LXX additions). The spectrum of verbs, already mentioned, which instill praising affirmations with the sense of "enhancing, enlarging, empowering" the name or majesty of God supports this notion, notably *gdl*, *rum*, and so on. Various other positive or negative expressions shed light on the dynamics of praise:

> I looked, but there was no helper;
> I stared, but there was no one to sustain me;
> so my own arm brought me victory,
> and my wrath sustained me. (Isa 63:5; cf. 59:16)

---

21. The word *hābû*, imperative of an unattested verb *yhb*, "to give" is neglected by two important theological dictionaries (*THAT* and *ThWAT*).

22. The grammatical construction *yôšēb těhillôt*, "the sitter of praise-songs" is not quite clear; however, see Gunkel and Begrich, *Einleitung*, 95 (emendation of text); Frank-Lothar Hossfeld and Erich Zenger, *Die Psalmen 1–50* (DNEB; Würzburg: Echter, 1993), 149 (a spiritual transformation of "sitting on cherubs," Pss 80:2; 99:1).

23. The interpretation of Ps 8 is difficult, especially as far as v. 3 is concerned (cf. Joel 2:16).

The absence of support for YHWH is contrasted by numerous implicit assertions to keep up with his praise and thus contribute to God's will and ability to help:

> I will bless YHWH at all times;
> his praise shall continually be in my mouth....
> O magnify YHWH with me,
> and let us exalt his name together. (Ps 34:2, 4)

It seems that the worshippers of YHWH, be they human or of other nature, by praising YHWH not only motivate him to take action but also contribute to him essential power for his activity. Just as the human monarch gains strength by acknowledgement and veneration bestowed on him by his subjects, ancient gods thrive on the laudatory songs of their worshippers (cf. "Sing to YHWH a new song," Pss 33:3; 96:1; 98:1; 144:9; 149:1; Isa 42:10; "blessed/praised"[24] be YHWH," Pss 28:6; 31:22; 41:14; 66:20; 68:20.36; 72:18.19; 89:53, etc.). Praise of God is not only a grateful and overwhelming acknowledgement of majesty and graciousness but, even more, a creative act of generating those beneficial forces and transferring them to the deity, or offering them as due tribute.

This impression is strengthened by looking at Mesopotamian hymns and the functioning of their praise capacity. Most of all, Sumerian praise songs, dominating cultic ceremonies for more than a full millennium even after the language had given way in daily and worldly affairs to Akkadian idioms (around 2000 B.C.E.), give us vivid pictures of gods *receiving* eulogies and they themselves *spending* good words, destinies, and blessings on each other and on terrestrial entities, human as well as natural, religious, or cultural phenomena. Along this vein we meet, for instance, in one of the most ancient hymns, Enlil speaking "in praise" (*zà-mí*) of Keš, thus attributing divine powers to the temple.[25] The high priestess of Inana, in a famous poem (ETCSL 4.07.2, lines 60–65) recites a holy praise song which is tantamount to enumerating and fortifying the divine powers of

---

24. There is a fundamental discussion about an alleged "magic" force of the *bārûk*-formula. See J. Scharbert, "ברך," *ThWAT* 1:817; James K. Aitken, *The Semantics of Blessing and Cursing in Ancient Hebrew* (ANESSupS 23; Leuven: Peeters, 2007); Martin Leuenberger, *Segen und Segenstheologien im alten Israel* (AThANT 90; Zürich: Theologischer Verlag, 2008).

25. ETCSL 4.80.2 line 9.

the goddess (= ME). Šulgi, second king of the Ur III-dynasty, places great emphasis on hymn singing on his own behalf; he craftily indulges in the specific genre of "self-praise." One of his texts (Šulgi E, ETCSL 2.4.2.05) urges posterity not to forget those strengthening cultic performances in order to keep up the king's name and existence. In short, there is a very broad testimony in the corpus of Sumerian praise songs, as well as in later ancient Near Eastern specimens of praise texts, of the vital part they played in the upkeep of the good world order, natural as well as just societal processes, or let us say, life and history on earth. Hymn singing sustains all beings, conferring strength to everything and everybody in need of it. Small wonder that hymns in the Sumerian tradition are very much aligned with or directed to those divine powers (ME) that permeate the whole universe and which, strangely for us to acknowledge, are not identical with personalized divinities. The ME can work on their own, although they are also considered "properties" of deities, temples, and possibly kings. They may be conferred from one to other entities, and they even can be given away or stolen from their holders, as the mythical story of Inana and Enki (ETCSL 1.3.1) shows. But if we look closely at the Bible, we may discover traces of similar impersonal forces such as "Justice," "Truth," "Wisdom," and so on (Pss 36:6–7; 43:3; 85:11–12; 89:15; 117:2) in our Scriptures.

Recognition of competing powers everywhere in the existing world, which may be influenced by strong and determined expressions of powerful praise after and beside the Sumerian example, can be followed through the history of Mesopotamian psalm singing.[26] Old Testament hymns take part in the Mesopotamian, Levantine, and Egyptian traditions, as past research has proven many times.[27] It may be affirmed also for the hymnic genres, therefore, what Aitken proposes for blessing and curse: "Words are power-laden," not per se, but because of the semantic conventions in which they are embedded.[28] The decisive difference which we may discover in the ancient Near Eastern texts may be exactly the one hinted at before: hymnic

---

26. Groneberg, for example, has collected young-Babylonian materials (cf. Groneberg, *Syntax*). She distinguishes between "incantations," "sacral lyrics" (being of private, edifying nature), "cult hymns," and "narrative literature." Sacral lyrics are her field of investigation.

27. In a model kind of elaboration Patrick D. Miller Jr. (*They Cried to the Lord*), has demonstrated the close relationship of Israel's prayers to ancient Near Eastern supplication and praise. He cites many relevant studies pointing in exactly this direction.

28. Aitken, *Semantics*, 21.

language of old may not (as in our Western protestant theological perception) open up a binary rift between divine and human being—in fostering poetic, conceptual, theological, or intellectual juxtapositions—but rather may emphasize the unity of all existence and a common responsibility for order and justice by recognizing participation of all agents in the universal power play. Synergism, so much abhorred in Christian doctrine, was natural to old Mesopotamians and probably also to most Old Testament witnesses. YHWH's words, deeds, bodily parts, and properties, after all, are in many texts of the Hebrew Bible agents in their own rights (see his "arms," "hands," "utterances," "love," "justice," "glory," "presence," "face," "wings," "angel (messenger)," "wrath," "dwelling," "authority," "strength," "plan," "foresight," "commandment," "aura," "house," etc.).

Conclusions

Poetic language in the ancient Mesopotamian world, as a refined means of articulation, is not content with descriptive and ordering speech; it always approaches borderlines of world interpretation penetrating into the mechanisms of all human and transhuman affairs. Praise rhetoric, in particular, visualizes the world in flux. It recognizes leading global players, known and unknown, personal or impersonal, which must be identified in their responsibilities. By enhancing the positive powers of the acting agents, the laudations presented to them in high moods of festive joy and awe, supported by music (and sacrifices?), praise oratory becomes a meaningful part of promoting world order and well-being of people and environments. It seems less the innate capacity of verbal expressions that makes poetic praise language a suitable receptacle for powerful action, but the creative, ceremonial enactment of laudation resounding in human religious history that forms and transforms the world.

In this fashion, cultic laudation is more than an aesthetic performance or an expression of theological exuberance, more also than a thanksgiving response to God's actions. Gerhard von Rad had a wonderful notion that Israel's hymnic praise was considered continually necessary for the upkeep of wholesome and blessed life.[29] What we may add and perhaps

---

29. See von Rad, *Theologie*, 1:353–54: "Unceasingly Israel gave praise to Yahweh. That late period which finally nominated the Psalter in Hebrew "*tehillim,*" even comprehended the whole supplicatory discourse of Israel including numerous complaints and laments and those didactically meditating psalms as one single, multi-voiced

modify in this concept of "hymnic necessity" is on the one hand the fact that Israel was fully embedded in and taken along by the broad stream of ancient Near Eastern traditions of singing praises to the agents of power. The other insight may be that, together with other hymnologies, Old Testament praise rhetoric is based on what is, from our perspective, quite an unorthodox concept of God and humanity. Even the most high deity is deeply entangled with all the active forces in this world, including nature and human beings, rivers, earth, and beasts. They, too, it seems to be expected, should step in to articulate, implement, and promote the generative dominion of the benign forces for all beings. The adequacy of poetic communication with the Divine is neither questioned, nor analyzed, nor reflected upon. It is taken for granted and practiced in jubilant songs.

Letting go of idealistic bifurcations of being, we may say that poetry, especially of the hymnic types, propels history to the better. As Natan Sznaider, a sociologist in Tel Aviv, Israel, states it, referring to a German expressionist writer: "Paul Celan called a poem once a 'bottled message, to be posted in perils of drowning, hopefully to be carried to the heart-soul-land.' 'Poems,' continues Celan, 'are also on their way in this fashion: They are aiming at something. What are they aiming at? At something receptive, something to be occupied, maybe at an open minded You, or a sensitive reality.' "[30]

BIBLIOGRAPHY

Aitken, James K. *The Semantics of Blessing and Cursing in Ancient Hebrew.* ANESSupS 23. Leuven: Peeters, 2007.
Alonso Schökel, Luis. *A Manual of Hebrew Poetics.* SubBi 11. Rome: Pontificio Istituto Biblico, 1988.

---

eulogy of Yahweh." And see 359: "Creation and sustenance of the world by Yahweh certainly was one of the noblest topics in Old Testament hymns, but surely not their last word. Singing praises included still another special knowledge about this world. Because it has been created by Yahweh so miraculously and is wondrously sustained by him, the world possesses such a glory, that it radiates all by itself praise and testimony; in other words: The world is not only an object of laudation but a performing subject as well."

30. Natan Sznaider, "Das moralische Gefühl," *Frankfurter Rundschau* 262 (10 November 2010): 32. Translated by E. S. Gerstenberger.

Berlin, Adele. "Poetry, Hebrew Bible." Pages 290–96 in vol. 2 of *Dictionary of Biblical Interpretation*. 2 vols. Edited by John H. Hayes. Nashville: Abingdon, 1999.

Black, Jeremy. "Poesie/Poetry." *Reallexicon der Assyriologie* 10 (2003–2005): 593–97.

———. *Reading Sumerian Poetry*. London: Athlone, 1998.

Bowra, Maurice C. *Primitive Song*. Cleveland: World, 1962.

Brueggemann, Walter. *Israel's Praise: Doxology against Idolatry and Ideology*. Philadelphia: Fortress, 1988.

Elliot, Dale E. "Toward a Grammar of Exclamations." *Foundations of Language* 11 (1974): 231–46.

Groneberg, Brigitte R. M. *Syntax, Morphologie, und Stil der jungbabylonischen "hymnischen" Literatur*. 2 vols. FAOS 14. Stuttgart: Steiner, 1987.

Gunkel, Hermann, and Joachim Begrich. *Einleitung in die Psalmen: Die Gattungen der religiösen Lyrik Israels*. Göttingen: Vandenhoeck, 1933. Repr. 1985. Translated by James Nogalski as *Introduction to the Psalms*. Atlanta: Mercer University Press, 1998.

Hossfeld, Frank-Lothar, and Erich Zenger. *Die Psalmen 1–50*. DNEB. Würzburg: Echter, 1993.

Leuenberger, Martin. *Segen und Segenstheologien im alten Israel:Untersuchungen zu ihren religions-und theologiegeschichtlichen Konstellationen und Transformationen*. AThANT 90. Zürich: Theologischer, 2008.

Michalowski, Piotr. "Ancient Poetics." Pages 141–53 in *Mesopotamian Poetic Language*. Edited by Marianna E. Vogelzang and H. L. J. Vanstiphout. Groningen: STYX, 1996.

Miller, Patrick D. Jr. *They Cried to the Lord: The Form and Theology of Biblical Prayer*. Minneapolis: Fortress, 1994.

———. "The Theological Significance of Poetry." Pages 225–30 in *Language, Theology, and the Bible*. Edited by Samuel B. Balentine and John Barton. Oxford: Clarendon, 1994.

Mowinckel, Sigmund. *Psalmenstudien* . Kristiania: SNVAO, 1921, 1922. Repr. 1961.

———. *The Psalms in Israel's Worship*. 2 vols. Nashville: Abingdon, 1962.

Rad, Gerhard von. *Theologie des Alten Testaments*. 2 vols. Munich: Chr. Kaiser, 1957.

Ringgren, Helmer. "*hll* I und II," in *ThWAT* 2:433–41.

Rosengren, Inger. "Zur Grammatik und Pragmatik der Exklamation." Pages 263–306 in vol. 1 of *Satz und Illokution*. Edited by Inger Rosengren. Linguistische Arbeiten 278. Tübingen: Niemeyer, 1992.

Scharbert, J. *ThWAT* 1:817.

Sznaider, Natan. "Das moralische Gefühl." *Frankfurter Rundschau* 262 (10 Nov 2010): 32. Translated by E. S. Gerstenberger.

Vogelzang, Marianna E., and Herman L. J. Vanstiphout, eds. *Mesopotamian Poetic Language: Sumerian and Akkadian: Proceedings of the Groningen Group for the Study of Mesopotamian Literature*, vol. 2. CM 6. Groningen: STYX, 1996.

Wendt, Herbert, and Norbert Loacker, eds., *Kindlers Enzyklopädie: Der Mensch*. 10 vols. Zürich: Kindler, 1981–1985.

Westermann, Claus. *Lob und Klage in den Psalmen*. 5th ed. Göttingen: Vandenhoeck, 1977. Translated by Keith R. Crim and Richard N. Soulen as *Praise and Lament in the Psalms*. Atlanta: John Knox, 1981.

Wilcke, Claus. "Formale Gesichtspunkte in der sumerischen Literatur." Pages 205–316 in *Sumerological Studies in Honour of Thorkild Jacobsen on the Occasion of His Seventieth Birthday*. AS 20. Edited by Stephen J. Lieberman. Chicago: University of Chicago Press, 1974.

Philosophical Perspectives on Religious Diversity as Emergent Property in the Redaction/Composition of the Psalter*

Jaco Gericke

Introduction

There is a humorous Zen story that alludes, among other things, to the philosophical problem of religious diversity in relation to the question of truth:

> In a monastery, two monks argued about one point regarding their master's teaching. One said yes and the other said no. Finally, they came in front of their master telling their understanding of the teaching. After the first monk explained why he said yes, the master nodded his head and said that he was correct. The first monk was then very happy and went away. The other monk, of course, was not happy. He also explained to the master why he said no. Thinking for a while, the master also nodded his head and said that he was also correct. The monk was then satisfied and went away. A little monk who was sitting beside the master was very puzzled. He said to his master, "Master, I do not understand. They cannot be both right. The master replied with a smile, "You are correct too!"[1]

On many religious-philosophical issues, different views exist among different subjects, despite the fact that they might be equally knowledgeable and sincere. Those who have access to the same information and are equally

---

* This paper was originally presented as part of the ProPsalm 2012 proceedings at the University of Pretoria, South Africa.

1. This anecdote, which exists in many versions, was retrieved from "You Are Correct Too," *Zen Story*. Online: http://www.buddhistdoor.com/OldWeb/bdoor/archive/zen_story/zen7.htm.

interested in the truth often hold contradictory perspectives on many topics related to religious thought. This phenomenon is called religious diversity or pluralism[2] and can fruitfully be explored in many ways—for instance, from psychological, anthropological, or historical perspectives.[3] In the context of the composition and redaction of the Psalter, instances of religious diversity have likewise been noted in discussions of the plurality of theologies in that corpus.[4] A plurality of theologies emerges as a result of particular compositional and redaction processes in the Psalter's history. Conspicuously absent from research on this latter topic, however, is the involvement of analytic philosophy of religion.[5] In that current we find an emphasis on the problem of diversity, not only between different religions but also within and between traditions in the same religion:

> While it is still somewhat popular in philosophical circles today to focus on diversity among basic theistic systems, there is a growing awareness that the same basic questions (and responses) that apply to inter-system diversity … apply just as clearly, and in exactly the same sense, to intra-system diversity.[6]

Given this, we are in a position to pose the questions that constitute the research problem of the discussion to follow. Supposing we see the psalms as characterized by intrasystem diversity, what examples of theological pluralism do we encounter there? What kind of property does such pluralism instantiate in relation to the composition and redaction of the Psalter? What perspectives are available when theological pluralism in the psalms

---

2. The reference to pluralism here and elsewhere in this chapter is, unless otherwise specified, understood to be synonymous with the concept of religious diversity, i.e., the fact that in a given society there exist multiple religious perspectives. I do not use the term pluralism in any of its other popular senses, i.e., pluralism as referring to religious inclusivism, religious tolerance, or religious ecumenism.

3. See David Basinger, "Religious Diversity (Pluralism)," *The Stanford Encyclopedia of Philosophy (Spring 2012 Edition)*. Online: http://plato.stanford.edu/archives/spr2012/entries/religious-pluralism/.

4. See Erhard Gerstenberger, "Theologies in the Book of Psalms," in *The Book of Psalms: Composition and Reception* (ed. Peter Flint and Patrick D. Miller Jr.; Leiden: Brill, 2005), 603–26.

5. For an introduction, see the discussion in Phillip Quinn, "Religious Diversity: Familiar Problems, Novel Opportunities," in *The Oxford Handbook of Philosophy of Religion* (ed. William Wainwright; Oxford: Oxford University Press, 2005), 392–417.

6. Basinger, "Religious Diversity (Pluralism)."

is considered in relation to the question of truth or attitudes towards religious diversity? These are the questions that this chapter seeks to attend to. Clarification of the composition or redaction of particular psalms or of a part of the Psalter will be left to the other contributors to this volume.

With regard to objective, the aim of the presentation is to offer a descriptive philosophical perspective on intrareligious theological diversity as an emergent property of the Psalter in its format of being a redacted compositional whole. As for methodology, a historical and comparative philosophy of religion will be working in tandem with the history of religion to enable us to obtain an idiosyncratic elucidation of aspects of the conceptual contradictions between some of the theological propositions in a number of psalms. The hypothesis of this contribution is that the contradictions themselves are a direct result of the juxtaposing of divergent material through the redaction and composition of the Psalter as a quasi-unified whole. But before the discussion proper can follow, it is necessary to give some elementary, albeit relevant, background regarding the redactional/compositional turn in psalm studies.

THE REDACTIONAL/COMPOSITIONAL TURN IN THE STUDY OF THE PSALTER

It is by now common knowledge that during the heyday of historical criticism, the Psalter "was treated almost universally only as a disjointed assortment of diverse compositions that happened to be collected loosely together into what eventually became a canonical 'book' with no coherent structure and message."[7] During the last few decades, however, the prevailing interest in research on the psalms has shifted to questions concerning "the composition, editorial unity, and overall message of the Psalter as a *book*, i.e., as a literary and canonical entity that coheres with respect to structure and message, and with how individual psalms and collections fit together."[8] As David Howard notes:

> These studies diverge widely among themselves, but they can generally be categorized in two major groups: (1) those dealing with the macro-

---

7. David M. Howard, "Recent Trends in Psalms Studies," in *The Faces of Old Testament Studies: A Survey of Contemporary Approaches* (ed. Bill T. Arnold and David Baker; Grand Rapids: Baker Academic, 2005), 329, emphasis original.

8. Ibid., 330.

structure of the Psalter, i.e., overarching patterns and themes, and (2) those dealing with its microstructure, i.e., connections among smaller groupings of psalms, especially adjacent psalms. What they have in common is a renewed conviction that there are purposeful literary relationships between psalms and that the Psalter itself is a purposefully edited collection.[9]

Granting all of this, it must be remembered that the newly appreciated unity derived from the redaction and composition of the Psalter does not do away with the contradictions in the details of different psalms regarding a variety of theological subjects, as pointed out by historical criticism. What I mean by contradictions is not, as is popularly noted in discussions of theological pluralism, a plurality of social or historical contexts.[10] Nor is it identical to the crude lists of verbal discrepancies thrown up in popular atheist and fundamentalist apologetic discussions of "contradictions in the Bible." It is simply religious diversity that cannot be harmonized via an appeal to the fluidity and instabilities of metaphor and myth, since it involves mutually exclusive conceptual content.

Examples of such intra-Psalmic theological pluralism include the following cases:[11] whether or not YHWH sleeps (e.g., Pss 44:24 vs. 121:4), the role of the Leviathan/Rahab (e.g., Pss 74:13–14; 89:10 vs. 104:26), YHWH's relation to the dead (e.g., Pss 6:5; 88:10–12 vs. 139:8–10), contradictory images of the divine body, disagreements as to the existence of other gods (e.g., Pss 29:1; 58:1; 82:1; 97:7 vs. 96:5; 115:4–7), allusions to alternative accounts of creation (e.g., Pss 8:1–8; 33:6; 74:13–14; 104:24–26), different conceptions of the divine location (e.g., Pss 14:2; 115:3 vs. 139:8–10), discrepant beliefs concerning the relation between YHWH and moral evil (e.g., Pss 5:4 vs. 105:25), different accounts of historical chronological details (e.g., Pss 78:44–51 vs. 105:28–36), diverging views of the axiological status of royalty (e.g., Pss 45:7 vs. 146:3), conflicting beliefs about the nations (e.g., Pss 147:20 vs. 87:4–6), and a variety of anthropologies (e.g., Pss 8:5, vs. 103:14–16).

If the psalms featuring the motifs mentioned above stood by themselves, no contradictions would arise, despite the fact that contradictions

---

9. Ibid.

10. Gerstenberger, *Theologies in the Book of Psalms*, 603–26.

11. Of course, many more examples of contradictions could be given without making the point any clearer.

can occur within a single psalm as a result of redactional activity (e.g., Ps 89). This means that it is in fact the same processes of redaction and composition which was intended to unify the Psalter that led to the juxtaposing of radically divergent theological motifs between individual Psalms. Given the gaps in our knowledge of the world behind the text, the theological pluralism is of such a nature as cannot be neatly formalized via the logic of belief revision. What can be said, from a philosophical perspective, however, is that the discrepancies between theological propositions on the synchronic level instantiate themselves as religious diversity as emergent property on the diachronic level following centuries of ongoing redactional and compositional activities in the construction of the canonical Psalter.

Religious Diversity as an Emergent Property in the Psalter's Redaction/Composition

Emergence, according to one philosophical outline of the phenomenon, is a notorious philosophical term of art. The concept has been in use since at least the time of Aristotle. In art, emergence is used to explore the origins of novelty, creativity, and authorship. Emergence is central to the theories of integrative levels and of complex systems.[12] In philosophy, "emergence is often understood in relation to the aetiology of a system's properties."[13] An emergent property of a system, like the religious diversity in the Psalter, is one that is "not a property of any component of that system, but a feature of the system as a whole."[14] Put differently,

> An emergent behaviour or emergent property can appear when a number of simple entities (agents) operate in an environment, forming more complex behaviors as a collective. If emergence happens over disparate size scales, then the reason is usually a causal relation across different scales. In other words there is often a form of top-down feedback in systems with emergent properties....[15]

---

12. Timothy O'Connor and Hong Yu Wong, "Emergent Properties," *The Stanford Encyclopedia of Philosophy (Spring 2012 Edition)*. Online: http://plato.stanford.edu/archives/spr2012/entries/properties-emergent/.

13. Ibid.

14. Ibid.

15. Ibid.

In the context of the discussion, I use the term *emergence* to refer to the way complex contradictions and religious diversity arise in the Psalter out of a multiplicity of relatively simple interactions between various psalms as a result of their redactional juxtaposing. This usage of the notion "emergence" with reference to the psalms and their redaction/composition can be classified according to the traditional category of "weak emergence."[16] Weak emergence is present in the religious diversity of the Psalter in the ways in which contradictions arise as a result of the interactions between individual psalms. Yet if it could also be demonstrated that the Psalter as a book has qualities not directly traceable to individual compositions, but rather to how those compositions interact due to meso-level (e.g., the Songs of Ascent) and macro-level (e.g., books 1–5) supervenience on its components (individual psalms), we can even speak of strong emergence.[17]

The general implication of redaction and composition criticism is that the theological pluralism in the psalms appeared when a number of simple elements in the redaction/ composition began to operate in a context in which more complex behaviors were formed that manifested themselves within the collective. In this regard, it is useful to borrow and reapply terms from Connor and Wong's discussion of emergent properties and to distinguish the following three forms of emergent structures in the psalms.[18]

1. A first-order emergent structure occurred as a result of synchronic conceptual interactions between individual psalms.
2. A second-order emergent structure involved diachronic conceptual interactions played out sequentially over time.
3. A third-order emergent structure was a consequence of synchronic, diachronic, and editorial (redactional/compositional) interactions.

The processes from which religious diversity as emergent property may have occurred in the psalms can be identified by their patterns of accumulating change or growth. Pluralism as emergent behavior occurred as a result of intricate causal relations across different compositional and redactional scales, that is, interconnectivity. Religious diversity as an

---

16. Ibid.
17. Ibid.
18. Ibid.

emergent property in the psalms is therefore a systemic feature of the Psalter as a complex system that could not be predicted from the standpoint of a preemergent stage, despite the composers' and redactors' thorough knowledge of the features and their creation of structures governing the relations between various parts.

One reason why religious diversity as emergent property in the Psalter is hard to quantify is the indefinite number of interactions between compositional components of the Psalter, which also increased with the number of redactional components, thus potentially allowing for many new and subtle types of behavior to emerge. On the other hand, merely having a large number of interactions is not enough by itself to guarantee the presence of theological pluralism in the Psalms as emergent behavior. Many of the interactions may be negligible, or may cancel each other out, or a large number of interactions may even work against the emergence of religious diversity as a result of redactional harmonization.[19] A necessary condition for theological pluralism as emergent property, therefore, was the temporary repression or ignorance of its reality. Connections were allowed to coexist in contradictory states to encourage the emergence of theological pluralism; it was never just about the sheer number of connections between components.

Given this state of affairs, two pitfalls still claim victims in redaction and composition criticism whenever they attempt to read the Psalter as a unified whole: *a fallacy of division* occurs when one reasons logically that because something is true of the psalms as a whole it must also be true of all or some of its parts; and conversely, *a fallacy of composition* arises when one infers that something is true of the psalms as a whole from the fact that it is true of some *part* of the whole (or even of *every* proper part).

The implication of this is that there is no single theological perspective in the psalms regarding the details of most issues of interest to Old Testament theologians. Thus while redaction and composition criticism has stressed a return to the unity of the Psalter as a book, theological criticism is needed to remind us that this does nothing to refute the insights of the historical critics regarding the problem of religious diversity as emergent property in the synchronic and diachronic configurations of discourse in the psalms.

---

19. Ibid.

INTRA-PSALMIC RELIGIOUS DIVERSITY AND THE QUESTION OF TRUTH

It is only natural in the context of analytic philosophy of religion to ask about what theological pluralism implies for the question of truth (or meaningfulness) with regard to the propositions about YHWH in the God-talk of the Psalter. Our context is biblical scholarship and not philosophy proper. However, the question is not how individual composers of the Psalms or the redactors would have viewed the problem of pluralism in relation to truth. It would be presumptuous to assume that they were aware of all the contradictions of the final corpus. To be sure, we see attempted harmonies and bridges between individual psalms and between the five books, which presuppose an awareness of tensions. Yet these redactional activities appear to have been attempts to create topical coherence and narrative flow rather than ways with which to reconcile theological inconsistencies.

Again, because the context of our inquiry is biblical scholarship and not philosophy proper, neither is the objective here to be normative and prescriptive, that is, to assert what exactly the plurality of theologies in the Psalter are and what they are supposed to imply with regard to the truth (or untruth) of the psalms for readers today. Rather, in this section I shall seek simply to note various philosophical options available for how religious diversity in the Psalter could be conceptualized in relation to the question of truth. Basinger writes:

> One obvious response to religious diversity is to maintain that since there exists no divine reality—since the referent in all religious truth claims related to the divine is nonexistent—all such claims are false. Another possible response, put forth by religious relativists, is that there is no one truth when considering mutually incompatible religious claims about reality; more than one of the conflicting sets of specific truth-claims can be correct.... However, most current discussions of religious diversity presuppose a realist theory of truth—that there is a truth to the matter.[20]

If one assumes that there must be some truth to the Psalter's contradictory claims about YHWH then Raimundo Panikkar's construction of four major attitudes that can be adopted in inter- and intrareligious dialogue may be helpful for imagining a response to the religious diversity under

---

20. Basinger, "Religious Diversity (Pluralism)," *n.p.*

consideration: exclusivism, inclusivism, parallelism, and interpenetration.[21] The scheme is not without its shortcomings,[22] yet it might be considered functional for the purpose of clarifying possible states of affairs obtaining within the theological pluralism of the Psalter vis-à-vis truth-conditional classifications.[23]

Exclusivism can be construed as the simple, naive belief that one particular beloved psalm's theology is true. If that is the case then anything contradictory in other psalms must be false. Simple as this may seem, this view generates many problems, not least of which is the absence of an absolute standard internal to the Psalter. Moreover, it assumes a myopic view of truth—one dependent on classical logic, on top of epistemological naivete. If truth is multisided, then even if individual psalms offer a strictly exclusive language, it comes down to interpretation.[24]

Inclusivism involves the conditional claim that the truth of a given psalm is complete, while those of other psalms are partially true. An inclusivist attitude would therefore seek to reinterpret "apparent" discrepancies to make them more compatible. A bold contradiction will be papered over with explanations of different levels of truth. Thus, the inclusivist might appeal to formal or existential truths, rather than to an essential one. This seems magnanimous and grand—every psalmist follows his own path. Being inclusive may mean being at peace with pluralism. Its difficulty is a paradoxical concept of truth. It is paradoxical once the inclusive attitude becomes theory and practice. If the Psalter's truth is all-inclusive, then the truth of any given psalm's theology becomes relative and lacks truly independent intellectual content. Truth itself becomes one thing for one psalmist and something else for another. Yet the inclusivist assumes she is beyond the limitations of relative truth, and slots every psalm's theology in a place within the inclusivist's supersystem. She claims to a superior point of view, even if she insists that her view is one among many. At bottom

---

21. See Raimundo Panikkar, *The Intrareligious Dialogue* (New York: Paulist, 1999).

22. See Gwen Griffith-Dickson, *The Philosophy of Religion* (London: SCM, 2005), 8.

23. The following is indebted to and represents a reapplication of the generic summary in "Religious Attitudes," *The Galilean Magazine and Library*. Online: http://www.galilean-library.org/site/index.php/topic/3762-religious-attitudes/.

24. Ibid.

the inclusivist claims to a greater truth while all the others are limited to relative truths.[25]

Parallelism is the view that different theologies in the psalm run parallel towards the ultimate (knowledge of YHWH), despite deviations or tangential detours. Thus the Psalter consists of the parallel paths, and the redactors' respected alternative views as enriching their own tradition in order to finally meet at the finish line. This attitude is tolerant, both respectful and nonjudgmental, and there is no syncretism or eclecticism to blur the distinct parallel lines. All psalms are basically different paths that lead to the same summit. All are right, while using different means to gain the same goal. Of course, the difficulties with this view include the fact that parallelism clearly contradicts the historical experience of individual psalmists and ideological communities. It assumes that all traditions are part of a growth process, that every tradition is self-sufficient, and that there is no possible mutual learning, and it denies the possibility of walking a new path outside of them. It seems flattering to presume that the psalms have everything needed for religious maturity. Yet parallelism fragments the Psalter into fixed compartments and allows only for growth rather than mutation.[26]

Interpenetration maintains that all psalmists seek understanding, and that this search is a matter of interpenetration. It is the understanding that the existence of every psalmist's theology also implies another's, and thus everyone is related in many ways. More precisely, the beliefs of other psalms may challenge as well as enrich and lead to better understanding of what may be seen as complementary and sometimes supplementary. Many psalmists accept the ideas of others. Basically one psalm may not be understandable without a background understanding of the Psalter in general. Perhaps no religious consciousness in the Psalter could be distinguished without the existence of other religious consciousness in the same corpus. No psalm is utterly foreign. The problem with this view is of course its wishful thinking. Can contradictory psalms and concepts of YHWH truly "interpenetrate" one another? Or do they exclude? How can we interpret them? How is this not merely a small adjustment of the traditions themselves? Is this interpenetration of psalmic theologies a cherry-picking from the main traditions while skirting others? Is the psalmic

---

25. Ibid.
26. Ibid.

theological cosmos large enough to contain logically incommensurable ideas? [27]

It is not clear which, if any, of these views (or the objections to them) it is appropriate to adopt in the context of a purely descriptive philosophy of religion. Contrary to a popular liberal view, however, one cannot simply be anachronistically ecumenical and insist that the redacted Psalter operates with some fuzzy nonclassical logic in which both A and not-A can be affirmed because the composers and redactors were not themselves historical critics and might not even have been aware of or cared in the same sense we do for the full extent of the religious diversity in the psalms from which they constructed the Psalter as a book. From an evaluative perspective, however, things are certainly different and openended, and readers can and probably will decide for themselves how best to view the religious diversity in the psalms and whether it has anything to do with the question of truth in the logical sense. A look at the way in which the concept of truth is used in the psalms itself shows that its philosophical connotation is not the only available option.[28]

CONCLUSION

The aim of this essay is to clarify religious pluralism as emergent property in the redaction/composition of the Psalter. Though working philosophically, this paper simply sought to describe what is there and how it may be viewed. In doing so it offered no critical evaluative judgments to harmonize contradictory theologies for apologetic purposes in the quest for final answers or absolute truth. In this I sought to follow the tradition of the later Wittgenstein, who considered it the task of philosophy as clarification only, that is, to leave everything as it is.

---

27. Ibid.

28. See Jaco Gericke, "But Is It True? Philosophical Theories of Truth and the Interpretation of Psalms in the Book of Hebrews," in *Psalms and Hebrews: Studies in Reception* (ed. Dirk Human and G. Steyn; New York: T&T Clark, 2010), 27–51; see also Don Cupitt, *Philosophy's Own Religion* (London: SCM, 2001), 42, who made the same point with reference to the use of the concept of truth in the Gospel of John.

Bibliography

Basinger, David. "Religious Diversity (Pluralism)." *The Stanford Encyclope-dia of Philosophy (Spring 2012 Edition)*. Online: http://plato.stanford.edu/archives/spr2012/entries/religious-pluralism/.

Cupitt, Don. *Philosophy's Own Religion*. London: SCM, 2001.

Gericke, Jaco. "But Is It True? Philosophical Theories of Truth and the Interpretation of Psalms in the Book of Hebrews." Pages 27–51 in *Psalms and Hebrews: Studies in Reception*. Edited by Dirk Human and Gert Steyn. New York: T&T Clark, 2010.

Gerstenberger, Erhard. "Theologies in the Book of Psalms." Pages 603–26 in *The Book of Psalms: Composition and Reception*. Edited by Peter Flint and Patrick D. Miller Jr. Leiden: Brill, 2005.

Griffith-Dickson, Gwen. *The Philosophy of Religion*. London: SCM, 2005.

Howard, David M. "Recent Trends in Psalms Studies." Pages 329–68 in *The Face of Old Testament Studies: A Survey of Contemporary Approaches*. Edited by Bill T. Arnold and David Baker. Grand Rapids: Baker Academic, 2005.

O'Connor, Timothy, and Hong Yu Wong. "Emergent Properties." In *The Stanford Encyclopedia of Philosophy (Spring 2012 Edition)*. Online: http://plato.stanford.edu/archives/spr2012/entries/properties-emergent/.

Panikkar, Raimon. *The Intrareligious Dialogue*. New York: Paulist, 1999.

Quinn, Phillip. "Religious Diversity: Familiar Problems, Novel Opportunities." Pages 392–417 in *The Oxford Handbook of Philosophy of Religion*. Edited by William Wainwright. Oxford: Oxford University Press, 2005.

"Religious Attitudes." *The Galilean Magazine and Library*. Online: http://www.galilean-library.org/site/index.php/topic/3762-religious-attitudes/.

"You Are Correct Too." *Zen Story*. Online: http://www.buddhistdoor.com/OldWeb/bdoor/archive/zen_story/zen7.htm.

LET US CAST OFF THEIR ROPES FROM US:
THE EDITORIAL SIGNIFICANCE OF THE PORTRAYAL
OF FOREIGN NATIONS IN PSALMS 2 AND 149*

Derek E. Wittman

INTRODUCTION

The Hebrew Psalter's second and penultimate psalms (Pss 2 and 149) contain the collection's first and last words portraying God as a royal figure and its initial and final references to foreign nations. The juxtaposition of these topics in the introduction and conclusion of the Psalter is striking, particularly when one considers that both Pss 2 and 149 contain unflattering portrayals of foreign nations that specifically feature the humiliation of their kings. To the extent that one considers emphasis on God's kingship to be a key feature of the canonical Psalter's final shape, the vivid portrayal of the nations and their kings in these two psalms strongly suggests that a complete description of God's reign in the collection must take into account its implications for foreign nations. My purposes in this essay are to explore the rhetorical effect of the negative portrayal of foreign nations in Pss 2 and 149 and to describe how it relates to the emphasis on God's kingship in the Psalter. I contend that the rhetoric of these two psalms predisposes readers of the Psalter toward a negative evaluation of foreign nations and connects with the dominant motif of God's kingship in such a way that it causes the Psalter's affirmation of God's kingship to function as a statement of resistance against foreign occupiers.

---

* This paper was originally presented as part of a session of the Book of Psalms Section of the Society of Biblical Literature annual meeting on 20 November 2011 in San Francisco.

Previous Scholarship on Foreign Nations in the Psalms

Discussion of the topic of foreign nations in the Psalter has tended to focus on the degree to which the enemies referenced in it are non-Israelites.[1] Harris Birkeland identifies a typical pattern according to which psalmists characterize enemies, regardless of whether they specifically mention that the enemies are foreign.[2] On that basis, he surmises that all enemies mentioned in the individual laments are foreign.[3] Taking into account psalms of other genres, he concludes that the religious perspective of the Psalter is that of "the extreme, frequently fanatical, nationalistic line."[4] For him, Israelite religion as portrayed in the psalms consistently ascribes righteousness and piety to Israel while viewing foreign nations as the only evildoers mentioned in the Psalter.[5]

Hans-Joachim Kraus and Steven Croft maintain that foreign nations are generally portrayed as enemies when they appear in the Psalter, but that there are also enemies represented in it who are not foreign. Kraus observes that foreign nations constitute one of several categories of enemies in the collection. With regard to the royal psalms, he notes that the king's enemies are simultaneously the enemies of Israel, and they are considered to be military threats to the nation.[6] These psalms set up an opposition between God and foreign nations, and the king defeats them on God's behalf.[7] The king does not play such a prominent role in communal psalms, but the vocabulary used to describe foreign nations is

---

1. See my summary of this body of literature in Derek E. Wittman, "The Kingship of Yahweh and the Politics of Poverty and Oppression in the Hebrew Psalter" (Ph.D. diss., Baylor University, 2010), 85–92.

2. Harris Birkeland, *The Evildoers in the Book of Psalms* (Oslo: Dybwad, 1955), 17.

3. Ibid., 31.

4. Ibid., 57. See also the similar comments of Erhard Gerstenberger, who observes commonalities in the portrayals of enemies in individual and communal laments and notes that victory and royal psalms (including Pss 2, 45, 68, 72, and 110) share features in common with the communal laments as well, Erhard Gerstenberger, "Enemies and Evildoers in the Psalms: A Challenge to Christian Preaching," *HBT* 4 (1983): 64–66.

5. Birkeland, *The Evildoers in the Book of Psalms*, 60.

6. Hans-Joachim Kraus, *Theology of the Psalms* (trans. Keith Crim; Minneapolis: Augsburg, 1986), 126.

7. Ibid., 126–27.

unchanged. God opposes the ambitions of the nations and repels their attempts at invasion.[8]

Kraus conceives of the individual psalmist's enemies as people who come between God and those who are poor and weak,[9] but he does not specify that they are foreign. He also identifies mythical powers associated with the primeval forces of chaos as enemies.[10] For Kraus, then, foreign nations are hostile figures in the Psalter, but the psalmists also refer to other types of enemies.

Steven Croft also critiques the sweeping breadth of Birkeland's thesis. He notes psalms that function as counterexamples to it and observes that the nationalistic religion that Birkeland identifies in the Psalter is inconsistent with the broader theology of the Hebrew Bible, claiming that Birkeland's view of language is excessively rigid.[11] Croft acknowledges that many psalms overtly portray foreign nations as enemies. For example, he refers to the wicked (רשעים) in Pss 140, 125, and 129 as "foreign military enemies."[12] He also identifies twenty-four additional psalms as "war psalms" in which the enemies (איבים) are foreign nations.[13] He understands the enemies in Ps 106 to be foreign as well.[14] For Croft, then, the Psalter's portrayal of foreign nations is more complex than Birkeland claims, but the enemies are foreign in two of every three psalms that mention them.[15]

In *The God of Israel and the Nations*, Norbert Lohfink and Erich Zenger argue that several psalms reflect a positive and welcoming stance

---

8. Ibid., 127.

9. Ibid., 132–33.

10. Ibid., 134.

11. Steven J. L. Croft, *The Identity of the Individual in the Psalms* (JSOTSup 44; Sheffield: Sheffield Academic, 1987), 17–18.

12. Ibid., 32.

13. Croft's category of "war psalms" includes Pss 8, 18, 21, 27, 42–43, 44, 45, 56, 59, 61, 66, 69, 72, 74, 78, 80, 81, 83, 89, 102, 110, 132, 138, 143 (ibid., 34–40).

14. Ibid., 43.

15. Ibid., 48. The diversity of the category of enemies in the Psalter is further evident in light of Gerald Sheppard's demonstration that, in some psalms, "prayers are assumed to be overheard or, later, heard about by friends and enemies alike; and, furthermore, 'enemies' mentioned in these prayers belong to the very same social setting in which one prays." Gerald T. Sheppard, "'Enemies' and the Politics of Prayer in the Book of Psalms," in *The Bible and the Politics of Exegesis: Essays in Honor of Norman K. Gottwald on His Sixty-Fifth Birthday* (ed. David Jobling, Peggy L. Day, and Gerald T. Sheppard; Cleveland: Pilgrim, 1991), 72.

toward foreign nations. They undertake to enrich Jewish-Christian dialogue through theological analysis of the motifs of Torah, covenant, and the pilgrimage of the nations to Zion in Isaiah and the Psalter.[16] Lohfink's reading of Ps 25, for example, treats it as the prayer of a non-Israelite who prays for the well-being of Israel in verse 22.[17] In his reading of Ps 33, Lohfink argues that God's frustration of the plans of the peoples in verse 10 does not preclude the notion that God may have plans for a positive future for them,[18] and he notes the surprising lack of explicit reference to Israel in the covenantal language in verse 12.[19] He concludes that it is possible that the nations are included among God's chosen people in Ps 33.[20]

Zenger maintains that Ps 87 references a "world family" governed by God from Zion,[21] an image that differs markedly from God's judgment against the nations in Ps 83.[22] Further, Zenger views book 4 of the Psalter as an invitation to the nations to engage in a voluntary pilgrimage to Zion, the seat of God's reign, where they will experience peaceful coexistence with Israel.[23]

Lohfink's and Zenger's observations are helpful, but it seems to me that they have identified a handful of possible exceptions that prove a broader rule, particularly in light of the Psalter's ubiquitous explicit references to foreign nations as enemies to which both Birkeland and Croft call attention. Birkeland rightly identifies a consistent nationalistic tone in the Psalter, and he and Croft highlight a critical mass of explicit references to foreign nations as enemies in it. I also find persuasive the arguments of Croft and Kraus that not all of the enemies in the Psalter are foreign, but rather that they include mythic forces of chaos and even some enemies within Israel. The explicit polemic against foreign nations in the Psalter, however, is sufficiently frequent and consistent to warrant viewing it as being a significant concern in the editorial shaping of the collection. Significantly, Pss

---

16. Norbert Lohfink and Erich Zenger, *The God of Israel and the Nations: Studies in Isaiah and the Psalms* (Collegeville, Minn.: Liturgical, 2000), 34–36.

17. Ibid., 80.

18. Ibid., 116.

19. Ibid., 109.

20. Ibid., 116.

21. Ibid., 160.

22. Ibid., 148.

23. Ibid., 190.

2 and 149 link that polemic with the theme of God's kingship, so it is to the analysis of these psalms that I now turn.

PSALMS 2 AND 149: LITERARY RELATIONSHIP, PRIMACY, AND RECENCY

Various interpreters of the Psalter have observed a literary relationship between Pss 2 and 149. James Limburg notes that both share language that references Zion and kingship.[24] Nancy deClaissé-Walford suggests reading the fate of the nations in Ps 149 as the consequence of their failure to heed the command to fear and serve God that is issued to them at the end of Ps 2.[25] Robert Cole cites the psalms' shared references to nations, peoples, foreign kings, materials made of iron, and the act of binding.[26] Clinton McCann notes that the two psalms reference nations, peoples, kings, and especially divine sovereignty. He calls attention to the presence of a Davidic figure in Ps 2 that is absent from Ps 149, arguing that "Psalm 149 completes the movement of transferring the Davidic theology to the whole people, since after asserting God's sovereignty (vv. 1-3), it assigns to the 'faithful' the task of concretely implementing God's sovereignty in the world, a task Psalm 2 assigns to the monarchy."[27] This "democratization" of kingship is also noted in commentaries by James Mays, William Brown, and John Goldingay. [28] There thus appears to be ample justification for reading these psalms in relation to one another.

The canonical placement of Pss 2 and 149 in the Psalter's introduction (Pss 1-2) and conclusion (Pss 146-150) is significant. Dennis Tucker discusses these groupings as "strategic locations" that provide what he calls a "hermeneutical horizon" for the interpretation of the Psalter,[29] and such a

---

24. James Limburg, *Psalms* (Louisville: Westminster John Knox, 2000), 503.

25. Nancy deClaissé-Walford, *Reading from the Beginning: The Shaping of the Hebrew Psalter* (Macon, Ga.: Mercer University Press, 1997), 102.

26. Robert Cole, "An Integrated Reading of Psalms 1 and 2," *JSOT* 98 (2002): 80.

27. J. Clinton McCann Jr., "The Book of Psalms," in *The New Interpreter's Bible: A Commentary in Twelve Volumes* (ed. Leander E. Keck; Nashville: Abingdon, 1994), 4:1274.

28. James L. Mays, *Psalms* (IBC; Louisville: Westminster John Knox, 1994), 448; William P. Brown, *Psalms* (IBT; Nashville: Abingdon, 2010), 140; John Goldingay, *Psalms 90–150* (Grand Rapids: Baker Academic, 2008), 745.

29. W. Dennis Tucker Jr., "The Reign of God and the Theology of the Poor in the Final Shape of the Psalter" (Ph.D. diss., Southern Baptist Theological Seminary, 1997), 211–14. Zenger calls particular attention to these introductory and concluding groups

conclusion is warranted in light of the phenomena known as the primacy and recency effects.[30] Shlomith Rimmon-Kenan describes the primacy effect as a phenomenon in which material appearing at the beginning of a text creates in the reader a tendency to interpret the text in light of that material for as long as such an interpretation can be maintained.[31] In an essay entitled "Reading from the Beginning (Again)," W. H. Bellinger Jr. addresses the primacy effect in his discussion of the Psalter's introduction.[32]

Rimmon-Kenan also discusses the recency effect, whereby readers of a text tend to revise their readings on the basis of material presented last.[33] She conceives of the process of reading to be one of forming, testing, and revising hypotheses about the text,[34] leading to a retrospective reading that can give rise to a refinement or rejection of material presented in the past.[35] Menakhem Perry writes, "The literary text, then, *exploits* the 'powers' of the primacy effect, but it ordinarily sets up a mechanism to oppose them, giving rise, rather, to a recency effect. Its terminal point, the point at which all the words which have hitherto remained 'open' are sealed, is the decisive one."[36] Thus, the Psalter's introduction suggests to the reader a point of view from which to read the psalms that follow while its conclusion provides a framework for a retrospective assessment of the collection's message.

---

of psalms in support of his case that the Psalter functions as an anti-imperial document ("Der jüdische Psalter—ein anti-imperiales Buch?" in *Religion und Gesellschaft: Studien zu ihrer Wechselbeziehung in den Kulturen des Antiken Vorderen Orients* [ed. Rainer Albertz and Susanne Otto; Münster: Ugarit, 1997], 99–105).

30. For a similar articulation of the importance of Pss 2 and 149 for understanding the Psalter's portrayal of foreign nations in light of the primacy and recency effects, see my discussion in Wittman, " Kingship of Yahweh," 93–97.

31. Shlomith Rimmon-Kenan, *Narrative Fiction: Contemporary Poetics* (2nd ed.; London: Routledge, 2002), 121.

32. W. H. Bellinger Jr., "Reading from the Beginning (Again): The Shape of Book I of the Psalter," in *Diachronic and Synchronic: Reading the Psalms in Real Time: Proceedings of the Baylor Symposium on the Book of Psalms* (ed. Joel S. Burnett et al.; LHBOTS 488; New York: T&T Clark, 2007), 114–15.

33. Rimmon-Kenan, *Narrative Fiction*, 121.

34. Ibid., 122.

35. Ibid., 122–23.

36. Menakhem Perry, "Literary Dynamics: How the Order of a Text Creates Its Meanings," *Poetics Today* 1 (1979): 57.

FOREIGN NATIONS AND THE KINGSHIP OF GOD IN PSALMS 2 AND 149

The primacy effect, applied to an analysis of Ps 2, predisposes readers toward a negative evaluation of foreign nations. In verse 1, the psalmist asks why the nations are in a tumult and why the peoples utter vanity. In verse 2, the inquiry is extended to the kings of the earth who take their stand and the rulers who sit together in conclave, all of which is undertaken in opposition to God and God's anointed one. Cole argues that the use of the root יצב to denote the nations' taking of their stand has military connotations, as it does in Josh 1:5.[37]

God's response to their rebellion comes in verses 4–5, in which God laughs, mocks, speaks angrily and terrifies them.[38] Further, in verses 8–9 God offers to give the nations to the Davidic king as a hereditary possession that he may break with an iron rod and smash like pottery.[39] The psalm concludes in verses 10–12 with an admonition to the nations and the rulers of the earth to act prudently, to listen to reason, and to serve God with fear and trembling, or else God will become angry and they will perish in the way. The image of the nations and their kings in Ps 2 is that of people who are subjugated and humiliated because of their conspiracy against and opposition to God and the Davidic king.

The portrayal of the nations in Ps 2 is reinforced by the literary relationship between this psalm and Ps 1. Cole notes that the repetition of the אשרי formula in 1:2 and 2:12 acts as an *inclusio* around the two psalms, that the verbal root הגה is used in 1:2 and 2:1, that the root אבד is paired with the noun דרך in 1:6 and 2:12, and that both psalms lack a superscription.[40] He maintains, in addition, that the wicked of Ps 1 and the insubordinate kings of Ps 2 are one and the same.[41] Brown, McCann, and Patrick Miller all draw the same inference.[42] Specifically, for McCann, Ps

---

37. Cole, "An Integrated Reading," 78.

38. This contrast between God and the nations is noted in Artur Weiser, *The Psalms* (OTL; Philadelphia: Westminster, 1962), 112.

39. See Peter Craigie's observation of the contrast between strength of the king's iron rod and weakness implied in figurative portrayal of the nations as pottery in Peter C. Craigie, *Psalms 1–50* (ed. James D. W. Watts; WBC 19; Waco, Tex.: Word Books, 1983), 67.

40. Cole, "An Integrated Reading," 77.

41. Ibid., 79.

42. Brown, *Psalms*, 115; J. Clinton McCann Jr., *A Theological Introduction to the Book of Psalms: The Psalms as Torah* (Nashville: Abingdon, 1993), 42; Patrick D. Miller

2 expresses corporately what Ps 1 expresses individually.[43] The Psalter's introduction portrays the nations and their kings as concrete members of the general category of the "wicked" discussed in Ps 1. This portrayal attaches a presumption of wickedness to the nations that the reader carries along in the journey through the remainder of the collection.

The reader also first encounters the use of royal imagery with reference to God in Ps 2. In verse 4, the psalmist identifies the one laughing as יושב בשמים (the one enthroned in heaven). The root ישב (dwell) frequently has royal overtones, especially when it is used describe divine activity. According to Walter Kaiser, "In places where the Lord is said to dwell in heaven or in Zion, the thought is that he is enthroned."[44] He adds that, even when it describes human action, the term is often used to refer to judges sitting in judgment or kings sitting on thrones.[45] McCann argues that the psalm is, in fact, more concerned with God's kingship than with the Davidic monarchy, and that it functions to introduce the concept of God's reign into the Psalter.[46] DeClaissé-Walford asserts that the introduction of this concept into the collection is "precisely the role of Psalm 2 in the Psalter."[47] Gerald Wilson identifies the theme of God's kingship as the concept around which the Psalter in its final, edited form is organized.[48] Mays and McCann both identify it as the Psalter's theological core.[49] Its introduction in Ps 2, at the very moment when the nations make such a disastrous debut onto the Psalter's stage, heightens the read-

---

Jr., "The Beginning of the Psalter," in *The Shape and Shaping of the Hebrew Psalter* (ed. J. Clinton McCann Jr.; JSOTSup 159; Sheffield: Sheffield Academic, 1993), 87.

43. McCann, *Theological Introduction*, 42.

44. Walter C. Kaiser, "ישב," *TWOT* 1:411–13. For another affirmation of the royal connotations of this root, see Gerald Wilson's remarks on its function of describing God's "sitting enthroned" or dwelling in heaven. He notes Pss 2:4, 29:10, and 113:5 as instances of this usage of the term. He also mentions the use of it to describe God as being enthroned "between the cherubim" (Gerald Wilson, "ישב," *NIDOTTE* 2:550–52). See also Wittman, "Kingship of Yahweh," 108–9, for a similar discussion.

45. Kaiser, "ישב," 1:412.

46. McCann, *Theological Introduction*, 44.

47. See deClaissé-Walford, *Reading from the Beginning*, 47.

48. Gerald Wilson, "Shaping the Psalter: A Consideration of Editorial Linkage in the Book of Psalms," in *The Shape and Shaping of the Psalter* (ed. J. Clinton McCann Jr.; JSOTSup 159; Sheffield: Sheffield Academic, 1993), 81.

49. McCann, "The Book of Psalms," 1274; James L. Mays, "The Centre of the Psalms," in *Language, Theology, and the Bible: Essays in Honour of James Barr* (ed. Samuel E. Balentine and John Barton; Oxford: Clarendon, 1994), 232.

er's sensitivity to the nations' opposition to God's reign when reading the psalms that follow.

In Ps 149, the reader encounters the last portrayal of God as a royal figure in the Psalter. In verse 2 the psalmist calls upon Israel, the children of Zion, to rejoice in God, their maker and king.[50] The Psalter's last word on God's kingship associates it particularly with God's favor for Israel, and the psalmist states in verse 4 that God's delight is in God's own people, specifically identifying them as the lowly ones who are the recipients of God's salvation. The particularism expressed in Ps 149 resonates with the end of Ps 147, where the psalmist states in verses 19–20 that God's commands, statutes and judgments were given to Israel exclusively—not to any other nation.[51]

The second half of Ps 149 contains the Psalter's final word on foreign nations. In verses 6–9 the psalmist calls on the faithful ones (חסידים) to take up two-edged swords to carry out vengeance against the nations and punishment upon the peoples, and to bind their kings with chains and their honored ones with iron fetters, thus carrying out a written judgment against them. The psalmist thus portrays God as Israel's king who sides with them against the nations and their kings. These are to suffer vengeance, punishment, and imprisonment. This image is the Psalter's final, definitive expression of God's kingship in relationship to foreign nations. As in Ps 2, God's delegated royal power is exercised on behalf of Israel and in opposition to foreign nations, who are subject to punitive action. The impression of the nations that the reader forms at the beginning of the Psalter is reinforced and confirmed at its end, and this negative portrayal is as inextricably linked with God's kingship in the Psalter's conclusion as it is in the beginning.

IMPLICATIONS FOR THE CANONICAL PSALTER'S RHETORICAL FUNCTION

It remains to reflect on what might be the function of a Psalter that it is bracketed at its beginning and its end by affirmations of God's kingship over and against foreign nations and their kings. It is instructive first to

---

50. Mays notes that in Ps 149 "The LORD is identified without exception in relation to Israel" (Mays, *Psalms*, 446).

51. Zenger argues that Pss 147 and 149 correspond to one another in the concentric structure that he identifies in Pss 146–150 in that they pertain to Israel's situation in a world filled with injustice and violence (Zenger, "Der jüdische Psalter," 103).

consider the sociopolitical situation out of which such rhetoric arises. In his comments on the violent imagery in Ps 149, McCann argues that it does not really reflect triumphalism, but rather locates vengeance within the context of justice.[52] It is thus appropriate that Israel is equated with the poor (עֲנָוִים) in 149:4. DeClaissé-Walford asserts that Ps 2 functions to call on the postexilic community to rely solely on God for deliverance from their oppressors, observing that they lived "as vassals of foreign nations, dependent for their future upon the policies of distant kings."[53] Tucker adds that "the Psalter wrestles with a world abounding in hostility, a world in which empires and enemies remain a perpetual threat to those who pray the psalms."[54] Notably, Zenger argues that the Psalter rejects the destructiveness of imperial power structures and embraces the notion that God will bring them to an end and establish a new order.[55] The strategic canonical placement of the rhetoric surrounding God's kingship in Pss 2 and 149 emerged out of a setting characterized by the threat of foreign domination.[56] The simultaneous affirmation of God's kingship and denunciation of foreign kings frames the Psalter's rhetoric of kingship as, above

---

52. McCann, "The Book of Psalms," 1276.

53. DeClaissé-Walford, *Reading from the Beginning*, 43–44.

54. W. Dennis Tucker, "Empires and Enemies in Book V of the Psalter," in *The Composition of the Book of Psalms* (ed. Erich Zenger; BETL 238; Leuven: Peeters, 2010), 723.

55. Zenger, "Der jüdische Psalter," 97.

56. The date at which the canonical Psalter reached its final form is the subject of some discussion. James Limburg notes that the final form must be dated after 587 B.C.E., because of the obvious reference to exile in Babylon in Ps 137 ("Psalms, Book of," *ABD* 5:526). Zenger prefers a date around 200 B.C.E. on the basis of references to the collection, and in particular to the introductory and concluding psalms of the Hebrew Psalter, in Sirach and contemporary Qumran texts (Zenger, "Der jüdische Psalter," 95–96, n. 2). David Mitchell argues for a date no later than 200 B.C.E. on the basis of the LXX evidence of the acceptance of "an MT-type Psalter" by that date (David C. Mitchell, *The Message of the Psalter: An Eschatological Programme in the Book of Psalms* [JSOTSup 252; Sheffield: Sheffield Academic, 1997], 81). Wilson, on the other hand, notes that the psalm scrolls at Qumran exhibit a state of flux in the arrangement of books 4–5 until after the mid-first century C.E. (Gerald Wilson, "A First Century C.E. Date for the Closing of the Book of Psalms?" *JBQ* 28 [2000]: 102–3). A setting characterized by the threat of foreign domination fits any date within this range of possibility—even the Hasmonean period, which emerged through rebellion against oppressive Hellenistic rule, the memory of which must have remained fresh throughout such a brief time of political independence.

all, a rejection of foreign rule, thus serving the anti-imperial purpose that Zenger identifies.

Other Jewish texts from the Second Temple period employ a similar rhetoric of kingship in the service of anti-imperial ends. Anathea Portier-Young's *Apocalypse against Empire* explores the similar anti-imperial function of Jewish apocalyptic literature. Some of her observations are of immense value in understanding the implications of the rhetoric of Pss 2 and 149. In her analysis of the eighth week of the Apocalypse of Weeks (1 En. 91:12–13), she notes that the righteous receive a sword with which to execute vengeance against the wicked, and then proceed to build a new temple for God, who is portrayed as a king.[57] She observes that, while the temple is of great importance in that text, no Davidic messiah is mentioned; rather, the emphasis is on divine sovereignty.[58] She writes, "By naming this order 'the kingdom of the Great One,' the apocalypse undercuts all other claims to power and rule and identifies God as the definitive measure of value. This vision of the future provided orientation for resistance to Antiochus's edict and persecution."[59] It seems that much the same could be said of the canonical Psalter in light of the rhetoric in Pss 2 and 149. Zion and the kingship of God figure prominently in both psalms, and the righteous in Ps 149 are given a sword with which to exact vengeance upon their enemies, while the Davidic figure in Ps 2 is given an iron rod with which to strike his enemies. These parallels strongly suggest reading the affirmation of God's kingship in the canonical Psalter as politically subversive rhetoric that functions in a manner similar to what Portier-Young describes as the function of early Jewish apocalypses.

We may also find an analogy to this rhetoric in Jewish wisdom literature. In his essay on Ben Sira's view of kingship, Benjamin Wright notes that the text's most basic claim is that "God reigns as sovereign over the cosmos."[60] Wright observes in particular that Ben Sira's view of God's kingship reflects the affirmation of divine rule in the Psalter.[61] Concerning Sir

---

57. Anathea E. Portier-Young, *Apocalypse against Empire: Theologies of Resistance in Early Judaism* (Grand Rapids: Eerdmans, 2011), 337–41.

58. Ibid., 344.

59. Ibid., 345.

60. Benjamin Wright, "Ben Sira on Kings and Kingship," in *Jewish Perspectives on Hellenistic Rulers* (ed. Tessa Rajak et al.; Berkeley: University of California Press, 2007), 78.

61. Ibid., 79.

10:1–5, which states that God holds the earth's governments in God's hand and appoints all of its rulers, Wright comments, "One could read these verses both as critical of foreign kings and as subversive of foreign rule because their message functions to cut any foreign ruler down to size."[62] He goes on to note the vivid imagery in Sir 10:14–17 in which God is said to uproot and destroy the nations, overturning their rulers' thrones and installing the poor and lowly in their place, calling this language a "critique through historical reminder" that recalls moments in Israel's history when God humbled haughty foreign rulers.[63] Additionally, he calls attention to the prayer for deliverance in Sir 36:1–22, noting that the prayer identifies the nations as ancient Israel's enemies and invites divine wrath upon their arrogant rulers. He states that Ben Sira "hopes for a revitalization of Israel, free from foreign domination and with God as its sovereign."[64] One finds in Sirach, then, rhetoric similar to that of Pss 2 and 149 in that it dovetails affirmations of God's kingship with negative portrayals of foreign nations that feature violent imagery and depict the humiliation of foreign kings. Wright's acknowledgement that this rhetoric undermines the legitimacy of foreign rulers mirrors Portier-Young's similar assessment of the Apocalypse of Weeks.

In light of the political subversion inherent in such rhetoric, it is appropriate to raise the question of the identity of the speaker in Ps 2:3. The text reads, "Let us tear apart their fetters and let us cast off their ropes from us." The traditional form-critical approach is to read the verse as the utterance of subjugated foreign rulers who are seeking to rebel against the Davidic king.[65] Thus the psalmist is quoting what the nations and their kings are saying to one another about Israel.

In light of the social and historical setting of the final form of the canonical Psalter, however, I maintain that it is best to read the verse as the psalmist's exhortation to an Israelite audience about the nations, functioning as a call to resist the power of foreign occupiers and their kings on the

---

62. Ibid., 82.

63. Ibid., 84.

64. Ibid., 85. See also Tucker's reference to this prayer as an example of a text that shares themes in common with the Psalter, participating in a common "anti-imperial ethos" (Tucker, "Empires and Enemies," 730–31).

65. See, for example, Weiser, *Psalms*, 109; Keith R. Crim, *The Royal Psalms* (Richmond: John Knox, 1962), 72; and J. H. Eaton, *Kingship and the Psalms* (SBT 32; London: SCM, 1976), 111.

basis of the complete superiority of Israel's divine king. Israel throws off the nations' ropes in Ps 2:3 and then proceeds to bind the kings of those nations with vastly stronger chains of iron in Ps 149:8.

Finally, the portrayal of kingship in Pss 2 and 149 has implications for how one conceives of the Psalter's editors' rhetorical opponents. Specifically, it constructs a primary and overriding opposition between divine rule and foreign rule. Accordingly, Mays writes, "In the rhetoric and theology of the Psalms, nations and their rulers are typically the opposition to the reign of God."[66] Similarly, McCann observes, "Psalm 2 and the whole Psalter recognize that the reign of God exists amid continuing opposition—from the nations and peoples (2:1), the kings and rulers of the earth (2:2), the wicked (Psalm 1)."[67]

Wilson's view, however, is that the Psalter was edited in such a way that it encourages reliance upon God's kingship as an alternative to Davidic rule in light of the failure of the Davidic covenant.[68] McCann lends support for this view by arguing that not only books 4–5 but also books 1–3 of the Psalter have been shaped in such a way that they demonstrate the failure of the Davidic covenant.[69]

Against Wilson's view, Mitchell notes that the theology of the Davidic covenant is manifestly present in book 5, specifically in Pss 110, 132, and 144.[70] He argues that the presence of royal psalms in a Psalter compiled after the fall of the Davidic monarchy suggests an editorial preference for their messianic interpretation.[71] For Jamie Grant, the affirmation of God's kingship in the Psalter should be viewed through the lens of the eschatological hope that God's reign will be made manifest through the messianic rule of "a restored Davidic leader."[72] Both Mitchell and Grant see in the Psalter's canonical shape a clear anticipation of the restoration of

---

66. Mays, *Psalms*, 447.

67. McCann, *Theological Introduction*, 44.

68. Gerald Wilson, "The Use of Royal Psalms at the 'Seams' of the Hebrew Psalter," *JSOT* 35 (1986): 92.

69. J. Clinton McCann Jr., "Books I–III and the Editorial Purpose of the Psalter," in *The Shape and Shaping of the Psalter* (ed. J. Clinton McCann Jr.; JSOTSup 159; Sheffield: Sheffield Academic, 1993), 104.

70. Mitchell, *The Message of the Psalter*, 79.

71. Ibid., 86.

72. Jamie A. Grant, *The King as Exemplar: The Function of Deuteronomy's Kingship Law in the Shaping of the Book of Psalms* (Atlanta: Society of Biblical Literature, 2004), 36.

Davidic rule, although Grant allows that the role of the Davidic king has been democratized to the extent that the king's obedience to Torah "is held up as an example for the people to follow."[73]

The emphasis that Wilson, Mitchell, and Grant place on Davidic kingship as part of the Psalter's editorial agenda seems overstated in light of the prominent role of foreign nations in Pss 2 and 149. The relative ambiguity about Davidic covenantal ideology in books 4–5 contrasts sharply with the clarity of the Psalter's celebration of God's kingship and its critique of foreign nations and their kings. It is instructive to compare the fortunes of the Davidic king with those of foreign kings in Pss 2 and 149. The Davidic king appears in Ps 2, and his power derives exclusively from God, whom the psalmist also portrays as king. By contrast, the Davidic king fades from view in Ps 149, and I find arguments that his role has been democratized and transferred to the people to be persuasive. Neither psalm exhibits dismay at the fall of the house of David nor expresses explicit opposition to its restoration, and in both, foreign kings receive a withering critique. God's kingship alone is affirmed in Ps 149, thus differing from all human kingship. Such rhetoric is likely directed primarily against Israel's foreign occupiers and their supporters. It is clear that affirming God's kingship is of central concern in the rhetoric of Pss 2 and 149, and undermining the legitimacy of the kings of the nations appears to be a much higher priority than affirming or opposing messianic hope for the restoration of Davidic kingship.

Conclusion

The affirmation of God's kingship that lies at the theological and editorial heart of the Psalter is more than a theological metaphor and more than a sapiential alternative to Davidic ideology. Above all, it is an inherently political utterance that strikes at the heart of the legitimacy of foreign occupiers to rule over Israel, and it constitutes a rallying cry for resistance to their dominion. To be sure, the enemies in the Psalms are a diverse group, and not all of them reside outside Israel's borders, yet psalmists display an overwhelming tendency to portray foreign nations in a negative light when they refer to them explicitly. Psalms 2 and 149 are strategically placed in the Psalter's introduction and conclusion. The literary

---

73. Ibid., 286.

relationship between them is strong, and they contain the Psalter's first and last references to God's kingship and to foreign nations. They create in the mind of the reader a lasting negative impression of foreign nations and their kings as enemies of Israel and opponents to God's reign. In a social and historical setting in which the Davidic monarchy existed only in the past, the Psalter's editors utilized the rhetoric of these psalms to point their readers toward God's kingship as a concept around which to organize resistance to oppressive foreign domination.

BIBLIOGRAPHY

Bellinger, W. H. Jr. "Reading from the Beginning (Again): The Shape of Book I of the Psalter." Pages 114–26 in *Diachronic and Synchronic: Reading the Psalms in Real Time: Proceedings of the Baylor Symposium on the Book of Psalms.* Edited by Joel S. Burnett, W. H. Bellinger Jr., and W. Dennis Tucker Jr. LHBOTS 488. New York: T&T Clark, 2007.

Birkeland, Harris. *The Evildoers in the Book of Psalms.* Oslo: Dybwad, 1955.

Brown, William P. *Psalms.* IBT. Nashville: Abingdon, 2010.

Cole, Robert. "An Integrated Reading of Psalms 1 and 2." *JSOT* 26 (2002): 75–88.

Craigie, Peter C. *Psalms 1–50.* WBC 19. Waco, Tex.: Word, 1983.

Crim, Keith R. *The Royal Psalms.* Richmond: John Knox Press, 1962.

Croft, Steven J. L. *The Identity of the Individual in the Psalms.* JSOTSup 44. Sheffield: Sheffield Academic, 1987.

DeClaissé-Walford, Nancy. *Reading from the Beginning: The Shaping of the Hebrew Psalter.* Macon, Ga.: Mercer University Press, 1997.

Eaton, J. H. *Kingship and the Psalms.* SBT 32. London: SCM, 1976.

Gerstenberger, Erhard. "Enemies and Evildoers in the Psalms: A Challenge to Christian Preaching," *HBT* 4 (1983): 61–77.

Goldingay, John. *Psalms 90–150.* Grand Rapids: Baker Academic, 2008.

Grant, Jamie A. *The King as Exemplar: The Function of Deuteronomy's Kingship Law in the Shaping of the Book of Psalms.* Atlanta: Society of Biblical Literature, 2004.

Kaiser, Walter C. "ישׁב." *TWOT* 1:411–13.

Kraus, Hans-Joachim. *Theology of the Psalms.* Translated by Keith Crim. Minneapolis: Augsburg, 1986.

Limburg, James. *Psalms.* Louisville: Westminster John Knox, 2000.

———. "Psalms, Book of." *ABD* 5:526.

Lohfink, Norbert, and Erich Zenger. *The God of Israel and the Nations: Studies in Isaiah and the Psalms*. Collegeville, Minn.: Liturgical, 2000.

Mays, James L. "The Centre of the Psalms." Pages 2331–46 in *Language, Theology, and the Bible: Essays in Honour of James Barr*. Edited by Samuel E. Balentine and John Barton. Oxford: Clarendon, 1994.

———. *Psalms*. IBC. Louisville: Westminster John Knox, 1994.

McCann, J. Clinton Jr. "The Book of Psalms." Pages 641–1280 in vol. 4 of *The New Interpreter's Bible: A Commentary in Twelve Volumes*. Edited by Leander E. Keck. Nashville: Abingdon, 1994.

———. "Books I–III and the Editorial Purpose of the Psalter." Pages 93–107 in *The Shape and Shaping of the Psalter*. Edited by J. Clinton McCann Jr. JSOTSup 159. Sheffield: Sheffield Academic, 1993.

———. *A Theological Introduction to the Book of Psalms: The Psalms as Torah*. Nashville: Abingdon, 1993.

Miller, Patrick D. Jr. "The Beginning of the Psalter." Pages 83–92 in *The Shape and Shaping of the Hebrew Psalter*. Edited by J. Clinton McCann Jr. JSOTSup 159. Sheffield: Sheffield Academic, 1993.

Mitchell, David C. *The Message of the Psalter: An Eschatological Programme in the Book of Psalms*. JSOTSup 252. Sheffield: Sheffield Academic, 1997.

Perry, Menakhem. "Literary Dynamics: How the Order of a Text Creates Its Meanings." *Poetics Today* 1 (1979): 35–64.

Portier-Young, Anathea E. *Apocalypse against Empire: Theologies of Resistance in Early Judaism*. Grand Rapids: Eerdmans, 2011.

Rimmon-Kenan, Shlomith. *Narrative Fiction: Contemporary Poetics*. 2nd ed. London: Routledge, 2002.

Sheppard, Gerald T. "'Enemies' and the Politics of Prayer in the Book of Psalms." Pages 61–83 in *The Bible and the Politics of Exegesis: Essays in Honor of Norman K. Gottwald on His Sixty-Fifth Birthday*. Edited by David Jobling, Peggy L. Day, and Gerald T. Sheppard. Cleveland: Pilgrim, 1991.

Tucker, W. Dennis, Jr. "The Reign of God and the Theology of the Poor in the Final Shape of the Psalter." Ph.D. diss., Southern Baptist Theological Seminary, 1997.

———. "Empires and Enemies in Book V of the Psalter." Pages 721–33 in *The Composition of the Book of Psalms*. Edited by Erich Zenger. BETL 238. Leuven: Peeters, 2010.

Weiser, Artur. *The Psalms*. OTL. Philadelphia: Westminster, 1962.

Wilson, Gerald. "ישׁב." *NIDOTTE* 2:550–52.

————. "A First Century C.E. Date for the Closing of the Book of Psalms?" *JBQ* 28 (2000): 102–10.

————. "Shaping the Psalter: A Consideration of Editorial Linkage in the Book of Psalms." Pages 72–82 in *The Shape and Shaping of the Psalter*. Edited by J. Clinton McCann Jr. JSOTSup 159. Sheffield: Sheffield Academic, 1993.

————. "The Use of Royal Psalms at the 'Seams' of the Hebrew Psalter," *JSOT* 35 (1986): 85–94.

Wittman, Derek E. "The Kingship of Yahweh and the Politics of Poverty and Oppression in the Hebrew Psalter." Ph.D. diss., Baylor University, 2010.

Wright, Benjamin. "Ben Sira on Kings and Kingship." Pages 76–91 in *Jewish Perspectives on Hellenistic Rulers*. Edited by Tessa Rajak, Sarah Pearce, James Aitken, and Jennifer Dines. Berkeley: University of California Press, 2007.

Zenger, Erich. "Der jüdische Psalter—ein anti-imperiales Buch?" Pages 95–108 in *Religion und Gesellschaft: Studien zu ihrer Wechselbeziehung in den Kulturen des Antiken Vorderen Orients*. Edited by Rainer Albertz and Susanne Otto. Münster: Ugarit, 1997.

THE MESSAGE OF THE ASAPHITE COLLECTION AND ITS ROLE IN THE PSALTER[*]

Christine Brown Jones

INTRODUCTION

The Asaph Psalms are located in a pivotal place in the Psalter. Not only are they the first psalms of book 3, the middle book of the five-book Psalter, but they are also located in the numeric middle of the Psalter. They also seem to react to a very critical point in Israel's history, the exile.[1]

Is there, though, any insight to be gained by understanding how these psalms of assorted genre are arranged? Following the examples of Wilson, who suggests there is purposeful arrangement in the final Psalter,[2] and McCann, who has begun to look at arrangement within the books themselves,[3] its seems a worthwhile endeavor to look for arrangement within smaller collections, especially a collection that exhibits such unity. The following discussion will suggest an answer to McCann's question, "Is it possible that Psalms 73–83 in particular were not collected randomly but were selected and arranged to address a crisis in the national life?"[4]

---

* This paper was originally presented as part of a session of the Psalms Section of the Society of Biblical Literature annual meeting on 19 November 2011 in San Francisco.

1. J. Clinton McCann Jr. suggests that all of book 3 responds to the exile ("Books I–III and the Editorial Purpose of the Psalter," in *The Shape and Shaping of the Psalter* [ed. J. Clinton McCann Jr.; JSOTSup 159; Sheffield: Sheffield Academic, 1993], 96).

2. Gerald H. Wilson, *The Editing of the Hebrew Psalter* (SBLDS 76; Chico, Calif.: Scholars Press, 1985).

3. McCann, "Books I–III," 93.

4. Ibid.

Methodology

My study of the Asaphite collection employs various methods. This project, though, is primarily canonical in its approach. Ultimately, all of the methodological tools are utilized in order to read the psalms of the collection together and within the larger context of the Psalter. I begin with the assumption that the Asaph Psalms are held together by more than their common title. The unique use of divine names, the concern for history, and the judicial nature of the collection bind them together in a unique way and strengthen the connection first established by the common title. I am not suggesting, however, that the psalms were composed at the same time or that they were composed by the same person. Rather, when collected, the psalms were grouped in a way that displays unity.

In my 2009 dissertation I studied the Asaphite collection with attention to linguistic similarities as well as thematic links in an effort to understand the purpose of the collection.[5] Linguistic and thematic similarities abound in the collection and provide a sense of unity to the collection. Previous scholars have sifted through much of this information in an effort to understand the author(s) of the collection, the setting of the writing/recitation, and the history of the collecting of various psalms into the Asaphite collection.[6] These scholars have focused, however, only on the linguistic and thematic aspects that are unique to this collection. Thus, if a theme or linguistic link occurred elsewhere in the Psalter, it was not useful to them in the study of this collection. My research did not discount such occurrences, but studied the unique aspects as well as those more common in an effort to understand this collection's place within the Psalter.

One important aspect of my research was to understand the impact of linguistic and thematic links and arrangement upon the reader. By reader, I assume a knowledgeable, careful reader of the text who lived

---

5. Christine Brown Jones, "The Psalms of Asaph: A Study of the Function of a Psalm Collection" (Ph.D. diss., Baylor University, 2009).

6. See Franz Delitzsch, *Biblical Commentary on the Psalms* (3 vols.; Edinburgh: T&T Clark, 1908), 1:10–11; Martin Buss, "The Psalms of Asaph and Korah," *JBL* 82 (1963): 382–92; Ivan Engnell, "The Book of Psalms," in *A Rigid Scrutiny* (trans. and ed. John T. Willis; Nashville: Vanderbilt University Press, 1969), 68–122; Karl-Johan Illman, *Thema und Tradition in den Asaf-Psalmen* (Abo: Abo Akademi, 1976); Harry Nasuti, "Tradition History and the Psalms of Asaph" (Ph.D. diss., University of Michigan, 1985); Michael Goulder, *The Psalms of Asaph and the Pentateuch: Studies in the Psalter, III* (JSOTSup 233; Sheffield: Sheffield Academic, 1996).

during or shortly after the exile and was deeply influenced by and concerned about the fate of Judah. Communication occurs in the interaction between text and reader, and thus a major question for me is, "What message is being communicated?"

God in the Asaph Psalms

In order to more fully understand the message of collection, it is important to look closely at the portrayal of God and the faithful in the collection. We begin with linguistic and thematic links concerning God. Psalm 50, the first psalm in the collection, presents the concept of God as judge, which recurs in several psalms that follow, especially Pss 75, 76, and 82.[7] God's judgments come in God's time (Ps 75) and are longed for, as they will bring salvation to the oppressed (Ps 76:10), and yet they are feared (Ps 76). Psalm 82 establishes God as the only judge capable of judging justly. One of God's prominent roles in the Psalms of Asaph is to act as judge. The reader of the Asaphite collection understands that God alone is the righteous judge of all, a message communicated not only through the words of the psalms, that is, Ps 50:6, "The heavens declare God's righteousness, for God is the one who judges," but also through the overall message of the psalms.

Another prevalent theme of the Asaphite collection is God's dissatisfaction with the behavior of the people, which has resulted in anger with them. The people associate God's lack of action during the destruction of the temple (Ps 74), God's lack of compassion during their time of trouble, and God's ongoing lack of intervention (Ps 79) with God's anger. In Pss 76 and 79, they ask God to turn that anger toward their enemies. Psalm 78, on the other hand, seems to deal with God's anger toward previous generations and more specifically the Ephraimites/Israelites. God's anger is not a problem for the people when it is turned upon those who seem deserving. At other times God is provoked to anger, God is furious, and God fumes.[8] The collection also communicates God's anger in tacit ways, especially as God deals with the wicked in Ps 50. The final judgment upon

---

7. Many scholars have pointed out the judicial character and tone of the collection as a means of establishing unity within the collection. See especially Delitzsch, *Psalms*, 2:142; and Goulder, *Psalms of Asaph*, 19–20.

8. In Ps 78:58 the people provoke God to anger (*hiphil* of כעס) and in v. 62 God becomes furious (*hithpael* of עבר) with them. In Ps 80:5, God fumes over (עשׁן) the prayers of the people.

them is dire—the ones who forget God will be torn apart with no hope of deliverance (v. 22). Though Ps 50:22 does not mention God's wrath or anger, the metaphorical use of tearing implies anger.[9]

Taking these two traits, God's just judgment and God's anger, into consideration as one approaches the collection, it is interesting that judgment and anger together are only referred to in the same psalm once, Ps 76.[10] God and judgment are found in Pss 50, 75, 76, and 82,[11] while God's anger is prominent in Pss 74, 76, 77, 78, 79, and 80. Though in other places in the Psalter God's anger is associated with righteous judgment (e.g., Ps 7), this collection seems to distinguish between judgment and anger. The psalms referring to God's anger are surrounded by those referring to God as judge. What impact, then, does this have upon the reader of these psalms? First, it distinguishes between God's ability to judge and the actions of God (or lack thereof) that the people perceived to be connected with God's anger. Second, it communicates the tension that the exilic and postexilic people must have felt between their understanding of God as just judge and the reality of their situation of continued national turmoil. God may have been just in some judgments, but is God just in allowing the punishment to continue into subsequent generations? Third, God's anger toward the people is not the last image provided for the reader. The collection closes with the establishment of God as the one and only judge of the earth (Ps 82), and the call for God to take vengeance upon the nations who conspire against God's people (Ps 83). God's anger against the people is not permanent; it will be turned upon the enemy in due time.

God's judgment and anger are not the only aspects of God described in this collection. God as savior, redeemer, and deliverer is referenced more often than either judgment or anger. As with judgment and anger, the theme of God's salvific action on behalf of the people is not limited to the Asaphite collection, but when read as a collection, the prominence of this theme is powerful. God's salvation (ישע) is promised to the faithful (Ps 50:23) and withheld from those who do not trust in God's salvation

---

9. See Job 16:9 and Amos 1:11.

10. Not including the tacit expression of anger in Ps 50, which focuses on God as judge.

11. Ps 73:14 contains יכח, a word linked with judgment, as noted above. But it has been left off this list because God is not clearly noted as the one doing the reproving. Ps 83, though not containing any words of judgment, seems to be an explanation of what the people expect of God after calling on God to judge the earth in Ps 82:8.

(Ps 78:22). When the psalmist cries for God to act in Ps 79:9, it is with the understanding that God is a God of salvation.

In Ps 76:10 God's justice upon the earth is paralleled with the salvation of the oppressed of the earth. God's concern for just judgment motivates God's salvific activity, and the remembrance of these actions motivates the people to call upon God to act again. After affirming God's sovereignty in Ps 80:2, the people call upon God in v. 3 to awaken (עוּר, *poel*) and come to their salvation. They do not call, however, for salvation for their own sakes; rather they tie salvation to a long-standing relationship (vv. 15–19) with God and to God's reputation.

Deliverance (נצל) is another salvific term of the collection. While Ps 50:22 attributes God's lack of deliverance as part of God's judgment, Pss 79 and 82 state that deliverance belongs to those who remember God and to the weak and needy, a reassuring thought to the faithful after the exile. A final term used to describe God's salvific activity is גאל, redeemer. In the Asaphite collection, this activity is specifically tied to bringing the people out of Egypt (Pss 74 and 77).

Words related to God's salvific activity are found in all but three of the Asaph Psalms.[12] These words refer to God's past deeds, especially in the remembrance of the exodus. They are applied to the present situation both in cries of the people for deliverance and in God's call for the people to seek only God for such deliverance. They are applied to the hope that God will act again and restore the people for God's name's sake. The hope of salvation is offered to the people and to the earth, but is withdrawn from the wicked and the enemies. In a collection where judgment is the first and last word (Pss 50, 82–83) and anger is prominent in the middle (Pss 74, 77–80), the remembrance of and hope for salvation assures the reader that God is capable and willing to deliver once again.

The last theme in the Asaphite collection is the creation and the created elements. God creates (Ps 74:12–17), establishes, and later steadies

---

12. Pss 73, 75, 83. In Ps 73 God's salvific activity is not referred to directly, but God's role as guide (v. 24) and refuge (v. 28) are often tied with salvific activity, especially in relation to the exodus (William P. Brown, *Seeing the Psalms: A Theology of Metaphor* [Louisville: Westminster John Knox, 2002], 48). Ps 75 is a psalm of judgment upon the wicked and no salvation is offered. Likewise, Ps 83 is a call for God's vengeance upon God's enemies and the people wish no salvation for them as the destruction of the enemy will likely result in the deliverance of the people.

the tottering earth (Ps 75:4).[13] God is sovereign over the created order (Ps 50), summons the entire earth (Ps 50:1), and calls to the heavens and the earth, commanding that they gather the faithful so that God may judge them (Ps 50:5).

Theophanies are also present in the Asaphite collection. In Ps 50:3 God's appearance is preceded by fire and surrounded by the tempest.[14] A more extensive description is found in Ps 77:17–21, an account of God's presence before Israel as they crossed the Reed Sea. Here a thunderstorm announces the power and presence of God, imagery used again in Ps 83:16, this time in the form of a request by God's people for God to pursue the enemy with God's tempest and hurricane.

God's power over the created world is evident in special ways in stories of the exodus and wilderness wandering. Psalm 78, with its unique recitation of Israel's past,[15] highlights the marvelous deeds of God. God made the waters stand like a heap (נֵד)[16] so that the people might pass through (v. 13), split rocks and made streams of water flow from them (vv. 15–16), and miraculously provided bread and meat until the people were filled (vv. 23–29).

The way in which God's sovereignty over creation is recounted in the Psalms of Asaph communicates several things to the reader: (1) it helps to establish that God is the sovereign God over all creation, not only the sovereign of God's chosen people; (2) it highlights God's great power; (3) God is able to command created elements in a way that suits God's purposes; and (4) the earth and all that is in it belongs to God (Ps 50:12). The exilic and postexilic communities surely would have questioned the sovereignty of God. By highlighting God's role in the creation not only of Israel, God's chosen people, but of the entire cosmos, the Asaphite collec-

---

13. Ps 75:4 falls within Illman's "bringing forth of the cosmos" category (*Thema und Tradition*, 18–19).

14. Gerald Wilson, *Psalms, Volume 1* (NIV Application Commentary; Grand Rapids: Zondervan, 2002), 761.

15. Unique in the sense that the accounts are not in chronological order, some plagues are omitted, and the psalm includes the otherwise untold account of battle at the fields of Zoan (Hans-Joachim Kraus, *Psalms 60–150* [CC; trans. Hilton C. Oswald; Minneapolis: Fortress, 1989], 127, 129).

16. נֵד in connection with water is used twice of the Sea (Exod 15:8; Ps 78:13) and three times of the Jordan River (Josh 3:13, 16; Ps 33:7), according to *BDB*, 622.

tion reminds the reader that God is sovereign over all[17] and God remains powerful despite the defeat of the nation.

What then does the collection in its entirety communicate about God? God is the only just judge of the entire world, judging the wicked and the righteous at the appointed time. Despite the fact that God's anger seems to have resulted in excessive punishment, God is still recognized as the source of salvation and redemption in the present situation. Underlying these assessments of God is the fact that God is sovereign over the world and as such has the power to carry out just judgment and miraculous salvific actions. Though the nation has faltered, the people can still trust in their God.

The Faithful in the Asaph Psalms

The faithful in the Asaphite collection are portrayed in two distinct roles: they recount God's great deeds of the past and they question God's present actions. As a response to the nearness of God, the psalmist and the other faithful recount (ספר) God's works (מלאכות, Ps 73:28) and wonderful acts (נפלאות, Ps 75:2). They also commit to telling (ספר) the coming generations about those wonderful acts of God (פלא, Ps 78:4). The psalmist not only speaks of these deeds (מעלל in Ps 78:12, פלא in vv. 12, 15, and פעל in v. 13), but meditates on them, presumably for reassurance in trying times (Ps 77:12–16). The recounting of God's deeds serves several functions: (1) to praise the God who did such things; (2) to prompt listeners to obey; and (3) to establish hope for the future.

Though accounts of God's miraculous deeds are often expressed by the faithful, one question resounds from the lips of the faithful: "How long?" (עד מתי in Pss 74:10; 80:5; and עד מה in Ps 79:5). How long will the enemy scoff (Ps 74:10)? How long will God's jealous wrath burn (Ps 79:5)? How long will God be angry with the people's prayers (Ps 80:5)? The question appears in expanded form in Ps 77:8–10 when the psalmist wonders if God will ever be favorable again or if God's promises have ended.

The deeds of God are recounted before and after the psalms that bear this difficult question. Psalms 73:28 and 75:2 surround Ps 74, assuring the psalmist of God's nearness. Psalm 79 is preceded by several stories of God's miraculous provision, which are retold in Ps 78. And though the tension

---

17. Elmer Smick, "Mythopoetic Language in the Psalms," *WTJ* 44 (1982): 88–98.

created by Ps 79 is not relieved in Ps 80, in Ps 81 God recounts previous instances when the people cried out and God answered, and God states that if the people will listen, God will again respond. The doubts of Ps 77:2–11 regarding God's promises are resolved within the psalm itself as the psalmist recalls God's redemption of the people. The question "How long?" is a fundamental question, and the collection does not downplay it or simply brush it aside, but the response given by the collection is not so much an answer to the question as it is instruction for enduring the wait. In the meantime, trust in your God who so ably and mercifully provided in the past.

THE ARRANGEMENT OF THE COLLECTION

A study of the arrangement of the Asaphite collection suggests that Ps 50 functions as a bridge between the Korahite collection of Pss 42–49 and the second Davidic collection of Pss 51–72, because of the thematic and linguistic links that occur between what comes before it and what follows.[18] Psalm 50 also introduces an important theme of the collection, God as judge. This theme is echoed in the intervening Davidic collection and reaches its crescendo in the Asaphite collection. Psalm 50 also establishes an idea that is uncertain at the beginning of the rest of the Asaphite collection—the wicked will be punished and the righteous will be rewarded.

Psalm 73 presents the underlying problem of the larger Asaphite collection: life is not as it should be. The reader is quickly ushered into the upside down world of the psalmist who sees the wicked thriving while the righteous languish. Despite the oracle of God in Ps 50 and the confidence of the Davidic collection, the reader now encounters a struggle with the fact that reality does not line up with what the tradition has taught.

The locus of change for the psalmist in Ps 73 is the sanctuary of God, but what the exilic reader knows is confirmed in Ps 74—the sanctuary has been destroyed. Psalm 74 elaborates on the confusion presented at the beginning of Ps 73 by communicating the distress of the people in the face of the destruction of the sanctuary. The temple, the place where one had gone to be in the presence of God, has been destroyed; thus the psalmist must turn to another source to find comfort. Psalm 74:13–18 states that that source is God's created order. God's rule was not destroyed

---

18. Jones, "Psalms of Asaph," 136–41.

when the temple was destroyed because God's rule is far older than the temple and God's rule stretches far beyond Jerusalem. Once the psalmist has (re)-established God's sovereignty, then the psalmist calls upon God to act according to God's promises.

Psalm 74, while ending with some confidence that God is capable of action, does not end with any assurance that God will act soon. Read by itself, there is no assurance that God will act, but when read with Ps 75, there is assurance. The transition from Ps 74 to 75 is abrupt; the reader encounters the final pleas of Ps 74 and then moves immediately to the jubilant thanksgiving of Ps 75. This shift is similar to the shift in many lament psalms where the psalmist quickly moves from lament to praise.[19] The assurance found in Ps 75 is based once again on the fact that God is a just judge who will put down the proud and will lift up the lowly.

The attitude of thanksgiving is further expanded with the praises of Ps 76. While Ps 76 does extend the more assured tone of Ps 75, the motive for its praise seems out of place to the reader of the collection, as it lauds God's definitive actions in establishing Zion as God's own dwelling. It seems out of place because of the utter destruction of the sanctuary recounted in Ps 74. Psalm 76, with its reminiscence of God's initial actions to secure Zion, functions to reassure the people once again. God chose Zion in the past and fought on her behalf; perhaps God will do so again.

The next three psalms, Pss 77–79, are the heart of the Asaphite collection, and as such present the resounding question of the people, "How long will God's anger keep God from acting?" These psalms also present the people with a way to maintain faith in the meantime by remembering the past. Psalm 77 begins this series of psalms with words that ponder the current situation and question God's faithfulness to God's promises. The initial conclusion is devastating: God must have changed. The psalmist is surely expressing the thoughts of many in this profound statement. The reader, however, is not allowed to linger in this assessment for long. The psalm sharply turns to recollecting God's mighty deeds in the past, highlighting one definitive act, the parting of the sea. The vivid image portrays God exhibiting complete control over the natural elements of water, clouds, lightning, thunder, and the earth.

---

19. Hermann Gunkel, *An Introduction to the Psalms: The Genres of the Religious Lyric of Israel* (completed by Joachim Begrich; trans. James D. Nogalski; Macon, Ga.: Mercer University Press, 1998), 93, 180–81.

Psalm 78 continues recalling the past in such a way that those in the present may learn from past mistakes, apply their learning to their current situations, and pass it down to the next generation. The purpose of recalling the past is twofold: (1) to help the people place their hope in God; and (2) to learn from the mistakes of their ancestors. A pattern is established in Ps 78: God acts graciously, the people forget and reject God, and God punishes the people. Though the psalm repeatedly mentions God's anger, it repeatedly speaks of God's compassion, graciousness, and willingness to give the people another opportunity. The pattern can provide considerable encouragement to the reader. It is time for God to act graciously again. The pattern also places major responsibility upon the reader to remember the past and not repeat it. The cycle can be broken.

Psalm 78 ends at the point when new opportunities are at hand with the appointment of David and the election of Zion. But the story does not end there. Psalm 79 carries the story further and lets the reader know that the people must have once again forgotten, because they are again in a devastating situation. The reader's suspicions are confirmed later in the psalm (vv. 6, 9); once again God is angry, and the people are pleading for God to show compassion. The psalmist pleads for compassion; the reader knows compassion is possible; and, according to the pattern of Ps 78, compassion should be forthcoming. Psalm 79 continues and the people cry out for God to forget their ancestors' iniquities and to act on their behalf. The psalm ends with a promise from the people to God. If God exacts revenge, then the people will give thanks and praise God forever.

Psalms 80 and 81 stand side by side as the people's plea for God to turn and as God's response and plea for the people to turn. Psalm 80 asks for God's swift action (v. 3), and ponders the longevity of God's anger (v. 5). The heart of the psalm returns the reader to the confusing reality of the people (vv. 9–14). God is the one who transplanted the people to a place where they could prosper. Why then has God allowed such destruction? The psalm itself does not reveal an answer to the question. But based on the previous psalms of the collection, the reader assumes one—disobedience. Whether because of disobedience or some other reason, God has turned against the people and the people can only plead for God to turn around and look down from heaven at their situation. The return of God's shining face is enough to rebuke the nations and save the people. In return for God's turning, the people promise never to turn their back to God.

Psalm 81 is God's response, not only to Ps 80, but also to Pss 77–79. In the midst of the sights and sounds of a festival day, God speaks and answers the questions of the people. God begins by recounting God's own role in their rescue from Egypt, an action initiated by the distressed cries of the people. God then admonishes them because, unlike God who hears their cries, the people are not listening. The only offense God mentions specifically is their worship of other gods. In this divine oracle it is clear that action against their enemies would be swift if the people would listen and walk in the ways of God. God has again heard the cries of the people and responds to the question "How long?" by placing the responsibility back on the people. "How long?" depends on when the people will turn back and follow God's ways.

Following God's response, Ps 82 returns again to the theme of God as judge. The collection has already established that God is a just judge who cares for the righteous. In this psalm, however, God is not judging humanity, but other deities. Psalm 82 takes the offense of Ps 81, the worship of other gods, and illustrates why it is misguided. God enters the divine council as judge to pronounce judgment on the other gods. Their task has been to provide justice and deliverance for the weak, but they have sided with the wicked instead, and for that they will perish. Because of the actions of these unjust gods, the foundations of the earth are shaken, but when the earth shakes, it is God who steadies it again (Ps 75:4). Reliance on those gods is useless, but reliance on God, who is just and righteous, is cause for confidence. It is with that confidence that the psalmist calls for God to judge the whole earth.

Psalm 83 points out where the psalmist thinks God's judgment of the earth should begin; it should begin with those who plan to wipe out God's people. The list of enemies is not related to the exilic or postexilic struggles, but does include numerous enemies of Israel's past. Any group whose goal is to wipe out Israel should be subject to God's judgment, including the present enemy who is not mentioned by name. Psalm 83 ends the Asaph collection with a call for God to assert divine sovereignty definitively. Throughout the collection God's sovereignty is announced in various ways — God is sovereign as just judge, as master of creation, and as mighty deliverer of the people. The psalmist knows that God is sovereign, the reader should know, and when God acts so will the entire earth.

The collection is an honest reflection of the confusion encountered after the destruction of the temple and the exile. On the one hand, the people embrace God's role as judge of the wicked and righteous. On the other hand, their present situation does not reflect a reality in which God is acting as such. The primary message of the collection is that the people should remain faithful and obedient. The basis of such a message is two-fold. First, God is the one just judge who will come to judge the wicked. Second, based on God's previous actions of salvation and deliverance, the people can be assured of God's faithfulness toward them. In Ps 81, God makes it clear that obedience is necessary in order for God to act. God has not abandoned the people and the people should not abandon God for the ways of the wicked.

Attempts to understand the Psalter as a whole are challenged in the Psalms of Asaph.[20] In these psalms the role of the Davidic king is greatly diminished when compared to the psalms before and after them.[21] The one place where David is mentioned (Ps 78:69–72) speaks of him as servant and shepherd, not specifically as king, and is tempered by the arrangement of Pss 78 and 79. God is only referred to as king once (Ps 74:12) and God's kingship is tied to God's creation of the earth rather than God's reign in Zion. God's dominant role in the Psalms of Asaph is judge, an aspect of divine kingship that is not often emphasized in the Psalms. It is as if the confusion over the loss of their earthly king has caused them to rethink that role altogether, at least for a time. Though God's role as judge is important in the Asaphite collection, especially in moving the people beyond a focus on God's anger, it does not continue to be a dominant theme in book 3. Book 3 comes back to the concept of

---

20. Recently several have attempted to locate a single or dominant theology or organizing principle of the Psalter. For God's sovereignty, see James L. Mays, *The Lord Reigns: A Theological Handbook to the Psalms* (Louisville: Westminster John Knox, 1994). For the destiny of the righteous, see Jerome F. D. Creach, *The Destiny of the Righteous in the Psalms* (St. Louis: Chalice, 2008). For God's justice and faithfulness, see J. Clinton McCann Jr., "The Single Most Important Text in the Entire Bible: Toward a Theology of the Psalms" in *Soundings in the Theology of the Psalms: Perspectives and Methods in Contemporary Scholarship* (ed. Rolf A. Jacobson; Minneapolis: Fortress, 2011), 63–75. For YHWH as faithful, see Rolf A. Jacobson, "'The Faithfulness of the Lord Endures Forever': The Theological Witness of the Psalter," in *Soundings in the Theology of the Psalms: Perspectives and Methods in Contemporary Scholarship* (ed. Rolf A. Jacobson; Minneapolis, Fortress, 2011), 111–37.

21. Admittedly, the concept of king does include ideas about the king as warrior, judge, and shepherd. By king, I am referring primarily to the office of king, which is highlighted both by the Davidic superscriptions of the psalms before the Asaphite collection and the content of the psalms following the collection in book 3 (Korahite collection).

king and laments greatly over the loss of the earthly king in the Korahite collection.

The present reality also threatens the people's perception of God's sovereignty, an issue that is in some ways tied to the idea of kingship, but encompasses more than the idea of the office of king. God, whose nearness had been felt most fully in the temple, is now without a physical dwelling place, since both the temple and Zion are destroyed. Perhaps it is for this reason that the psalmist continually points to God's cosmic sovereignty as creator and God's nearness as the shepherd of Israel. The people must expand their understanding of God's sovereignty in order to maintain their belief that God is capable of making things right.

Also tempered in the Asaphite collection is the faith of the righteous. At least twice in the collection (Pss 73:13 and 77:11), the psalmist comes to the verge of abandoning faith in light of the conflict between present reality and the promises of God. God's *ḥesed* is even questioned in Ps 77:9. The situation that the righteous are encountering is threatening every previously held assumption about God. Hope is offered to the readers, especially in the form of God's past actions, but the collection does not provide any indication that the people have actually taken up the hope. It is still in question.

The fact that the Asaphite collection seems to challenge attempts to define an overall concern or theology of the Psalter does not necessarily mean that those attempts are incorrect. In fact, it further illustrates the confusion that the people were feeling as a result of the destruction of the temple and the exile. Beliefs about God, the earthly king, and Zion have been severely undermined. The Asaphite collection represents one group's initial attempts to move forward, even though they do not seem altogether sure that God was moving with them. A failure to grapple with the confusion and to seek a way forward would have meant the end of their faithfulness and, as the psalms of the collection reflect, that was not an option they were willing to take.

Their attempts to move forward pave the way for the people to evaluate previous assumptions and create new ways of understanding God and God's purposes. Though the struggle of the exile is still present in the remainder of book 3, especially the struggle over the loss of the Davidic monarchy, the testimony of books 4 and 5 make it clear that the people did maintain their faith and they did find hope in God's universal sovereignty.

BIBLIOGRAPHY

Brown, William P. *Seeing the Psalms: A Theology of Metaphor*. Louisville: Westminster John Knox, 2002.

Brown Jones, Christine. "The Psalms of Asaph: A Study of the Function of a Psalm Collection." Ph.D. diss., Baylor University, 2009.

Buss, Martin. "The Psalms of Asaph and Korah." *JBL* 82 (1963): 382–92.

Creach, Jerome F. D. *The Destiny of the Righteous in the Psalms*. St. Louis: Chalice, 2008

Delitzsch, Franz. *Biblical Commentary on the Psalms*. 3 vols. Edinburgh: T&T Clark, 1908.

Engnell, Ivan. "The Book of Psalms." Pages 68–122 in *A Rigid Scrutiny*. Translated and edited by John T. Willis. Nashville: Vanderbilt University Press, 1969.

Goulder, Michael. *The Psalms of Asaph and the Pentateuch: Studies in the Psalter, III*. JSOTSup 233. Sheffield: Sheffield Academic, 1996.

Gunkel, Hermann. *An Introduction to the Psalms: The Genres of the Religious Lyric of Israel*. Completed by Joachim Begrich. Translated by James D. Nogalski. Macon: Mercer University Press, 1998.

Illman, Karl-Johan. *Thema und Tradition in den Asaf-Psalmen*. Abo: Abo Akademi, 1976.

Jacobson, Rolf A. "'The Faithfulness of the Lord Endures Forever': The Theological Witness of the Psalter." Pages 111–37 in *Soundings in the Theology of the Psalms: Perspectives and Methods in Contemporary Scholarship*. Edited by Rolf A. Jacobson. Minneapolis: Fortress, 2011.

Kraus, Hans-Joachim. *Psalms 60–150*. CC. Translated by Hilton C. Oswald. Minneapolis: Fortress, 1989.

Mays, James L. *The Lord Reigns: A Theological Handbook to the Psalms*. Louisville: Westminster John Knox, 1994.

McCann, J. Clinton Jr. "Books I–III and the Editorial Purpose of the Psalter." Pages 93–107 in *The Shape and Shaping of the Psalter*. Edited by J. Clinton McCann Jr. JSOTSup159. Sheffield: Sheffield Academic, 1993.

———. "The Single Most Important Text in the Entire Bible: Toward a Theology of the Psalms." Pages 63–75 in *Soundings in the Theology of the Psalms: Perspectives and Methods in Contemporary Scholarship*. Edited by Rolf A. Jacobson. Minneapolis: Fortress, 2011.

Nasuti, Harry. "Tradition History and the Psalms of Asaph." Ph.D. diss., University of Michigan, 1985.

Smick, Elmer. "Mythopoetic Language in the Psalms." *WTJ* 44 (1982): 88–98.

Wilson, Gerald H. *The Editing of the Hebrew Psalter.* SBLDS 76. Chico, Calif.: Scholars Press, 1985.

———. *Psalms, Volume 1.* NIV Application Commentary. Grand Rapids: Zondervan, 2002.

Instruction, Performance, and Prayer: The Didactic Function of Psalmic Wisdom

Catherine Petrany

In Ps 34:12, the pedagogical implications of the psalmist's declaration are explicit.

> Come, children, listen to me;
> I will teach you the fear of YHWH.[1]

This is an exhortation that passes between a human teacher and human students, with the teacher calling upon the students to receive the wisdom spoken to them through the act of hearing. It echoes a specific kind of address found in biblical wisdom literature, most prominently in the book of Proverbs.[2] This verse represents but one example of wisdom elements scattered throughout the book of Psalms, elements that invite the faithful to reflect and learn rather than to participate in the language of prayer and praise. Scholars have struggled with the question of this kind of psalmic wisdom precisely because it seems to stand outside the ritual or liturgical context that the psalms primarily evoke, and eludes characterization with regard to its setting.[3] Rather than a temple, psalmic wisdom suggests a

---

* I would like to thank Dr. Harry Nasuti for his suggestions and guidance in the writing of this essay.

1. All translations, unless otherwise stated, are my own and follow the versification of the MT.

2. This familial address, in concert with various imperatives, is found predominantly in the singular ("son/child"). See Prov 1:8, 10, 15; 2:1; 3:1, 11, 21; 4:10; Sir 2:1; 3:12; 4:1; etc. It is found also in the plural as in this psalm ("sons/children"). See Prov 4:1; Sir 3:1; 23: 7; 41:14.

3. Roland Murphy, "A Consideration of the Classification, 'Wisdom Psalms,'" *Congress Volume: Bonn, 1962* (ed. G. W. Anderson; VTSup 9; Leiden: Brill, 1963), 161.

school. Rather than a ritual, it suggests a proverbial pedagogy. Rather than a dialogue, it suggests a monologue.[4]

Wisdom elements in the Psalter can come in the form of entire psalms, but they can also emerge on a smaller scale as brief, potentially didactic reflections in the midst of other, more easily established genres.[5] The question of the degree of influence such wisdom components exert within the literary and theological confines of an individual psalm can provide a foundation for understanding the role of psalmic wisdom in the Psalter as a whole. Are wisdom elements in psalms of different genres didactic? If so, how do they teach? What do they teach? How does the interaction of wisdom elements with other kinds of psalmic speech determine the function of both?

What follows is an examination of three such psalms, each generally categorized according to a different genre, namely trust (Ps 62), thanksgiving (Ps 92), and lament (Ps 94).[6] From a form-critical point of view, however, all three psalms admit some uncertainty with regard to genre and

---

4. On the dialogic character of the lament psalms, see Carleen Mandolfo, *God in the Dock: Dialogic Tension in the Psalms of Lament* (JSOTSup 357; London: Sheffield Academic, 2002).

5. Roland Murphy ("Consideration of the Classification," 165), who provides a sober and influential voice in the debate about wisdom psalms, conservatively (though not exhaustively) identifies the following passages as wisdom elements in psalms of other genres: 25:8–10, 12–14 (individual lament); 31:24–25 (individual lament); 39:5–7 (individual lament); 40A:5–6 (thanksgiving); 62:9–11 (trust); 92:7–9 (thanksgiving); 94:8–15 (lament). It is possible to extend this list in a number of ways, depending on how one identifies a wisdom element in a nonwisdom psalm, and whether one distinguishes *wisdom* elements from *didactic* elements. Indeed, David G. Firth makes the point that "didactic intent" can manifest itself across form-critical boundaries, and is not simply found in wisdom psalms ("The Teaching of the Psalms," in *Interpreting the Psalms: Issues and Approaches* [ed. David Firth and Philip S. Johnston; Downers Grove, Ill.: InterVarsity Press, 2005], 164). Likewise, Mandolfo's examination of the "didactic voice" in the lament psalms is focused on grammatical, rather than formal, criteria (*God in the Dock*, 1, 5).

6. With regard to these three psalms, J. Kenneth Kuntz differs slightly from Murphy, recognizing 92:7–8, 13–15 and 94:8–11, 12–15 as wisdom elements without mentioning Ps 62. See J. Kenneth Kuntz, "Wisdom Psalms and the Shaping of the Hebrew Psalter," in *For a Later Generation: The Transforming of Tradition in Israel, Early Judaism, and Early Christianity* (ed. Randal Argall, Beverly Bow, and Rodney Werline; Harrisburg, Pa.: Trinity, 2003), 149.

contain a sapiential "moment," an element that by way of form, theme, or sensibility echoes biblical wisdom and suggests a didactic quality.

PSALM 62

Psalm 62 is a psalm of confidence or trust. Certain characteristics of the psalm, though, particularly its resonances with biblical wisdom, lend it a unique profile.[7] The psalm's emphasis lies on the God who is a refuge, who offers the psalmist a safe haven even in the midst of admitted and seemingly immediate uncertainties and dangers. The introduction of a wisdom moment in verses 9–12 does not stand out as a foreign element, but does initially represent a shift in focus.

> [9] Trust in him at all times, O people,
> pour out your hearts before him.
> God is our refuge. Selah.
> [10] Human beings are only a breath,
> The children of man are deception.
> Upon the scales,
> they are less than a breath all together.
> [11] Do not trust in extortion,
> or become vain by robbery,
> if wealth bears fruit pay it no mind.
> [12] One thing God has spoken;
> two things I have heard:
> that strength belongs to God.[8]

This passage resonates with biblical wisdom in several ways. Formally, it contains an "admonition" in verse 9, a "proverbial saying" in verse 10, a

---

7. Hermann Gunkel and Joachim Begrich, *Introduction to the Psalms: The Genres of the Religious Lyric of Israel* (trans. James D. Nogalski; Macon, Ga.: Mercer University Press, 1998), 190–91.

8. Scholars disagree about where the "wisdom element" begins and ends. Gunkel, *Introduction to the Psalms*, 297; Murphy, "Consideration of the Classification," 165; and Dahood, *Psalms II: 51–100* (AB 16; Garden City, N.Y.: Doubleday, 1968), 90 all cite vv. 9–11 as the wisdom section. In contrast, F. de Meyer, "La dimension sapientiale du Psaume 62," *Bijdragen* 42 (1982): 357; and Frank-Lothar Hossfeld and Erich Zenger, *Psalms 2* (ed. Klaus Baltzer; trans. Linda M. Maloney; Minneapolis: Fortress, 2005), 112 cite vv. 9–13 as the wisdom section. Here, I have not explicitly included v. 13 as part of the wisdom element for reasons that will become obvious below.

"negative warning" in verse 11, and a "numerical saying" in verse 12, all with ties to biblical wisdom.[9] With regard to content, verse 10 contains an anthropologically focused reflection on the futility and weightlessness of human life, underlined by the twofold use of the noun form of the root הבל (which we find again in verbal form in v. 11). This abstract reflection, conceptually akin to the thought-world of Qoheleth, cedes to an empirical focal point, namely the speaker's exhortation not to place one's trust in extortion, robbery, and wealth. So, while the passage does not explicitly identify a pupil, it does direct itself to a human audience and treat certain concrete realities of human life.[10] This is not a prayer speech addressed to God, but rather one that asks its plural human audience to reflect on a particular reality and adopt certain empirical behaviors.

But do these wisdom nuances and interhuman addresses concerning human life lend this passage a didactic function? If so, how does its interaction with other modes of speech in the psalm condition that function? This so-called wisdom passage says nothing about teaching or instruction. Moreover, it does not operate in isolation but rather in concert with the multifaceted and constantly transitioning modes of speech in the psalm as a whole. The characters involved and addressed throughout the psalm include the speaker, the speaker's adversaries (v. 4), the speaker's own soul (v. 6), the speaker's community (vv. 9, 11) and finally, the deity (v. 13).[11] Moreover, the psalm shifts in verse 9 with the first person plural affirmation "God is our refuge," which implies that the audience has joined the speaker in the act of trust. It is impossible to posit any kind of sustained monologue or cooptation of the psalm's communicative environment by the figure of a human teacher in these verses. Psalm 62 offers nothing like a lesson one might find in the instructions of Proverbs, in which the father/

---

9. Gunkel, *Introduction to the Psalms*, 300–301.

10. In her study of didactic "interjections" in lament psalms, Mandolfo (*God in the Dock*, 13) defines this didactic function according to a "horizontal dynamic," that is, "the human-to-human flow of information." Proverbial discourse exemplifies the dynamic she describes, and its presence in the psalms often coincides with other wisdom characteristics, though not always.

11. Derek Suderman, in an as yet unpublished dissertation, deals extensively with the grammatical identification and rhetorical significance of multiple addressees in the lament psalms. See his "Prayers Heard and Overheard: Shifting Address and Methodological Matrices in Psalms Scholarship" (Ph.D diss., Toronto School of Theology, 2007).

mother/teacher figure is the lone speaker, and the child/student the per-petually silent addressee.[12]

The psalm's series of shifting speakers and addressees reaches a cul-mination in the final verse that exerts a definitive influence over what pre-cedes it. Here, the speaker prays,

> Yours, Lord, is faithfulness,
> for you reward everyone according to their deeds. (Ps 62:13)

This direct address to God, the first and only of the psalm, absorbs the potentially pedagogical bent of the psalm's anthropologically focused wisdom moment. This verse explicitly ties together the thing learned in verses 9–12 with the divine addressee, who is the true focus of the psalm. The final prayer completes the substance of the "lesson": the lives of human beings are ephemeral and futile, and only God's actions confer meaning to life in the world. Thus, the interaction of the didactic and prayer moments has less to do with the acquisition of knowledge or the inculcation of a particular type of behavior, and rather more to do with faith.[13]

Indeed, the final shift in addressee in verse 13 lends definition to this conclusion. This prayerful finale reshapes the wisdom moment of the psalm, placing its contents within the context of the speaker's act of trust. The speaker understands and vocalizes the matters outlined in the psalm's wisdom moment not as a sage, that is, not due to his or her observation or experience of the world. Rather, the speaker arrives at these conclusions because of "One thing God has spoken; two things I have heard" (v. 12). Regardless of the formal implications of this statement, it explicitly places the insight of the wisdom moment within the context of the speaker's

---

12. On the "missing voice" of the proverbial student, see James L. Crenshaw, *Education in Ancient Israel: Across the Deadening Silence* (New York: Doubleday, 1998), 187–203. See also Carol Newsom, "Woman and the Discourse of Patriarchal Wisdom: A Study of Proverbs 1–9," in *Gender and Difference in Ancient Israel* (ed. Peggy L. Day; Minneapolis: Fortress, 1989), 142–60.

13. In his commentary on this psalm as a "*nachkultische*" composition, Fritz Stolz contrasts the experience of the everyday world expressed by the psalm's wisdom forms with the experience of faith that ultimately follows in the final verse. He argues that, unlike the experiential platform of wisdom discourse, which takes its cues from the observable world, the experience of faith is only verifiable through an act of trust. See Fritz Stolz, *Psalmen im nachkultischen Raum* (ThSt 129; Zurich: Theologischen, 1983), 53.

verbal interchange with God. The speaker has heard something from God, and now calls upon God in turn in verse 13. The didactic implications of the wisdom moment thereby take on a new dimension, conditioned by the speaker's own activity and shift towards God in speech. The human teacher's lesson to the human student on the vaporous character of life in the world in verses 10–11 is transformed by the turn to God in speech, an act which itself lends weight and meaning to the observable world. To finish the "lesson," to understand this conclusion, the student must not only listen, but also take up the speech, participate in the prayer.

PSALM 92

Psalm 92 does not contain the dramatic back and forth between shifting dialogue partners that one finds in Ps 62. The speaker's address to the divine "you," while not entirely consistent, dominates the psalm and lends its liturgical character a personal veneer that frequently characterizes psalms of thanksgiving.[14] Like Ps 62, Ps 92 includes a wisdom sensibility that radiates from particular moments of the psalm and stands in contrast with the psalm's strong emphasis on performance.

Indeed, Ps 92 begins with a description of a liturgical performance embedded in a direct address to God. The superscription, "song for the Sabbath day," initiates this emphasis, and in verses 2–3, the speaker describes the singing of hymns taking place in the morning and at night.[15] In verse 4, the speaker states that praise involves not only voices, but also instrumentation, including harp and lyre. Within this performance-oriented context, the psalm includes two moments that share an affinity with biblical wisdom and strike a more reflective note. Following the liturgical description of verses 2–4, the speaker directly addresses God in verses 5–6, vociferously praising the work of the divine. The psalm's first wisdom element then manifests in verses 7–8:

---

14. Sigmund Mowinckel, *The Psalms in Israel's Worship* (2 vols.; trans. D. R. Ap-Thomas; Oxford: Basil Blackwell, 1962), 2:32.

15. Despite the lack of an imperative in the psalm's opening, Peter L. Trudinger convincingly argues that v. 2 ("It is good to praise YHWH, to sing to your name, Most High") functions essentially as a command to take up the performance subsequently described. See Peter L. Trudinger, *The Psalms of the Tamid Service: A Liturgical Text from the Second Temple*, (VTSup; Leiden: Brill 2004), 152–53.

⁷ A brutish person does not know,
nor does a fool understand this:
⁸ the wicked sprout like grass,
and all troublemakers blossom,
in order to be destroyed forever. [16]

Following the continuance of the prayer and the relation of the speaker's personal experience in verses 10–12, the psalm concludes with a second wisdom element, which is dominated by ambiguous third person language rather than the first person account and direct address to God that prevailed in verses 5–6 and 9–12.

¹³ The righteous one sprouts like a palm tree,
like the cedar in Lebanon, he grows great.
¹⁴ Planted in the house of YHWH
they sprout in the courts of our God.
¹⁵ They still bear fruit in old age,
they are full of sap and freshness (Ps 92:13–15)

The emphasis on the righteous in contrast with the picture of the foolish painted in the psalm's first wisdom moment in verses 7–8 sets up a dichotomy common in the wisdom corpus. Terminologically, the parallel references to the "fool" (כסיל) and "brutish person" (איש־בער) bear a wisdom stamp and occur in other psalms with wisdom echoes.[17] The explicit references to the capacity to "know" and to "understand" in verse 7 recall the opening of the book of Proverbs, and suggest intellectual (rather than liturgical) activity, or lack thereof, on the part of the fool. Thematically, both passages taken together exhibit a "preoccupation" with moral

---

16. As noted above, Kuntz sees Ps 92 as an individual thanksgiving but, following Murphy, contends that vv. 7–9 are an "impersonal sapiential assertion" which contains "most" of the nine wisdom words he identifies in the psalm. See J. Kenneth Kuntz, "The Canonical Wisdom Psalms of Ancient Israel: Their Rhetorical, Thematic, and Formal Dimensions," in *Rhetorical Criticism: Essays in Honor of James Muilenberg* (ed. Jared Jackson and Martin Kessler; PTMS 1; Pittsburgh: Pickwick, 1974), 207. In contrast to Murphy, Kuntz also recognizes vv. 13–15 as sapiential. Moreover, in his later article, Kuntz cites vv. 7–8 (rather than 7–9) and vv. 13–15 as the psalm's wisdom elements ("Wisdom Psalms and the Shaping of the Hebrew Psalter," 149). Likewise, I have not included v. 9 as part of the wisdom element because it includes a direct address to God and no explicit wisdom features.

17. Gunkel, *Psalms*, 298. See also Pss 49:11; 94:8.

retribution, and the second includes the image of the righteous as a tree, which recalls Ps 1, and indicates a sapiential quality.[18] Moreover, both of the psalm's wisdom moments are anthropologically focused, third person reflections in which the speaker does not identify a particular audience. This suggests that the speaker has stepped out of his or her prayer with God, and into another kind of discourse, whether directed internally or directed toward another human. Indeed, what the speaker imparts is a deposit of knowledge that fools are incapable of recognizing. The one who hears this reflection is thus called to understand something about the respective fates of the wicked and the righteous. Taken together, these two wisdom moments represent an instructive meditation on the benefits of living a righteous life.

How does the interaction between these two wisdom elements and the psalm's other elements, namely the initial focus on liturgical performance and the prevailing divine address, shape the function of each? Despite the sapiential timbre of verses 7–8 and 13–15, each section also includes characteristics that distinguish it from biblical wisdom and a purely reflective aim, particularly when taken within the context of the psalm as a whole. The first section on the wicked in verses 7–8 is bracketed on either side by direct address to God in verses 6 and 9. This bracketing phenomenon suggests that the intervening wisdom moment is, to some degree, subsumed into the surrounding address to the divine "thou," which places the speaker's reflection within the context of prayer with the divine. If the psalm effects a shift in audience in these verses (toward a human addressee), it is not an explicit move. The confluence of explicit prayer address wrapped around an ambiguously directed third person reflection suggests a blurring of the lines between human-divine and interhuman address, which adds an additional nuance to verses 7–8, one that would not be present in proverbial discourse.[19]

---

18. Murphy, "Consideration of the Classification," 165–66.

19. The only prayer in the book of Proverbs occurs in 30:7–9. The addressee is never explicitly stated and the prayer concludes with a third person reference to God. See James L. Crenshaw, "The Restraint of Reason, the Humility of Prayer," in *The Echoes of Many Texts: Reflections on Jewish and Christian Traditions* (ed. William G. Dever and J. Edward Wright; BJS 313; Atlanta: Scholars Press, 1997), 81–97. Crenshaw demonstrates that a sustained attention to prayer only develops in the book of Sirach, which includes multiple references to prayer and two explicit examples of prayer in 22:27–23:6 and 36:1–22.

The second wisdom passage in verses 13–15 on the righteous is not part of this encounter between the speaker and God. Rather, it concludes the psalm and contains third person language *about* God rather than second-person address *to* God, technically excluding it from the "prayer" that prevails in the rest of the psalm.[20] Moreover, verse 13 includes a plural identification of "our God" as the God who blesses the righteous with prosperity. In other words, the speaker's singular "I," whose presence is explicit at various points throughout the psalm, transforms into the plural "we" who are called upon to respond and declare that "our God" blesses the fruitful righteous.

If we can call this a lesson learned, it is one that must ultimately be taken up in speech rather than silence. The proverbial "silent child," if present here, is called upon to lay claim to the discourse of the speaker by vocally taking it up rather than silently taking it in. Thus, neither so-called wisdom element promotes a purely reflective response: the first is grammatically encased by the prayer, and the second includes a first person plural which suggests the presence of an active congregation, invited to a vocal and perhaps liturgical reification of the speaker's main point about the way God works. Thus, what initially seems to be a clearly delineated juxtaposition of performance-oriented content and content of a more reflective nature in the psalm is not ultimately sustained because of the way it is shaped by the shifting character of speaker and audience. The emphasis on performance in the beginning of the psalm leads to the ritualization of reflection in its conclusion.

PSALM 94

Like Pss 62 and 92, Ps 94 does not strictly adhere to one particular form, but rather includes elements of different genres, including communal and individual lament as well as, of course, a wisdom section. In verses 1–7, the speaker issues an urgent, imperative complaint speech addressed to God, seeking divine retribution for the exultant wicked who litter the earth and oppress the voiceless widow, stranger and orphan. The psalm shifts in

---

20. Gunkel (*Psalms*, 298) writes that, "In general, even if not in every particular case, wisdom components (mostly sayings) stand out in the particular psalms by the fact that they speak about YHWH in the third person, and thus do not exhibit the form of a prayer."

verses 8–12, when the speaker turns his address from God to the "fools" who lack understanding. These verses state:

> [8] Understand, you brutes among the people,
> you fools, when will you have wisdom?
> [9] He who plants the ear, shall he not hear?
> He who forms the eye, shall he not see?
> [10] He who disciplines nations, shall he not rebuke,
> he who teaches humankind knowledge?
> [11] YHWH knows human thoughts, that they are breath.
> [12] Happy is the man whom you discipline, YHWH,
> the one whom you teach by your instruction,
> [13] to give him quietness from evil days,
> until a pit is dug for the wicked.
> [14] For YHWH will not leave his people,
> and he will not forsake his inheritance.
> [15] For justice will return to judgment,
> And all the upright will follow it. (Ps 94:8–15)

The wisdom resonances of this passage, as well as its explicitly didactic flavor, are immediately discernible.[21] Formally, the "admonition" in verse 8 and the *ʾašrê* clause of verse 12 are wisdom formulas. As in Ps 92, the psalm includes a dual reference to evildoers as "brutes" (בערים) and "fools" (כסילים), which occurs in other psalms associated with wisdom.[22] The references to teaching and instruction cohere with the main function of the wisdom literature as didactic material.[23] While the emphasis of the passage seems to be wholly theological, verses 8–11 represent another explicitly inter-human exchange, and furthermore include third person language about, rather than to, God. Thematically, the rhetorical questions in verse 9 echo the sensory appeals that often guide a prover-

---

21. Though Kuntz ("Canonical Wisdom Psalms," 202) formally designates Ps 94 as a lament, he follows Murphy in identifying vv. 8–15 as a wisdom element. He isolates fifteen "wisdom words" (taken from R. B. Y. Scott) in the psalm as a whole, twelve of which appear in vv. 8–15.

22. Pss 49:11; 92:7; cf. Ps 73:22.

23. The difficulty (if not impossibility) with establishing a viable inventory of wisdom terminology is well documented. See Roland E. Murphy, "Assumptions and Problems in OT Wisdom Research," *CBQ* 29 (1967): 410; James Crenshaw, "Wisdom Psalms?" *CurBS* 8 (2000): 12.

bial epistemology, the virtues of hearing and seeing in the cultivation of understanding.[24]

Despite these resonances with biblical wisdom and the potentially instructive nature of the inter-human discourse, however, it is impossible to simply characterize this passage as didactic. The speaker does not intend to instruct the "fools" to whom he or she speaks in verses 8–11, nor would a hearer of this speech likely identify himself or herself as one of these fools.[25] Rather, these fools seem to parallel the evildoers denounced in the first seven verses, regardless of whether that group represents an internal faction of Israel or an external group.[26] Moreover, this initial admonition of the "fools" is immediately connected with an ensuing question regarding the punishment of nations, with the image of God as both judge and instructor (v. 10). The speech in verses 8–11 is not a lesson for the wise, the righteous, or those seeking wisdom.[27] It is a proclamation of divine retribution against those who have imposed their wicked will on the widow, the orphan, and the stranger. The wisdom teaching is not a wisdom teaching at all, but a foreboding message of divine justice for those who seem to have escaped divine sight. It is a passionate performance of the speaker, who does not offer an intellectual reflection about life in the world. Rather, the speaker seeks to summon and bring about the "lesson" of divine wrath upon those who deny the divine teacher.[28]

---

24. Hossfeld and Zenger (*Psalms 2*, 454) cite Prov 20:12 in the background here, and see parallels between vs. 10 with Prov 8:10, 15, and between vss. 10b–11a with Prov 16:1–9, and v. 11b with the book of Qoheleth, concluding that "verse 7 is refuted by means of wisdom." For a less optimistic perspective on the value of seeing and hearing, see Qoh 1:8.

25. Trudinger, *Psalms of the Tamid Service*, 117.

26. Erhard S. Gerstenberger, for example, sees the evildoers/fools as a subgroup of the community. See *Psalms, Part 2, and Lamentations, with an Introduction to Cultic Poetry* (FOTL 15; Grand Rapids: Eerdmans, 2001), 178. Hossfeld and Zenger (*Psalms 2*, 454) admit that it remains unclear whether this group is internal or external to the community, but argue that the fools/brutes of v. 8 must be identified with the wicked of vv. 3–7.

27. Hans-Joachim Kraus argues the opposite. See his *Psalms 60–150* (Minneapolis: Augsburg Fortress, 1989), 243.

28. In a slightly different vein, Trudinger likewise argues that vv. 8–15 do not represent a "sapiential teaching" but, in contrast, sees these verses rather as a "consolation" for the righteous. (*Psalms of Tamid Service*, 118). For him, the primary audience of vss. 8–11 is not the explicitly identified audience (the fools), but rather the "faithful community."

Indeed, verse 12 substantiates this notion when the speaker shifts again and directly calls upon God. This effectively ends the inter-human dialogue between the speaker and the fools addressed in verses 8–11. Rather than taking up again the lament language of address to God that dominates verses 1–7, however, the speaker continues with the use of wisdom language but unites it with a direct address to God. This verse is still part of the wisdom element with regard to both form and vocabulary, but a distinct shift occurs. The subject matter remains essentially the same as in the previous two verses; God is the one who instructs, and disciplines. The address to the fools of the previous verses, however, now becomes a direct address to YHWH. It is no longer an indictment but rather a prayer speech which shifts the orientation of discourse while sustaining the use of wisdom forms and didactic terminology.

It is here, in the prayer and the following reflection in verses 13–15, that the lesson for those who would hear actually manifests. In verses 12–15, the object of God's so-called instruction has shifted from the fools to the one who ultimately benefits from God's hearing and sight, the righteous one who can rest in times of struggle knowing that God will devastate the wicked. This is a telling convergence of the functions of prayer and instruction because it reimagines God as the ultimate sage in the midst of a vertically inclined address which gently shifts into a third person reflection about God and the upright. It is a pedagogy of a different order, no longer simply imaged in the horizontal discourse spoken by a wise parent and received by a silent child. Rather, Ps 94 presents the divine teacher as one *addressed* by the human student in verse 12. Here we have a dramatic example of didacticism translated into a psalmic dialect, in which God is both the subject and ultimately the object of the speaker's words, and the act of divine instruction is both an indictment and a comfort to the wicked and righteous in their turn.

Conclusion

How can these individual and compact examples of psalmic wisdom contribute to the ongoing question of the shape of the Psalter as a whole? Studies on the shape of the Psalter as a whole often engage the question of the book's comprehensive function as either a hymnbook or a book for instruction.[29] A conceptual framework has developed that focuses on the

---

29. On different scholarly approaches to this question, see Susan E. Gillingham,

wisdom elements in the Psalter as signaling a shift from cultic origin to noncultic redaction.[30] Subsequently, questions on the shape of the Psalter have often focused on the role that wisdom circles played in the supposedly purposeful arrangement of the book.

A primary example of this move is represented in the influential work of Gerald Wilson. He argued for a set of competing frames that manifest at key points in the Psalter, namely a "royal-covenantal frame" and a "wisdom frame." The former, concentrated in the first three books of the Psalter, traces the initiation of the Davidic monarchy (Ps 2), the transmission of the monarchy to David's successors (Ps 72), and the failure of the Davidic hopes in the exile (Ps 89).[31] In contrast, the "wisdom frame" shapes books 4 and 5, beginning with Pss 90 and 91 and concluding with Ps 145. According to Wilson, both frames extend into the other, with the royal Ps 144 found in book 5 and the "wisdom frame" extending into the first three books at Ps 73 and Ps 1. For Wilson, the "wisdom frame" ultimately proves to be the dominant impulse within the Psalter's final form, and the key in the Psalter's transformation into a book of instruction.[32] He connects this developmental schema with particular historical processes

---

The Poems and Psalms of the Hebrew Bible (Oxford: Oxford University Press, 1994), 232–55; Harry P. Nasuti, "Redaction-Critical and Canonical Approaches to the Psalms and Psalter," in Cambridge Methods in Biblical Interpretation: The Book of Psalms (ed. Esther M. Menn; Cambridge: Cambridge University Press, forthcoming). For studies that emphasize the reflective or meditative function of the Psalter as a whole, see Georg P. Braulik, "Psalms and Liturgy: Their Reception and Contextualization," VE 24 (2003): 318–22; Norbert Lohfink, "Psalmen im Neuen Testament: Die Lieder in der Kindheitsgeschichte bei Lukas," in Neue Wege der Psalmenforschung (ed. K. Seybold and Erich Zenger; HBS 1; Freiburg: Herder, 1994), 106–7; Erich Zenger, "Psalmenforschung nach Hermann Gunkel und Sigmund Mowinckel," in Congress Volume: Oslo, 1998 (ed. A. Lemaire and M. Saebo; Leiden: Brill, 1981), 430.

30. See, for example, Joseph Reindl, "Weisheitliche Bearbeitung von Psalmen: Ein Beitrag zum Verständnis der Sammlung des Psalters," in Congress Volume: Vienna, 1980 (ed. John A. Emerton; Leiden: Brill, 1981) , 333–56. For scholars who take issue with this historical viewpoint, see Susan Gillingham, "The Zion Tradition and the Editing of the Hebrew Psalter," in Temple and Worship in Biblical Israel (ed. J. Day; London: T&T Clark, 2005), 310; and Katharine Dell, "'I Will Solve My Riddle to the Music of the Lyre' (Psalm XLIX 4 [5]): A Cultic Setting for Wisdom Psalms?" VT 54 (2004): 445.

31. Gerald Wilson, The Editing of the Hebrew Psalter (SBLDS 76; Chico, Calif.: Scholars Press, 1985).

32. Gerald Wilson, "The Shape of the Book of Psalms," Int 46 (1992): 134.

which culminated with the establishing of the final form of the Psalter in the first century C.E.[33]

Regardless of whether one accepts Wilson's argument, this brief example shows one way in which the isolation and functional significance of wisdom elements can be central for the question of the Psalter as a whole. But how does the question of the comprehensive role that psalmic wisdom plays in the Psalter relate to the role of psalmic wisdom on a small scale, in individual psalms?[34] Of course, in addition to isolated wisdom moments in psalms dominated by other kinds of language, the Psalter contains entire psalms that resonate with the wisdom literature and seemingly function in a didactic capacity. Psalm 1 represents the most obvious example of a psalm that does not contain any address to God or suggestion of performance, and remains entirely focused on evoking a reflective response from its recipient.[35] With regard to the book as a whole, the analysis of the interaction of wisdom elements with other kinds of speech in individual psalms might provide a kind of mirror, a small-scale reflection of the way that psalmic wisdom functions in the larger Psalter.

From this perspective, the role of psalmic wisdom would be downplayed as a streamlined marker of didactic import and the dominant influence in shaping the Psalter's comprehensive function from a theological standpoint. In each of the psalms examined here, two things became clear. First, resonances with wisdom in the psalms do not unilaterally imply a continuity of function among the diverse examples manifest in the Psalter. Not all identified wisdom elements in the psalms are simply didactic, nor do these elements inevitably call for a reflective or meditative response from the proverbial "silent child." While each psalm examined here has elements identified by scholars as bearing a wisdom signature, these elements function in distinct ways. The wisdom element of Ps 62 in no way parallels

33. Gerald Wilson, "A First Century C.E. Date for the Closing of the Hebrew Psalter?" *JBQ* 28:2 (2000): 102–10.

34. Firth ("The Teaching of the Psalms," 162–63) explicitly examines the instructional import of the psalms at both levels, namely individual compositions and the Psalter as a whole. As noted above, however, he emphasizes the development of patterns for prayer and behavior that emerge across form-critical boundaries rather than focusing on wisdom elements.

35. See also Pss 37, 112, and 128. Other psalms typically designated as wisdom psalms often include elements such as direct address to God (Ps 32) or references to performance (Pss 34, 49). I restrict this comment to psalms that Murphy (*Consideration of the Classification*, 161) identifies as wisdom psalms.

the rhetorical or theological effect of the wisdom element in Ps 94. Second, and relatedly, ritual and instructional language in the psalms and Psalter exist in a fundamental tension, each impulse constantly conditioning the other in the formation of a dynamic psalmic dialect. A linear understanding of the shape of the Psalter as a whole from a ritual to reflective function fails to capture the opposite tendency—the ritualization of reflection, the transformation of sapiential discourse into prayer and praise.

Each psalm examined shows the disparate manner in which wisdom moments appear and function in the Psalms. Each involves a unique mix of content in relation to shifting modes of address. Yet all three psalms also show the privileging of the spoken or performed dialogue between human beings and God as the unique "pedagogical" apparatus of the psalms. The human teacher and student appear and ruminate, but ultimately find themselves taken up into the language of worship, their reflections ritualized and placed within the "I-Thou" encounter that theologically prevails in the book of Psalms.

BIBLIOGRAPHY

Braulik, Georg P. "Psalms and Liturgy: Their Reception and Contextualization." *VE* 24 (2003): 309–32.

Crenshaw, James L. *Education in Ancient Israel: Across the Deadening Silence.* New York: Doubleday, 1998.

———. "The Restraint of Reason, the Humility of Prayer." Pages 81–97 in *The Echoes of Many Texts: Reflections on Jewish and Christian Traditions.* Edited by William G. Dever and J. Edward Wright. BJS 313. Atlanta: Scholars Press, 1997.

———. "Wisdom Psalms?" *CurBS* 8 (2000): 9–17.

Dahood, Mitchell, S.J. *Psalms II: 51–100.* AB. Garden City, N.Y.: Doubleday, 1968.

Dell, Katharine J. " 'I Will Solve My Riddle to the Music of the Lyre' (Psalm XLIX 4 [5]): A Cultic Setting for Wisdom Psalms?" *VT* 54 (2004): 445–58.

Firth, David. "The Teaching of the Psalms." Pages 159–74 in *Interpreting the Psalms: Issues and Approaches.* Edited by David Firth and Philip S. Johnston. Downers Grove, Ill.: InterVarsity Press, 2005.

Gerstenberger, Erhard S. *Psalms, Part 2, and Lamentations, with an Introduction to Cultic Poetry.* FOTL 15. Grand Rapids: Eerdmans, 2001.

Gillingham, Susan. *The Poems and Psalms of the Hebrew Bible*. Oxford: Oxford University Press, 1994.

———. "The Zion Tradition and the Editing of the Hebrew Psalter." Pages 308–41 in *Temple and Worship in Biblical Israel*. Edited by J. Day. London: T&T Clark, 2005.

Gunkel, Hermann, and Joachim Begrich. *Introduction to the Psalms: The Genres of the Religious Lyric of Israel*. Translated by James D. Nogalski. Macon, Ga.: Mercer University Press, 1998.

Hossfeld, Frank-Lothar, and Erich Zenger. *Psalms 2*. Edited by Klaus Baltzer. Translated by Linda M. Maloney. Minneapolis: Fortress, 2005.

Kraus, Hans-Joachim. *Psalms 60–150*. Minneapolis: Augsburg Fortress, 1989.

Kuntz, J. Kenneth. "The Canonical Wisdom Psalms of Ancient Israel: Their Rhetorical, Thematic, and Formal Dimensions." Pages 186–222 in *Rhetorical Criticism: Essays in Honor of James Muilenburg*. Edited by J. J. Jackson and M. Kessler. PTMS 1. Pittsburgh: Pickwick, 1974.

———. "Wisdom Psalms and the Shaping of the Hebrew Psalter." Pages 144–60 in *For a Later Generation: The Transformation of Tradition in Israel, Early Judaism, and Early Christianity*. Edited by Randal Argall, Beverly Bow, and Rodney Werline. Harrisburg: Trinity, 2000.

Lohfink, Norbert. "Psalmen im Neuen Testament: Die Lieder in der Kindheitsgeschichte bei Lukas." Pages 105–25 in *Neue Wege der Psalmenforschung*. Edited by K. Seybold and Erich Zenger. HBS 1. Freiburg: Herder, 1994.

Mandolfo, Carleen. *God in the Dock: Dialogic Tension in the Psalms of Lament*. JSOTSup 357. London: Sheffield Academic, 2002.

Meyer, F. de. "La Dimension Sapientiale Du Psaume 62." *Bijdragen* 42 (1982): 350–65.

Mowinckel, Sigmund. *The Psalms in Israel's Worship*. 2 vols. Translated by D. R. Ap-Thomas. Oxford: Basil Blackwell, 1962.

Murphy, Roland. "Assumptions and Problems in OT Wisdom Research." *CBQ* 29 (1967): 102–12.

———. "A Consideration of the Classification, 'Wisdom Psalms.'" Pages 156–67 in *Congress Volume: Bonn, 1962*. VTSup 9. Edited by G. W. Anderson. Leiden: Brill, 1963.

Nasuti, Harry P. "Redaction-Critical and Canonical Approaches to the Psalms and Psalter." Forthcoming in *Cambridge Methods in Biblical Interpretation: The Book of Psalms*. Edited by Esther M. Menn. Cambridge: Cambridge University Press.

Newsom, Carol. "Woman and the Discourse of Patriarchal Wisdom: A Study of Proverbs 1–9." Pages 43–57 in *Gender and Difference in Ancient Israel*. Edited by Peggy L. Day. Minneapolis: Fortress, 1989.

Reindl, Joseph. "Weisheitliche Bearbeitung von Psalmen: Ein Beitrag zum Verständnis der Sammlung des Psalters." Pages 333–56 in *Congress Volume: Vienna, 1980*. Edited by John A. Emerton. Leiden: Brill, 1981.

Stolz, Fritz. *Psalmen im nachkultischen Raum*. ThSt 129. Zurich: Theologischen, 1983.

Suderman, Weldon Derek. "Prayers Heard and Overheard: Shifting Address and Methodological Matrices in Psalms Scholarship." Ph.D. diss., Toronto School of Theology, 2007.

Trudinger, Peter L. *The Psalms of the Tamid Service: A Liturgical Text from the Second Temple*. VTSup. Leiden: Brill 2004.

Wilson, Gerald H. *The Editing of the Hebrew Psalter*. SBLDS 76. Chico, Calif.: Scholars Press, 1985.

———. "A First Century C.E. Date for the Closing of the Book of Psalms?" *JBQ* 28 (2000): 102–10.

———. "The Shape of the Book of Psalms." *Int* 46 (1992): 129–42.

Zenger, Erich. "Psalmenforschung nach Hermann Gunkel und Sigmund Mowinckel." Pages 399–435 in *Congress Volume: Oslo, 1998*. Edited by A. Lemaire and M. Saebo. Leiden: Brill, 1981.

"WEALTH AND RICHES ARE IN HIS HOUSE" (PS 112:3): ACROSTIC WISDOM PSALMS AND THE DEVELOPMENT OF ANTIMATERIALISM

Phil J. Botha

INTRODUCTION

"Materialism" is understood in this paper as the notion that wealth is more important than spiritual values; "antimaterialism" would then be a rejection of a money-oriented and greedy approach to life. At first glance it would not seem to make sense, therefore, to insert the above quote from Ps 112:3 in the title. The promise that "wealth and riches" are in the house of the righteous does indeed seem to represent a positive appraisal of material things. Yet I would like to argue in this paper that Ps 112, together with the other acrostic wisdom psalms, constitute a unified, authoritative voice against secularism, greed, and religious apostasy in the late Persian period. Since the alphabetic acrostic psalms were composed and inserted into the Psalter by its ultimate (or a penultimate) set of wisdom-inspired editors, this view probably also represents the perspective that those "final" editors wanted readers to find in the book of Psalms as a whole. The theme is therefore important for the study of the Psalter and its editing as well. In this introduction I will subsequently explain the claim about the importance of the acrostic wisdom psalms made above. I will then give a short résumé on the battle against poverty and materialism in the postexilic Jewish society, and finally, introduce Ps 112 itself in order to argue that it should be read as a wisdom intertext, a text meant to be understood in terms of other wisdom texts. From a comparison with Proverbs and other acrostic wisdom psalms, the view of the editors of the Psalter on poverty, wealth, and riches and the threat of secularism should become clearer.

I have stated above that the alphabetic acrostic psalms in the Psalter were intended to give direction to the understanding of the book of Psalms as a whole. The *dimensions* of the alphabetic acrostic psalms already claim an important role for them—the undisputed members of this group comprise about 12 percent of the Psalms.[1] But their *placement* is even more important than their extent. Their composers, who probably were also the same people who decisively edited the Psalter from a wisdom perspective, selected special positions for them.[2] So, for instance, were Pss 25 and 34[3] used as "bookends" to encapsulate a mirror-like symmetrical collection of psalms. It seems logical that they were specifically composed for this purpose, since they are interrelated through the theme of poor piety (25:9, 16, 18, and 21; 34:3, 7, and 19); have the same peculiar alphabetic form; and fit together as a kind of supplication-cum-thanksgiving pair. Through their placement they thus stamp the cocooned collection with a wisdom perspective of poor piety.[4] Psalms 111–112 and 119 in turn are Torah wisdom psalms that together encapsulate the collection of Egyptian Hallel psalms, Pss 113–118,[5] and therefore stamp them with a peculiar form of Torah piety that echoes (inter alia) the perspective on being poor and pious or

---

1. 302 out of 2,527 verses.

2. A similar function was given, possibly earlier in the process of editing the Psalter, to the royal psalms. See in this regard Markus Saur, "Die theologische Funktion der Königspsalmen innerhalb der Komposition des Psalters," in *The Composition of the Book of Psalms* (ed. Erich Zenger; BETL 238; Leuven: Peeters, 2010), 689–700.

3. Similar alphabetic acrostics that lack *vav* and have an additional *pe*-line constitute a prayer for deliverance; as a supplication and a thanksgiving for the answer to the prayer, they correspond to one another. See Frank-Lothar Hossfeld and Erich Zenger, *Die Psalmen I: Psalm 1–50* (DNEB 29; Würzburg: Echter, 1993), 13.

4. Ulrich Berges ("Die Knechte im Psalter: Ein Beitrag zu seiner Kompositionsgeschichte," *Bib* 81 [2000]: 153–78) thinks that a servants redaction was responsible for the second-to-last phase of editing of the Psalter and that they made use of the compositions of the poor-piety group: "Gehören die Knechte im Buch Jesaja zu den letzten Gestaltern der tragenden Gesamtkomposition, so im Psalter zu den vorletzten." He understands Torah-piety to be the last. The prevalence of verses dealing with deprivation in the alphabetic acrostics (which are all Torah psalms) and the self-designation of the author of Ps 119 as "your servant" in fourteen verses make one wonder, however, whether such a clear distinction is necessary.

5. Yair Zakovitch ("The Interpretative Significance of the Sequence of Psalms 111–112.113–118.119," in *The Composition of the Book of Psalms* [ed. Erich Zenger; BETL 238; Leuven: Peeters, 2010], 220), thinks that Pss 113–118 were inserted between Pss 111–112 and 119 which were, at that stage, juxtaposed. This is improbable in view of

rich and arrogant found in Pss 25, 34, and 37.[6] Psalm 145 is another alphabetic acrostic psalm in a prominent position, since it concludes the book of Psalms just before the epilogue found in the final Hallel consisting of Pss 146–150.

Not only the variegated alphabetic acrostics themselves,[7] but also other *alphabetizing* psalms belong to the group of wisdom-inspired psalms, as well as some *nonalphabetic* acrostics.[8] According to Zenger, a special form of alphabetic acrostic is found in Ps 1, where the first word of the psalm begins with א and the last word begins with ת. According to him, this was meant to suggest that the psalm contains instructions for living one's life from A–Z, but it also subtly points to the great Torah psalm 119, which contains a *complete* instruction for living one's life, and seems to suggest that Ps 1 is meant as a résumé of Ps 119.[9] Little needs to

---

other wisdom compositions serving as "bookstands," for instance, 1 Sam 2 and 2 Sam 22 having been inserted as a hermeneutic horizon for the books of Samuel.

6. The rescue of the poor/oppressed (with motifs echoed in 1 Sam 2:1–10 and 2 Sam 22) and the constituting of a community of righteousness serve in this collection as a revelation of the unique divinity of YHWH in contrast to the powerless idols. See Erich Zenger, "Exkurs: Die Komposition des Ägyptischen Hallel bzw. Pessach-Hallel Ps 113–118," in *Psalmen 101–150* (ed. Frank-Lothar Hossfeld and Erich Zenger; HTKAT; Freiburg: Herder, 2008), 246.

7. The alphabet (with a number of smaller deviations) is distributed over twenty-two verse lines (Pss 25 and 34); forty verse lines (Ps 37); ten verse lines (Pss 111 and 112); 176 verse lines (Ps 119) or twenty-one verse lines (Ps 145). Zenger would like to include Pss 9–10 as a strophic alphabetic acrostic, arguing that the first stich of a strophe of four stichs was in each case dedicated to a letter of the alphabet (the first strophe is an exception in that each of the four stichs begins with א). The incomplete present state of the acrostic he adduces to the textual transmission. See Erich Zenger, "Exkurs: Akrostichie im Psalter," in Hossfeld and Zenger, eds., *Psalmen 101–150*, 217.

8. Psalms in which the alphabet of 22 letters is represented through the number of bicola or parallelisms, e.g., Pss 33, 38, 94, and 103. K. Seybold has also pointed out the existence of nonalphabetic acrostics, in which different patterns than the sequence of the letters of the alphabet were used to segment parts of the poem. In Ps 121, for instance, the first and third verse lines begin with the letter א, the fifth to eighth verse lines begin with the letter י. This demarcates four strophes in two main parts, according to Seybold (Klaus Seybold, *Poetik der Psalmen* [Stuttgart: Kohlhammer, 2003], 78).

9. Zenger, "Exkurs: Akrostichie im Psalter," 216–18. My own position is that the author of Ps 119 consulted Ps 1 or else that both were composed at more or less the same time by the same person or group of persons. For the connections among Pss 1, 19, 37, and 119, see Phil J. Botha, "Interpreting 'Torah' in Ps 1 in the light of Ps 119," *HTS* 68 (2012). Online: http://www.hts.org.za/index.php/HTS/article/view/1274/2588.

be said about the influential position of Ps 1. It serves as an introduction to the whole book of Psalms[10] and thus also forms part of a (large) frame, together with Ps 145, the last alphabetic acrostic in the Psalter. Regarding the function of the alphabetic acrostic form, the important principle seems to have been the prominence given to order.[11] The alphabet not only represents completeness from A–Z, as it were, but reflects the order in the universe in general and thus highlights the absence of all chaos in the presence of YHWH. The perfect, mirror-like symmetry with which many of these and related psalms were composed, as well as the symmetry of some collections encapsulated by them, seem to be factors that strengthen this notion.[12]

This paper will thus proceed from the assumption that the alphabetic acrostic psalms were composed and inserted by the wisdom-inspired editors of the Psalter to influence the way we have to understand the Psalms. They were probably composed in a relatively short span of time by the same person or persons.[13] This state of affairs is suggested by the similari-

---

10. Many researchers consider it to have been composed specifically for this position. See Christoph Levin, "Das Gebetbuch der Gerechten: Literaturgeschichtliche Beobachtungen am Psalter," *ZTK* 90 (1993): 355–81 (359). About the role of Ps 1 in the Psalms, see Beat Weber, "Psalm 1 and its Function as a Directive into the Psalter and towards a Biblical Theology," *OTE* 19 (2006): 237–60.

11. The alphabetic structure first of all was meant to suggest completeness from A–Z, coherence, and order. See Zenger, "Exkurs: Akrostichie im Psalter," 217.

12. Examples of such symmetry are provided inter alia by Pss 1, 26, and 33. For the structure of Ps 33, see Phil J. Botha and J. Henk Potgieter, "'The Word of Yahweh is Right': Psalm 33 as a Torah-Psalm," *VE* 31 (2010): 1–8. Pss 26–33 form a symmetric collection, while Pss 113–118 constitute two triptychs which each has a symmetric form, while the two collections also form a compositional parallel. For the details of this, see Zenger, "Exkurs: Die Komposition des Ägyptischen Hallel," 246. The same editors were probably also responsible for inserting the wisdom poem in 1 Sam 2:1–10 (the "Song of Hannah") and a copy of Ps 18 in 2 Sam 22:1–51 as a "frame" for the books of Samuel. In both compositions, humility is praised and arrogance denounced.

13. Contrary to this notion, Zenger ("Psalm 112," 234) does not even accept that Pss 111 and 112 have been composed by the same person ("wegen stilistischer Differenzen"). The same group of ancient intellectuals probably also composed and inserted other psalms as a whole (e.g., Pss 12, 26, 49, 52, 73), while they most probably edited a great number of already existing compositions to enhance the definition of the righteous and the wicked. See in this regard Levin, "Das Gebetbuch der Gerechten." For the wisdom connections of Ps 12, see Phil J. Botha, "Pride and the Suffering of the Poor in the Persian Period: Psalm 12 in its Post-exilic Context," *OTE* 25 (2012): 40–56.

ties they share, all having been influenced by the attempt to promulgate the book of Proverbs as the Torah or "teaching" of YHWH and to explicate this teaching for those who have a yearning to live an upright life of humility, dedication to the Torah (the Books of Moses), trust in YHWH, and willingness to wait for him to intervene on their behalf. Psalm 112 will be chosen as an example and the theme of wealth and poverty in the alphabetic acrostic psalms will be investigated to demonstrate how they relate to one another and collectively throw light on one another and on the circumstances under which they were produced.

In his important article on Pss 15, 49 and 112, Erich Zenger summarizes the role of money in creating societal antagonisms in Israelite and Jewish society.[14] The Hebrew Bible *in toto* suggests that there was a massive economical antagonism between rich and poor (also manifesting as the opposition between powerful and powerless people).[15] This reality was linked in many instances to the common Ancient Near Eastern system of money lending, disproportionate high interest rates asked, the taking of pledges, and debt slavery. This state of affairs is for example expressed in Prov 22:7: "The rich rules over the poor, the borrower is a slave of the lender."[16] Because of this system, many people lost their freedom or were forced to trade their children for their debt, and many more lost their inherited land and economic independence.[17] This happened already during the time of the monarchy (see Amos 2:6; 8:6), but the problem intensified in the Persian period when money was introduced for the first time and taxes had to be paid to the government in monetary form.[18]

The injustices and discrepancies caused by the insensitive and immoral abuse of the system brought about various responses and attempts to rectify imbalances. The theological response was that systematic impoverishment of a part of the people of YHWH could not be tolerated in view of the confession that YHWH gave freedom and land out of free grace.[19] The response in the *Bundesbuch*, Deuteronomic Law and Holiness Code can be viewed as progressively more emphatic and theologically stronger

---

14. Erich Zenger, "Geld als Lebensmittel? Über die Wertung des Reichtums im Psalter (Psalmen 15.49.112)," *JBTh* 21 (2006): 73–96.

15. Ibid., 73.

16. Ibid.

17. Ibid., 74.

18. Zenger, "Geld als Lebensmittel?" 75.

19. Ibid., 76.

motivated.[20] In Exod 21:2–6, temporal limits of six years are proscribed to debt slavery. Deuteronomy 15:12–18 makes an addition: Believers should give the impoverished neighbor some capital to begin anew and links this impetus to the theological program of YHWH as the God who liberates from slavery, Israel as a community of siblings, and wealth as a blessing from YHWH that must be shared. Leviticus 25:39–43 goes even further and practically abolishes debt slavery. In its place comes wage labor, which would not only provide a regular income and sustenance to the poor, but also the possibility of buying back land lost through debt and, eventually, of regaining independence.[21]

Zenger points out that those ideals unfortunately did not reflect reality. The *Bundesbuch* in Exod 22:24–26 rejects the system of interest and taking of sureties, but Deut 23:20–21 does not only plead for borrowing without interest, it also rejects any form of profit. Not only extortionate interest is proscribed, not only from the poor, but any form of interest.[22] Borrowing money is not something that one can be charged for, since it is linked to the divine blessing. The taking of securities is also practically abolished in Deut 24:6, 10–13, and 17–18.[23] Lev 25:35–38 defines the interest-free lending of money as "life sustenance" or "life nourishment." In these verses the generous handling of wealth and money becomes a medium through which YHWH can realize his being God in Israel.[24] The correct attitude towards money is the praxis of reverence for God and a continuation of the redemption history of Israel, begun by YHWH, the God of the Exodus.[25]

This development has then led to the view that wealth and money should be perceived as a blessing from YHWH; money should consequently not become an instrument of impoverishment, but be used as nourishment—not only for individual poor persons, but for Israel as the united people of YHWH as a whole.[26]

---

20. Ibid., 77.
21. Ibid.
22. Ibid., 78.
23. Ibid.
24. Ibid., 79.
25. Ibid.
26. Ibid.

In the diptych formed by Pss 111–112, the handling of money is described as an *imitatio dei*.[27] Psalm 111 is a song of praise for the creative power of YHWH and his righteous care for Israel during a long history of redemption. Psalm 112 is a wisdom teaching psalm in which wealth is described as the blessing of the person who lives his or her life in reverence of YHWH, imitating the righteousness of YHWH in Ps 111.[28] Wealth becomes a way to a happy life if it is shared with others by lending without interest and by gracefully giving to the poor. This twin pair of psalms together teaches that the gracious and charitable rich person becomes an "imitator" of the righteous and caring God of Israel.

What remains to be done in this paper is to give a short description of the form and message of Ps 112; determine its literary context; and investigate its relationship with other wisdom (more specific acrostic wisdom) psalms addressing the same problem, in order for us to gain some insight into the issues with which the editors of the Psalter had to grapple.

THE TEXT AND ORGANIZATION OF PSALM 112

Psalm 112 can be defined as a wisdom teaching song that aims to restore faith in the Proverbs torah of retribution for the arrogant wicked and, in contrast to this, YHWH's graceful gift of material blessings, honor, a good remembrance, and prosperity for those who show reverence for him and who trust in him by obeying the Torah (of Moses) to aid the poor and destitute, as well as an extended grace for their offspring. As such, the psalm conveys the same message as other wisdom psalms. Variations in the portrayal of this dogma should not be lightly interpreted as discrepancies or theological developments. I would like to argue the case for this by comparing Ps 112 with Proverbs and the other alphabetic acrostic psalms as a group.

The text of Ps 112 has been preserved remarkably well (see the table on pp. 112–13). It was found in exactly the same consonantal form at Qum-

---

27. Ibid., 80.
28. "Ps 111 beschreibt und feiert die göttliche Gerechtigkeit, Ps 112 beschreibt und empfiehlt die menschliche Gerechtigkeit" (Zenger, "Geld als Lebensmittel?" 82–33).

I	A			¹ Praise YHWH!
		1	הַלְלוּ יָהּ ׀	Blessed is the man who fears YHWH,
			אַשְׁרֵי־אִישׁ יָרֵא אֶת־יְהוָה	who greatly <u>delights</u> in his commandments.
			בְּמִצְוֺתָיו חָפֵץ מְאֹד׃	
		2	גִּבּוֹר בָּאָרֶץ יִהְיֶה זַרְעוֹ	² His offspring will be <u>powerful</u> in the land,
			דּוֹר יְשָׁרִים יְבֹרָךְ׃	(as) the generation of upright he will be <u>blessed</u>.
	B	3	הוֹן־וָעֹשֶׁר בְּבֵיתוֹ	³ Wealth and <u>riches</u> are in his house;
			וְצִדְקָתוֹ עֹמֶדֶת לָעַד׃	<u>and his righteousness endures forever.</u>
		4	זָרַח בַּחֹשֶׁךְ אוֹר לַיְשָׁרִים	⁴ He* shines as a light in the darkness for the upright,
			חַנּוּן וְרַחוּם וְצַדִּיק׃	**merciful and compassionate and just.**
	C	5	טוֹב־אִישׁ חוֹנֵן וּמַלְוֶה	⁵ It goes well with the one who shows <u>compassion and lends out,</u>
			יְכַלְכֵּל דְּבָרָיו בְּמִשְׁפָּט׃	and conducts his business **honestly**.
		6	כִּי־לְעוֹלָם לֹא־יִמּוֹט	⁶ For he will *never* be moved;
			לְזֵכֶר עוֹלָם יִהְיֶה צַדִּיק׃	the righteous will be an everlasting remembrance.

II	D	7	מִשְּׁמוּעָה רָעָה לֹא יִירָא	7 He does *not* fear bad news;
			נָכוֹן לִבּוֹ בָּטֻחַ בַּיהוָה׃	his heart is sure, trusting in YHWH.
		8	סָמוּךְ לִבּוֹ לֹא יִירָא	8 His heart is sustained, he will *not* fear
			עַד אֲשֶׁר־יִרְאֶה בְצָרָיו׃	until he looks down on his enemies.
	E	9	פִּזַּר ׀ נָתַן לָאֶבְיוֹנִים	9 He gives lavishly to the <u>poor</u>;
			צִדְקָתוֹ עֹמֶדֶת לָעַד	<u>his righteousness endures forever,</u>
			קַרְנוֹ תָּרוּם בְּכָבוֹד׃	his horn will be exalted in honor.
	F	10	רָשָׁע יִרְאֶה ׀ וְכָעָס	10 The wicked will see it and be <u>distressed</u>;
			שִׁנָּיו יַחֲרֹק וְנָמָס	he will gnash his teeth and <u>become weak</u>;
			תַּאֲוַת רְשָׁעִים תֹּאבֵד׃	the craving of the wicked people will <u>perish</u>.

* See the discussion and eventual choice for this interpretation in Zenger, "Psalm 112," 233. The righteous is also represented as a light in Prov 4:18 and 13:9. The righteous is represented by being described as merciful, compassionate, and just, and as replicating the qualities of YHWH (cf. Ps 111:3–4) and thus a kind of theophany (cf. Isa 58:8).

ran.[29] Psalm 112 has an asymmetric mirror-like structure.[30] The alphabet is used as a structuring principle not only in the acrostic form where each subsequent colon begins with the next letter of the alphabet, but the first and last words also begin with א and ת, respectively, and constitute antithesis on top of that: אשרי ("blessed") is the opposite of תאבד ("will perish").[31] Strophe A is therefore contrasted with strophe F and this is worked out in the contents of the strophes also, since the man who fears YHWH is said to be *blessed* and his offspring to become *powerful* in the land (A), while the wicked will become *weak* and their craving or desire will *perish* (F). Strophe A itself is bound together by the semantic inclusion formed by "blessed" (אשרי) and "be blessed" (יברך) (the first and last words). It is further composed with two pairs of parallelism (he **fears** YHWH; he **delights** in his commandments; his *offspring* will be powerful, his *generation* will be blessed). Strophe F is shorter, consisting of one tricolon, but is also bound together through a (chiastic) parallel: *The wicked* will be distressed; *he* will become weak and *the craving of the wicked* will perish. In contrasting strophe A and F, the author(s) also symbolize(s) the importance of the subject matter by giving less space to the wicked than to the one who fears YHWH. "Become powerful" in 2a also creates antithesis with "will become weak" in 10b.

Strophe B, the second poetic unit, in turn is related to strophe E, the second to last poetic unit. This time the two strophes form a parallel rather than antithesis as with strophes A and F. Cola 3b and 9b are almost exactly the same, drawing attention to the connection between the two strophes. The "riches" mentioned in 3a seem to form a contrast with the "poor" mentioned in 9a, but the last mentioned describes the role that the "wealth and riches" that are found in the house of the God-fearing person play in

29. 4QPs^w frgs. 1–2 contain the whole psalm; 4QPs^b co. XXVI: frg. 25 iii contains v. 4 and part of v. 5. See Eugene Ulrich, ed., *The Biblical Qumran Scrolls: Transcriptions and Textual Variants* (VTSup 134; Leiden: Brill, 2010), 676.

30. Zenger ("Psalm 112," 239) proposes the following structure: I (1–3); II A (4–6); II B (7–9); III (10). Yair Zakovitch ("The Sequence of Psalms 111–119," 216) has exactly the same segmentation as this for both Pss 111 and 112. The structure is not without merit and reflects the symmetry which was probably intended by the author to be noticed. Section II A in Zenger's scheme is, however, called "Erster Hauptteil: Die Gerechtichkeit des JHWH-Fürchtigen," but v. 3, which specifically mentions the "righteousness" of the righteous person, falls outside this unit.

31. This contrasting of the righteous person and the wicked person is a "watermark" of the authors also found in Ps 1, and played upon in Ps 119 as well.

his life—they are used to give lavishly to the poor (9a). The rhyme of הוֹן and אֶבְיוֹן (even though the plural form of אביון is used) thus draws attention to the connection between "riches" and poor people. It is because the one who fears YHWH "shines as a light in the darkness for the upright" (4a) that his horn will be "exalted in honor" (9c). Internally, strophe B forms a parallel (ABAB pattern in the four cola). Strophe E contains an extended grammatical parallel: Masculine verb + preposition לְ; suffix 3rd masculine singular + feminine verb + preposition לְ; suffix 3rd masculine singular + feminine verb + preposition בְּ.

The two middle strophes, C and D, also have a special connection. The presence of prosperity or success (טוב) in the life of the generous person (5a) has a direct bearing on his not fearing "bad news" (רעה) (7a). Although "good" and "bad" form an antithesis and thus draw attention to the connection between the two strophes, the presence of לא in 7a changes them into synonymous pronouncements. These two strophes are also the only two where negative particles are found, all of them used to describe the positive aspects of the life of the god-fearing man: He will *never* be moved (6a); he does *not* fear bad news (7a); he will *not* fear (8a). The repetition of לא יירא in 7a and 8a, and the wordplay with יראה in 8b, bind 7 and 8 together as a strophe.

The psalm thus clearly displays the characteristics of a literary wisdom composition. It was devised as a teaching song aimed at reinforcing the dogma that the righteous (identified as a צדיק in the structural middle of the poem, 6b) will be blessed and the wicked (identified as a רשע at the end,10a) will lose power and "melt" (10b). The contribution that the psalm makes to this theology is defining the righteous not only as one who fears YHWH and delights in his Torah but who *consequently* uses his prosperity to replicate the actions of YHWH in a merciful, compassionate, generous, and honest style of living and *therefore* does not have to fear calamity or an enemy. The decline of the wicked is also described as a *consequence* of the prosperity of the righteous, which seems to be a novel idea.

PSALM 112 IN THE CONTEXT OF WISDOM WRITINGS

As has been explained earlier, Ps 112 forms a diptych with its twin, Ps 111, and should be read and understood within this context.[32] Through this

---

32. For a summary of the relationship, see the overview of Erich Zenger, "Geld

juxtaposition, which will not be explored further here, however, a special relationship is established between Ps 112 and Prov 31:10–31.[33] Psalm 112 also has a special relationship with Pss 1 and 119, and in addition to this seems like a summary of Ps 37. Like the other psalms mentioned in the same breath, it must have been cultivated in the fertile soil of Proverbs.[34]

PSALM 112 AND PROVERBS

Bernard Gosse[35] finds the connection between Ps 112 and Proverbs first and foremost in the enduring justice of the person who fears YHWH (see the repetition of "his righteousness endures forever" in 3b and 9b). The following is a list of his comments on the connections between Ps 112 and Proverbs, with some notes of my own:

- Concerning Ps 112:1, "Blessed is the one who fears YHWH, who greatly delights in his commandments," Gosse remarks that one here encounters the theme of the "fear of YHWH" originating from the book of Proverbs; the beatitude of Ps 1:1;

---

als Lebensmittel?" 80–86, and the commentary of Zenger, "Psalm 112," 242–45. Zakovitch ("The Sequence of Psalms 111–119," 216–18) also has a fine comparison. These descriptions have taken into account *inter alia* Hans-Peter Mathys, *Dichter und Beter: Theologen aus spätalttestamentlicher Zeit* (OBO 132; Göttingen: Vandenhoeck & Ruprecht, 1994), 256–59; and Walter Zimmerli, "Zwillingspsalmen," in *Wort, Lied, und Gottesspruch: Beiträge zu Psalmen und Propheten* (ed. Josef Schreiner; Würzburg: Echter, 1972), 105–13.

33. The alphabetic acrostic poem in Prov 31:10–31 represents the ideal of a feminine *imitatio dei* of the divine actions of Lady Wisdom in Prov 1–9; in the same way Ps 112 represents the ideal of a masculine *imitatio dei* of the divine actions of YHWH in Ps 111. In this regard, see Zenger, "Psalm 112," 245.

34. It would be a mistake to deny that the same group of editors who inserted wisdom psalms into the Psalter could not also have edited the book of Proverbs – similarities between the acrostic psalms and Proverbs could in many cases be attributed to their having been composed by the same people. This possibility is not investigated in this paper, but see in this regard the work of Christoph Levin, "Das Gebetbuch der Gerechten," 372–74.

35. Bernard Gosse, *L'influence du livre des Proverbes sur les rédactions bibliques à l'époque perse* (Paris: Gabalda, 2008), 88–89. The following summary of Gosse's views is extracted from this description.

as well as the usage of מצוה which occurs in the Psalter based on its occurrence in Prov 3:1.[36]

- With regard to Ps 112:2, "His offspring (זרעו) will be powerful in the land, (as) the generation of upright he will be blessed," Gosse remarks that this verse conforms to the doctrine of Prov 20:7: "The righteous who walks in his integrity—blessed are his children after him!" In my view, this verse represents a doctrine of "extended retribution" which is also carefully formulated in Prov 11:21, "You can be sure that the evil person will not go unpunished, but the offspring (זרע) of the righteous will escape."

- With regard to Ps 112:3, "Wealth and riches are in his house; and his uprightness endures forever," Gosse refers to the three single occurrences of wealth (הון) in the Psalter (in Pss 44:13; 112:3; and 119:14), in contrast to its eighteen occurrences in Proverbs. The word for riches (עשר) is also found only in Pss 49:7; 52:9; and 112:3 in the Psalms, but nine times in Proverbs. By implication, this points to its context of origin being Proverbs. In addition to this, it would seem that Ps 112:3 was formulated in antithesis to and thus alluding to Prov 1:13, where the sinners are said to attempt to seduce people with the promise of finding *precious goods* (כל-הון יקר) and spoil with which they will fill their (our) *houses* (בתינו).

- According to Gosse, Ps 112:4, "He shines as a light in the darkness for the upright, merciful and compassionate and just," should be compared to Prov 13:9: "The light of the upright (אור צדיקים) rejoices, but the lamp of the wicked will be extinguished." There is, in my view, a special connection of this verse with Prov 4:18, which will be discussed below.

- Concerning Ps 112:6, "For he will never be moved (לא-ימוט); the righteous will be an everlasting remembrance (יהיה צדיק לזכר עולם)," Gosse notes that this calls to mind Prov 10:7: "The memory of the righteous is a blessing (זכר צדיק לברכה); but the name of the wicked will rot." The first half of the verse should, however, be read especially against the background

---

36. "My son, do not forget my Torah, but let your heart keep my commandments (מצותי)."

of Prov 10:30 and 12:3. Both these verses teach the doctrine
often repeated in acrostic and other wisdom psalms that "the
righteous shall never be moved (בל־ימוט), but the wicked
shall not dwell in the land."[37]

- Finally, Ps 112:9, "He gives lavishly to the poor (פזר נתן
  לאביונים); his righteousness endures forever, his horn will
  be exalted in honor," reminds one in the view of Gosse of
  the same design of retribution which is found in Prov 22:9:
  "Whoever has a bountiful eye shall be blessed; for he gives of
  his bread to the poor (כי־נתן מלחמו לדל)." To this should be
  added, however, that Ps 112 as a whole serves as an explica-
  tion and confirmation of Prov 11:24, "One distributes freely
  (יש מפזר), yet gains even more; another withholds unjustly,
  but comes to poverty (למחסור)." From this background it is
  clear that the "wealth and riches" in the house of the righteous
  are thought of as having accrued through his munificent attitude towards material possessions.[38]

PSALM 112 AND THE OTHER WISDOM ACROSTIC PSALMS

Psalm 112 seems to be especially closely related to Ps 1. As has been noted
earlier, a *structural* connection between Ps 112 and Ps 1 is found in the fact
that both psalms begin with אשרי and end with תאבד. In both psalms a
person who finds *delight* in the *teaching* of YHWH (in Ps 1:2 it is someone
who has חֵפֶץ in YHWH's תורה; in Ps 112:1 it is a person who "delights"
[חָפֵץ] in his מצות) is called "blessed." Something is also said to "perish" at
the end of both psalms. In the case of Ps 1:6 it is the *"way of the wicked"*
that will perish; in the case of Ps 112:10 it is the *"desire of the wicked"*

---

37. Prov 10:30 is quoted. Prov 12:3 has, "No one can be established through wickedness, but the root of the righteous shall not be moved." This verse has probably
contributed to the metaphor of the righteous being like a tree "planted" in Ps 1:3, while
it definitely played a role in the composition of Ps 52:7 and 10. See Pss 34:16; 37:9, 11,
22, 29, 34; 52:7.

38. Almost all occurrences of חנן in Proverbs refer to compassion with regard to
the poor or oppressed, cf. Prov 14:21 and 31; 19:17; 21:10; and 28:8. The only exception seems to be Prov 26:25. According to R. Norman Whybray (*Wealth and Poverty
in the Book of Proverbs* [JSOTSup 99; Sheffield: JSOT, 1990], 13), more than 120 verses
out of a total of 513 in Proverbs refer to wealth, a comfortable existence, or positions
of power and influence, showing how important this theme is in the book as a whole.

which will perish.[39] This may seem to suggest that Ps 112:10 addresses the problem of materialism while Ps 1 is more general, but this is not the case. Both speak from one mouth: The "road" of the wicked in Ps 1:6 also refers (indirectly) to the problem of greed, since it relates to the "road" of sinners spoken of in Ps 1:1, and this "road" in turn is defined in Prov 1:10–15 (on which Ps 1:1 is based)[40] as the road of sinners who spill blood and ambush people *to accumulate precious goods out of greed* (see the advice to refrain from "going" with the "sinners" on their "road" in Prov 1:15 and the description "greedy for unjust gain, בצע בצע" in Prov 1:19).

This corresponding antithesis between the being "blessed" of the upright and the "self-destruction" of evildoers in the two psalms is no coincidence, since the dogma was inspired by Proverbs and used by the editors of the Psalter to establish a link also between Pss 1 and 112.[41] It is said, for instance, in Prov 1:32, "the apostasy of the simple will kill them, and the complacency of fools *destroy* (תאבדם) them," while Prov 3:13 teaches, "*blessed* (אשרי) is the man who finds wisdom." Proverbs 10:28 also describes the contrast between the "wicked" and the "righteous" by using the verb אבד: "The hope of the righteous is joy, but the expectation (תקוה) of the wicked will perish (תאבד)." This is echoed not only in Pss 1 and 112, but also elsewhere. Psalm 9 (which incidentally also begins with a word in א) links to this verse by formulating an in-verse aphorism in its third last verse-line (9:19): "For the needy shall not always be forgotten, and the hope (תקוה) of the *poor* shall *not* perish (תאבד) forever." The אשרי-formula at the beginning and a form of אבד in the last verse line is also a feature of Pss 119 and 143, while the verb אבד seems to have been used (or was inserted) also often in more or less the middle verse-line of a number of psalms: it is found in the middle verse-line of Ps 5, the middle

---

39. In the words of Christoph Levin ("Das Gebetbuch der Gerechten," 370), "Ps 112 liest sich wie eine alphabetische Fassung von Ps 1."

40. It is therefore not surprising that Ps 1 defines the righteous at the beginning in negative terms—what he does *not* do—since it replicates the introduction to Proverbs. It is not necessary to deduce from this that appreciation of the Torah plays a secondary role in the poem as, e.g., Christoph Levin ("Das Gebetbuch der Gerechten," 360–61) does.

41. It is also possible that the authors of the acrostic wisdom psalms were also the authors of the introduction to Proverbs, which would also explain the connections. What speaks against this being the case is the substitution of חכמה with the תורה in the Psalter.

verse-line of Ps 31 (הייתי ככלי אבד),[42] and the middle verse-line of Ps 49. Psalms 31, 119, and 143 are known wisdom compositions.[43]

Psalm 112 is thus in line with Ps 1 in terms of the description of the righteous person, using terminology borrowed from Proverbs, as someone who *fears* YHWH and *delights* in his teaching. A similar definition is found in Ps 119:47, which speaks of "*delight*" in the "*commandments*" of YHWH, but uses the *hithpalpel* of שעע instead of חפץ.

But is Ps 112 not unique among the wisdom acrostics in emphasizing the *prosperity* of the righteous? This is indeed not the case. Although it is formulated more carefully and in relative terms, the other alphabetic acrostics also assert that the "being blessed" of the righteous person includes material prosperity and possession of the land. Psalm 25:13, for instance, says that the one who fears YHWH will "himself (נפשו) dwell in what is good (thus enjoy prosperity), and his offspring (וזרעו) will inherit the land." "Great prosperity" (רֹב שָׁלוֹם) is also promised to the humble (ענוים) in Ps 37, a prosperity that will result from possession of the land (Ps 37:11). The promise of occupation of the land by the righteous is often repeated, using different verbs to express it.[44] Psalm 112:2 shows similarity to Ps 25:13 in that this promise is extended to the *descendants* of the righteous: "his *offspring* (זרעו) will be powerful[45] in the land."

In the same vein, Ps 37 contrasts the "offspring (זרעו)" of the righteous, who has never been observed to beg for food (v. 25) and the "offspring (זֶרַע)" of the wicked, which will be exterminated (v. 28).[46] In Ps 37,

---

42. Ps 31:13, "I have become like something lost." Cf. the fine artistry of the author of Ps 119:176, who replicates the sound of this with "I have gone astray like a lost sheep (תעיתי כשׂה אבד)."

43. Concerning the wisdom connections of Ps 31, see my article "Freedom to Roam in a Wide Open Space: Ps 31 Read in Conjunction with the History of David in the Books of Samuel and the Psalms," in *Seitenblicke: Literarische und historische Studien zu Nebenfiguren im zweiten Samuelbuch* (ed. Walter Dietrich; OBO 249; Göttingen: Vandenhoeck & Ruprecht, 2011), 424–42.

44. Pss 25:13 לין; 37:3 and 29 שׁכן; 37:9, 11, 22, 29 and 34 ירשׁ.

45. In other words, influential. This is a blessing within a blessing, since it means that the children of the righteous will still be faithful to YHWH.

46. This "extermination" is not mentioned in Ps 112, but if one knows Ps 37:34, it is clear that this is what is hinted at in Ps 112:8. Ps 37:34b says, "when the wicked are cut off, you will see it (בהכרת רשעים תראה)." This is the background for Ps 112:8, "His heart is sustained, he will not fear until he looks down on his enemies (עד אשׁר־ יראה בצריו)."

the righteous are also promised possession of the land and everlasting residence in it (cf. Ps 37:29). It would seem that Pss 34 and 37 do not explicitly promise wealth, but rather the absence of poverty. Psalm 34:10 gives the assurance that those who fear YHWH "have no lack" and the next verse that those who seek YHWH "shall not want any good thing." The same psalm is willing to acknowledge that the righteous do not always enjoy prosperity, since it says that "many are the afflictions of the righteous" (34:20), but it nevertheless asserts that YHWH delivers the righteous from them all and "keeps all his bones" (34:21). And yet, Ps 37:4 promises that YHWH will give the "desires" of the heart to those who "delight" (hithpael of ענג) themselves in YHWH. This pronouncement is not far removed in theory from the "wealth and riches" promised in Ps 112:3. The important thing is that Ps 37:16 emphasises that the relationship with YHWH is more important than material possessions: "What little the righteous possesses is better than the abundance (המון) of many wicked people." Psalm 112, in turn, focuses on the other side of the coin. Its message can be described as, "No matter how much the righteous possesses, by sharing it with poor people, he displays his attachment to YHWH." In both Ps 37 and Ps 112, the righteous is defined as someone who depends on YHWH: Ps 37:17 says, "For the arms of the wicked shall be broken, but YHWH *supports* (סומך) the righteous." This concurs with Ps 112:8, which says of the righteous "His heart is *sustained* (סָמוּךְ); he will not fear." If the righteous is sustained, it means that he trusts in YHWH, and this, in distinction from those who trust in riches, is the characteristic of the righteous.[47] Although Ps 37 allows for the possibility that "evil times" may come over the righteous, even in the time of famine they will be "satisfied" (ישׂבעו, Ps 37:19).

To sum up, then: Ps 112 is more explicit in its promise of "wealth and riches" being included in the blessings of the YHWH fearer, but the other acrostic psalms also promise (relative) prosperity and the absence of destitution. The author of Ps 112 is not as naïve as some interpreters have thought:[48] True blessedness and happiness are described as consisting of finding joy in the Torah (v. 1), serving as a light for fellow believers (v. 4), imitating YHWH's compassion and mercy by caring for others (vv. 5, 9), experiencing confidence in YHWH's continued protection (vv. 7–8), and

---

47. Cf. Prov 11:28, "He who trusts in his riches (בעשׁרו) will fall, but the righteous will flourish like a green leaf." See also the discussion in Whybray, *Wealth and Poverty*," 39–40.

48. So also Zenger, "Psalm 112," 241.

being honored by one's in-group (vv. 2, 9). The open-handedness of the righteous person serves as proof that the Torah of YHWH and a personal relationship with him are more important than the accrual of riches.

At first sight, Ps 119 seems to offer a different view. "Wealth," "gold and silver," and "great spoil" are mentioned in the psalm, but these are consistently compared anti-materialistically to the greater wealth of the Torah. Psalm 119:14 says, "I have rejoiced in the way of your testimonies as (much as) in all riches (כל־הון)." Verse 36 prays in line with this, "Incline my heart to your testimonies and not to (greedy) gain (בצע)," taking a cue from Prov 1:19. And yet, when Ps 119:72 praises the Torah as being better than "thousands of pieces of gold and silver," or when verse 127 says that the suppliant loves the commandments "more than gold, even very fine gold," or verse 162 compares the suppliant's joy in the promise of YHWH with that of someone who finds "great spoil" (taking a cue from Prov 1:13 this time), there is no real difference with the promise of wealth and riches for the righteous in Ps 112:3, since the corresponding verse in the second half of Ps 112 (112:9) says "he gives lavishly to the poor." The inspiration for both Ps 112:3 and Ps 119:162 comes from Prov 1:13, and the two verses thus present basically the same view. Psalm 112:3b and 9b both assert that the *righteousness* of the righteous person "endures" forever. The wealthy righteous person who lavishly gives to the poor therefore does not differ from the suppliant of Ps 119 who values the Torah so much, since the Torah teaches precisely this, that one should lavishly give to the poor. The righteous beneficiary of Ps 112 is, in fact, the same person as the oppressed worshipper of Ps 119. He displays the very quality of YHWH himself and therefore also the quality of the Torah, since Ps 119:42 says that the righteousness of YHWH endures forever (cf. the similar pronouncement in Ps 111:3) and Ps 119:144 that the "testimonies" of YHWH are "righteous forever." YHWH and his Torah thus have the same quality as the righteous person of Ps 112. The last alphabetic acrostic in the Psalter similarly states that YHWH is "merciful and compassionate" (Ps 145:8), and these are also exactly the same qualities ascribed to the righteous wealthy person in Ps 112:4.

For the author of Ps 119, possession of the land does not seem to be an option any longer. He describes himself as a "sojourner" in the land.[49]

---

49. "I am a sojourner in the land" (Ps 119:19); "the house of my sojourning" (Ps 119:54).

In addition to this, his "heritage" is a spiritual one, not an estate: "Your testimonies are my heritage (נחלתי) forever" (Ps 119:111). If this is read in conjunction with Prov 8:21, "so that I (Lady Wisdom) may cause those who love me to inherit (להנחיל) property, and that I may fill their treasuries," the author seems to take a dim view of material possessions also. But this is a way of describing his personal dedication to the Torah and not an expression of his belief in retribution. The predominant style reflected in Ps 119 is that of a lament about oppression caused by arrogant, insolent people[50] who mock the supplicant about his dedication to the Torah,[51] leaving no room for a confession of personal blessing or connection with the Promised Land because of his dedication to the Torah.

When Ps 112:4a describes the effect of the righteous wealthy person by stating that he "shines as a light in the darkness for the upright," it is also the *righteousness* of that person that is highlighted. There is another connection with Ps 37 in this description, since Ps 37:6 promises that YHWH will "bring out" (*hiphil* of יצא) the righteousness (צדק) of the righteous as the light (כאור), and his justice (משפט) as the noonday." Compare in this regard the description of the righteous rich person in Ps 112:5 as one who "conducts his business honestly (במשפט)." Gosse sees a connection with Prov 13:9 in this verse of Ps 112, but Prov 4:18 probably served as the inspiration of both Ps 37:6 and Ps 112:5, for it says that the road of the righteous is (in contrast to that of the wicked which is associated with wickedness and violence, and therefore darkness)[52] "as the light of dawn which shines brighter and brighter until full day." The righteous person of Ps 112 is therefore the same person as the righteous person of Ps 37. This can also be seen in the fact that Ps 37:26 also defines the righteous in terms of his compassion and his willingness to lend money without reserve: "The whole day he *shows compassion and lends* out (חונן ומלוה), and his offspring is a blessing." This is exactly the same expression used in

---

50. The noun זֵד, "insolent person," appears six times in Ps 119 and only seven times elsewhere in the Hebrew Bible. Its occurrence in Mal 3:15 provides a good description of the problems the authors of the alphabetic acrostics had to contend with: "Now we consider the arrogant happy; indeed, those who practice wickedness prosper; indeed, they put God to the test and get away with it."

51. The connection between arrogant people who mock others is also expressed in Prov 21:24.

52. Cf. Prov 4:17 and 4:19.

Ps 112:5, "It goes well with the man who shows compassion and lends out (חונן ומלוה)."[53]

I claimed earlier that Ps 112 presents a novel idea when it states that the prosperity and honor of the righteous will be the cause of the disappearance of the wicked (cf. Ps 112:10). It would seem that the opposite possibility is expressed in Ps 37:1, since the righteous are there reprimanded not to fret because of evildoers nor to be envious of them. In Ps 37:8 the warning is even more pertinent: "Refrain from anger and forsake wrath; do not get excited—that only leads to evil." The two psalms, however, present the two sides of the same coin from Proverbs, since the wicked are merely depicted as being foolish and suffering from the consequences of this state.[54] The idea that evil, and hatred of the righteous, will kill the wicked, is also expressed in Ps 34:22.[55] There is a collection of admonitions in Proverbs that warns against quick temper, for example Prov 14:17, 29; 16:32; 19:11; 22:24; and 24:19. This last mentioned text has served as the direct inspiration for Ps 37:1, and the author of Ps 112 has inserted a hint in his composition that he also authored or had an intimate knowledge of Ps 37, since Ps 37:12[56] is alluded to in Ps 112:10.[57]

This investigation began with a comparison between Ps 112 and Ps 1. The similarities between the two, namely the first word being אשרי and the last word תאבד; the righteous being described in both psalms as someone who "fears" YHWH and who finds delight (with חפץ) in his "teaching"; and the fact that Ps 1, being based on Proverbs 1, also addresses the problem of materialism. To conclude this comparison between Ps 112 and the acrostic wisdom psalms, one further remark may be needed. It would seem that Ps 1 also applauds the generosity of the righteous person, and that Ps 112 helps us to understand this. The YHWH-fearer is compared in Ps 1 to a tree that "bears its fruit in season" (Ps 1:3). Fruit-bearing is a wisdom motif of retribution, and Prov 1:31 very likely played a role in the

---

53. In Ps 37:21, the conduct of the wicked who "borrows and does not give back" is contrasted to that of the righteous who "shows compassion and gives (חונן ונותן)." Cf. the use of נתן in a similar context in Ps 112:9.

54. Cf. Prov 1:32 which warns that the complacency of fools destroys them.

55. "Evil will kill the wicked, and those who hate the righteous will be condemned."

56. "The wicked plots against the righteous and gnashes his teeth at him (וחרק עליו שניו)."

57. "He will gnash his teeth (שניו יחרק)."

author of Ps 1 having chosen the tree metaphor—it concerns the "scoffers"[58] and "fools" having to eat the "fruit of their way" as a consequence of their complacency. Failing to choose wisdom leads to one being forced to eat the fruit of one's actions. But Prov 11:30 most certainly also contributed to the choice of the metaphor of a tree in Ps 1. It says, "The fruit of the righteous is a tree of life, and the one who saves lives is wise."[59] Understood against this background, Ps 1 thus also applauds the righteous person who has been blessed by YHWH and who consequently becomes a tree of life, giving "its fruit in its season," particularly in the form of shared blessings for fellow Israelites.

CONCLUSION: ISSUES WITH WHICH THE AUTHORS OF THE ACROSTIC WISDOM PSALMS WERE CONCERNED

In addition to their endeavour to create finely balanced compositions, it seems safe to contend that the authors of the acrostic wisdom psalms consciously attempted to produce wisdom intertexts.[60] That is, they fashioned their compositions as homilies on Proverbs and the Torah proper, alluding to and reinterpreting the wisdom teaching of Proverbs as referring to the teaching or Torah of YHWH (both that in the Pentateuch and Proverbs), since the ABC of knowledge, wisdom, and instruction was in any case considered to be the fear of YHWH (Prov 1:7). They furthermore seem to have composed each wisdom acrostic psalm also in such a way that it would contain allusions to various other members of the group, elucidating one another.[61] When these psalms, which they located at important

---

58. The author of Psalm 1 has borrowed the concept of "scoffers (לֵצִים)" from Prov 1:22. The idea of "canals" in Ps 1:3 could possibly relate to the "spirit" Lady Wisdom is said to "let gush out (*hiphil* of נבע)" in Prov 1:23, and the "wind" in Ps 1:4 relates to the "storm" and "whirlwind" which is used as a metaphor for judgement in Prov 1:27. "Perish (תאבד)" in Ps 1:6 is definitely derived from the idea of the complacency of fools "destroying" (תאבדם) them in Prov 1:32.

59. One of the few Bible translations that correctly understands this verse, especially the phrase ולקח נפשות חכם, is the New International Version (2011).

60. They not only composed a large number of psalms themselves but also revised others in what Alfons Deissler called "eine Art 'Wiederlesung' (in französisch: relecture) von einem neuen Verstehenshorizont her." See Alfons Deissler, *Die Psalmen* (2nd ed; Düsseldorf: Patmos, 1964), 14.

61. Zenger ("Psalm 112," 242) similarly suggests that Ps 37 should be used "als interpretatorischen Hintergrund" for Ps 112.

junctions in the Psalter, were perceived to speak in unison (they probably thought), the message would be so much more effective. In spite of seeming differences, these psalms do present a unified front when the intertextual connections with Proverbs are taken into account.

What was the message they wanted to convey? They wanted to draw a clear distinction between the righteous and the wicked, so that the reader or hearer would experience these psalms as exhortations to a certain style of living.[62] The wicked were those arrogant, irreverent, rich Judeans who did not hesitate to exploit the powerless and impoverished members of their own community so as to rob them eventually of their land. It was therefore first of all necessary to encourage the pious, poor Judeans who led an upright life of devotion to the Torah (but were beginning to lose faith in the doctrine of retribution) to persist with this kind of piety. The authors of the wisdom psalms consequently insisted that faithfulness to the Torah would be rewarded and the wicked would be punished.[63] According to Ps 112, those faithful who lived according to the Torah by being generous, by lending without interest, and by graciously and lavishly sharing the blessings they had received would be blessed even more through receiving honor and being remembered honorably. They did not need to fear a sudden calamity and could rest assured that their descendants would enjoy the same benefits and would be able to hold onto the land they would inherit. But even more importantly, those who did these things, the acrostic wisdom psalms taught, would enjoy riches which could not be taken away. They had entered a Promised Land which would prove to be an everlasting home, while the impetuous impious would sooner or later disappear from their world.

---

62. See the description of the history and intended effect of the Gattung of a beatitude in Zenger, "Psalm 112," 237–38. The purpose of Ps 112 would be, according to him, to define what reverence for YHWH constitutes, and promise true fulfilment for those who live their life accordingly.

63. As Walter Beyerlin has convincingly argued in the case of Ps 52, which must have been composed in more or less the same period as the alphabetic acrostics, the Sitz im Leben must have been the Second Temple. See in this regard Walter Beyerlin, *Der 52. Psalm: Studien zu seiner Einordnung* (BWANT 111; Stuttgart: Kohlhammer, 1980), 111. The message was intended for both the righteous and the "wicked" members of the community; it was meant to change attitudes and behavior. It is improbable that it was restricted to conventicles and small rooms, meant for Bible study alone. See the description of Christoph Levin, "Das Gebetbuch der Gerechten," 371, of the acrostic psalms.

Bibliography

Berges, Ulrich. "Die Knechte im Psalter: Ein Beitrag zu seiner Kompositionsgeschichte." *Bib* 81 (2000): 153–78.

Beyerlin, Walter. *Der 52. Psalm: Studien zu seiner Einordnung.* BWANT 111. Stuttgart: Kohlhammer, 1980.

Botha, Phil J. "Freedom to Roam in a Wide Open Space: Psalm 31 Read in Conjunction with the History of David in the Books of Samuel and the Psalms." Pages 424–42 in *Seitenblicke: Literarische und historische Studien zu Nebenfiguren im zweiten Samuelbuch.* Edited by Walter Dietrich. OBO 249. Göttingen: Vandenhoeck & Ruprecht, 2011.

———. "Interpreting 'Torah' in Ps 1 in the Light of Ps 119," *HTS* 68 (2012). Online: http://www.hts.org.za/index.php/HTS/article/view/1274/2588.

———. "Pride and the Suffering of the Poor in the Persian Period: Psalm 12 in its Post-exilic Context." *OTE* 25 (2012): 40–56.

Botha, Phil J., and J. Henk Potgieter. " 'The Word of Yahweh is Right': Psalm 33 as a Torah-Psalm." *VE* 31 (2010): 1–8.

Deissler, Alfons. *Die Psalmen.* 2nd ed. Düsseldorf: Patmos, 1964.

Gosse, Bernard. *L'influence du livre des Proverbes sur les rédactions bibliques à l'époque perse.* Paris: Gabalda, 2008.

Hossfeld, Frank-Lothar, and Erich Zenger. *Die Psalmen I: Psalm 1–50.* DNEB 29. Würzburg: Echter, 1993.

Levin, Christoph. "Das Gebetbuch der Gerechten: Literaturgeschichtliche Beobachtungen am Psalter." *ZTK* 90 (1993): 355–81.

Mathys, Hans-Peter. *Dichter und Beter: Theologen aus spätalttestamentlicher Zeit.* OBO 132. Göttingen: Vandenhoeck & Ruprecht, 1994.

Saur, Markus. "Die theologische Funktion der Königspsalmen innerhalb der Komposition des Psalters." Pages 689–700 in *The Composition of the Book of Psalms.* Edited by Erich Zenger. BETL 238; Leuven: Peeters, 2010.

Seybold, Klaus. *Poetik der Psalmen.* Stuttgart: Kohlhammer, 2003.

Ulrich, Eugene, ed. *The Biblical Qumran Scrolls: Transcriptions and Textual Variants.* VTSup 134. Leiden: Brill, 2010.

Weber, Beat. "Psalm 1 and its Function as a Directive into the Psalter and towards a Biblical Theology." *OTE* 19 (2006): 237–60.

Whybray, R. Norman. *Wealth and Poverty in the Book of Proverbs.* JSOTSup 99. Sheffield: JSOT Press, 1990.

Zakovitch, Yair. "The Interpretative Significance of the Sequence of Psalms 111–112.113–118.119." Pages 215–28 in *The Composition of the Book of Psalms*. Edited by Erich Zenger. BETL 238. Leuven: Peeters, 2010.

Zenger, Erich. "Exkurs: Akrostichie im Psalter." Pages 216–18 in *Psalmen 101–150*. Edited by Frank-Lothar Hossfeld and Erich Zenger. HTKAT. Freiburg: Herder, 2008.

———. "Exkurs: Die Komposition des Ägyptischen Hallel bzw. Pessach-Hallel Ps 113–118." Pages 245–47 in *Psalmen 101–150*. Edited by Frank-Lothar Hossfeld and Erich Zenger. HTKAT. Freiburg: Herder, 2008.

———. "Geld als Lebensmittel? Über die Wertung des Reichtums im Psalter (Psalmen 15.49.112)." *JBTh* 21 (2006): 73–96.

Zimmerli, Walter. "Zwillingspsalmen." Pages 105–13 in *Wort, Lied, und Gottesspruch: Beiträge zu Psalmen und Propheten*. Edited by Josef Schreiner. Würzburg: Echter, 1972.

Perhaps YHWH Is Sleeping:
"Awake" and "Contend" in the
Book of Psalms*

Karl N. Jacobson

Introduction

One of the key contributions of Gerald Wilson (and others) in the shape and shaping movement in Psalms study is in drawing the interpreter's attention to the character of the Psalter *as book*, and not just a collection of individual psalms (with the occasional paired psalms). This observation is one that is simple and perhaps obvious, but one that remains necessary, as it is so often undervalued. As Wilson noted when discussing the designation of the collection as a hymnbook, "the designation evidences our tendency over the last 150 years of Psalms study to focus almost exclusively on individual psalms to the neglect of the whole ensemble."[1] This insight is indicative of the deep and meaningful reflection on the interconnectedness of the cultic poetry, not only within groups which share common superscriptions—whether regarding authorship, such as Asaph (Pss 50, 73–83), or regarding musical setting or cultic *Sitz-im-Leben*—but across a wider spectrum both of form and putative function that the shape and shaping school has empowered.

What follows is not strictly a study in the shape and shaping of the psalms, but one shaped in part by it. Its essential contribution is to read

---

* This paper is dedicated with deep appreciation to James Limburg, Professor Emeritus of Old Testament at Luther Seminary in St. Paul, Minn., who first introduced me to the shape and shaping movement in the interpretation of the Psalms.

1. Gerald H. Wilson, "Shaping the Psalter: A Consideration of Editorial Linkage in the Book of Psalms," in *The Shape and Shaping of the Psalter* (ed. J. Clinton McCann Jr.; JSOT 159; Sheffield Academic, 1993), 72.

selections from the collection with the context of that collection still firmly in mind. This chapter explores the themes of divine rest, divine warfare, and the rousing of the divine through an intertextual study of selected psalms. The goal is to explore how the image of God as Divine Warrior is shaped, understood, and employed uniquely within the psalm of complaint. This study is not so much a diachronic approach, which is essentially evolutionary, wherein themes within the collection are studied with an eye to reconstructing development over time, but a synchronic approach that seeks to evaluate the overall impact of those themes when taken together.

THE PROBLEM OF A SLEEPING GOD

Does God sleep? Psalm 121:3–4 says quite clearly that the answer is "no," God neither slumbers nor sleeps:

> [God] will not let your foot tremble;
>> the one who keeps you will not slumber.
> The one who keeps Israel will neither slumber nor sleep.[2]

Furthermore, there are several examples of what appear to be tangentially significant assumptions that because God will not sleep, the one praying the psalm may sleep peacefully:

> I lie down and sleep;
>> I wake again, for YHWH sustains me (Ps 3:5).
> I will both lie down and sleep in peace;
>> for you alone, O YHWH, make me lie down in safety (Ps 4:8).
> [YHWH] gives sleep to his beloved (Ps 127:2).

Even Ps 46:5 seems to suggest that at—or perhaps even before—the final breaking of the dawn God has already won the victory:

> God is in the midst of the city;
>> it shall not be moved;
>> God will help it as morning breaks.[3]

---

2. Cf. Job 33:14–18, where, while mortals "slumber and sleep," God is active, sending visions and speaking to mortals.

3. NRSV has "*when* the morning breaks," but in the Hebrew there is no temporal

As Marc Brettler has noted, divine strength often vitiates human strength in the Psalms; here it is human rest that is vitiated by divine restlessness.[4] The psalmist finds comfort in that, while she is not able to keep watch during sleep, God sustains, protects, and knows all even in the dark of night. Thus God's gracious gift is of confident, restful slumber untroubled by dreams of want or nightmare visions of danger; the wisdom of the proverb notwithstanding, "a little sleep, a slumber, a little folding of the hands to rest" is in fact a good thing.[5]

This may constitute one theologically distinctive aspect of the God of the Hebrew Bible, compared to whom other gods are not only prone to slumber, but are *fast* asleep, sleeping the sleep of death, or the idyllic (read: idolic) resting on the shelf.[6]

It is in this spirit that in one of the great examples of biblical trash-talking Elijah mocks the prophets of Baal as prayers to their god go unanswered, "Cry aloud! Surely he is a god; perhaps he is meditating, or he has wandered away, or he is on a journey, or perhaps he is asleep and must be awakened" (1 Kgs 18:27). This is a picture of a sleepy, senile, straying god. In contrast, while Baal sleeps, YHWH answers.

The question remains a problem, however, or at least an open question. God rests, to be sure, after the exertions of creation (Gen 2:2–3), but does God sleep? Despite the dissent of Ps 121, other psalms seem to suggest that God *does* sleep. Psalm 44:23 [24] asks God, "Why do you sleep?" (לָמָּה תִישַׁן). Psalm 35:23 calls upon God to "Wake up!" (הָקִיצָה), a call that Ps 59 echoes (v. 5 [6] "awake to punish").

Psalm 78:65 even seems to suggest that God falls into the "big sleep," due to a bellyful of wine: "Then YHWH awoke as from sleep, like a war-

---

marker: יַעְזְרֶהָ אֱלֹהִים לִפְנוֹת בֹּקֶר. The Divine Warrior here wins victory before the dawning of the day, allowing the Israelite warrior to rest, and not to have to rise for dawn's muster. See Marc Brettler, "Images of Yhwh the Warrior in Psalms," in *Women, War, and Metaphor: Language and Society in the Study of the Hebrew Bible* (ed. Claudia V. Camp and Carole R. Fontaine; *Semeia* 61 (1993): 160.

4. Ibid., 153.

5. Cf. Prov 6:10–11, in which slumber and sleep are the locus of humankind's undoing, "A little sleep, a little slumber, a little folding of the hands to rest, and poverty will come upon you like a robber, and want, like an armed warrior."

6. Ps 115 goes so far as to suggest that those who worship idols—which have mouths, eyes, ears, noses, hands, and feet, but do not speak, hear, smell, feels or walk—will be just like them; i.e., they are doomed to death.

rior drunk because of wine" (מִיַּיִן כְּגִבּוֹר מִתְרוֹנֵן)[7]; not unlike El who, in the binge drinking banquet described in the Ugaritic text (KTU 1.114)[8], gets, in the words of Cal Naughton Jr. in the movie *Talledega Nights*, "hammered drunk." So perhaps the jury is still out; according to a few of the psalms YHWH does in fact appear to sleep—even "sleeping one off" occasionally.

"Awake" and "Contend" in the Psalms: A Brief Overview

For the psalmist, God needs to be aroused to the fullness of the godhead, out of cessation into participation in the life of the psalmist. What is interesting to note in this cultic wakeup call is that God is called to awaken to a particular kind of action. The call is to awaken or arise (עוּרָה), in order to contend (רִיב).

Neither of these words is common in the Psalter. עוּרָה occurs some nine times; of those nine, five are addressed as imperatives to God to awaken or rise up (Pss 7:6 [7]; 35:23; 44:23 [24]; 59:5; 80:2 [3]).[9]

רִיב also occurs in nine places in the Psalter, and in a number of cases the psalmist urges God to argue a particular case, to defend the cause of the psalmist (Pss 43:1; 119:154), or to plead God's own cause, in which the psalmist has a stake (Ps 74:22).[10]

---

7. Perhaps "recovering from" (JPS) is better; however, the OG has κεκραιπαληκώς, which echoes the drunkenness described in Isa 24:20; 29:9.

8. "El sat, he assembled his drinking feast; / El sat in his marzeaḥ. / El drank wine to satiety, / New wine to drunkenness. / El went to his house, / He stumbled to his court. / Thukamuna and Shunama supported him. / The "creeper" approached him, / The one having two horns and a tail. / He floundered in his (own) feces and urine, / El collapsed like the dead, / El was like those who descend to the underworld" (John L. McLaughlin, *The Marzeaḥ in the Prophetic Literature: References and Allusions in Light of the Extra-biblical Evidence* [VTSup 86; Leiden: Brill, 2001], 24–26).

9. The other examples all have to do with the same basic semantic function, arising from sleep or being stirred to wakefulness, but are simply indicative, not imperative; see Ps 57:8 [9], "Awake, my soul! Awake, O harp and lyre! I will awake the dawn"; cf. Ps 108:2 [3]; Ps 73:20, "They are like a dream when one awakes; on awaking you despise their phantoms"; Ps 78:38, "Yet [God], being compassionate, forgave their iniquity, and did not destroy them; often he restrained his anger, and did not stir up all his wrath."

10. Ps 18:43 [44] addresses strife with other people (in the context of a psalm celebrating the Divine Warrior); Ps 31:20 [21] speaks of those with "contentious tongues"; Ps 55:9 [10] of strife in the city.

What is of particular interest in an intertextual reading of psalms that employ these two words is that in every case in which an imperative form of the verb עוּר is employed, where God is called upon—commanded—to awaken, to rise up, there is clear indication of a "contention" with God, an accusation leveled against God; in other words these psalms entail a רִיב carried out (in a reversal of the motif as it is found in the eighth-century prophets), even when the word itself does not occur. Furthermore, in every case this רִיב is set in tension with the portrayal of YHWH as Divine Warrior—not primarily in the cosmogonic battle with the forces of chaos, nor even mostly with the nation in mind, but in the life of the psalmist.[11]

So while neither term is very common, both are striking in their usage, and reveal a particular element of the theology of complaint when explored either independently or together, and against the backdrop of the motif of Divine Warrior.

Interestingly, these two words appear in the same psalm just once, in Ps 35—though Ps 74 does something similar in verse 22—and it is from Ps 35 that I take my lead. I turn first to what I see as an interdependence of language and imagery that has its provenance in national, corporate application, and that in turn shapes the prayer of the individual. I then explore the intersection of stirring prayer, "courtroom" contention, and the Divine Warrior motif.

"Awake" in Psalms 44 and 7

There is not space enough here to explore in detail all the occurrences of עוּרָה in the psalms, but I will make note of two in particular—Pss 44 and 7. Psalm 44:23–26 [24–27] reads

> Awake! [עוּרָה] Why do you sleep, O Lord?
>   Wake up! [הָקִיצָה] Do not reject us forever!
> Why do you hide your face?
>   [and] forget our affliction and oppression?

---

11. Cf. Patrick Miller Jr.: "Yahweh and his armies go forth to fight not Tiamat, Mot, Yamm, and other divine beings, but the Canaanites, the Amorites, the Amalekites, and all the other people who stand in the way of Israel's acquisition of her promised heritage. To be sure, the battle of Yahweh against mythological forces appears at points, but it is always a subordinate event fused with the more political, historical aspect of the warrior God's activity – defeat of Israel's enemies" (*The Divine Warrior in Early Israel* [Cambridge, Mass.: Harvard University Press, 1973], 162).

For we sink down to the dust;
> our bodies cling to the ground.
Rise up! [קוּמָה] Come to our help.
> Redeem us for the sake of your steadfast love.

Psalm 7:6 [7] reads,

Rise up! [קוּמָה] O YHWH, in your anger;
> lift yourself up [הִנָּשֵׂא] against the fury of my enemies;
awake [וְעוּרָה], O my God; you have appointed a judgment.

Both psalms call upon God to awaken or rise up [עוּרָה], and while Ps 7 does not explicitly connect this petition to the problem of divine sleep as does Ps 44:23, for the purposes of this study I am holding them together under that sense.

What image of God is part and parcel of these wakeup calls? it is the Divine Warrior. The observation of the language and imagery related to the Divine Warrior in Ps 44 is fairly widespread. H. Wayne Ballard has correctly noted that the whole of the psalm has the Divine Warrior, "Judge, Warrior and Corrector of Injustices," as its backdrop.[12] Psalm 7:6, which calls to God to rise up and awaken to judgment (in favor of) the psalmist, leads into the next four verses, which bear unequivocally the imagery of the Divine Warrior:

God is my *shield*,
> who saves the upright in heart.
God is a righteous judge,
> and a God who has indignation every day.
If one does not repent, God will whet his *sword*;
> he has bent and strung his *bow*;
he has prepared his *deadly weapons*,
> making his arrows *flaming shafts* (vv. 10–13).

Shield, sword, bow, deadly weapons, and flaming arrows are the tools of the trade of the Divine Warrior, whom the psalmist summons to take up his side.

---

12. H. Wayne Ballard Jr., *The Divine Warrior Motif in the Psalms* (BIBAL Dissertation Series; North Richland Hills, Tex.: D&F Scott, 1999), 46.

Kraus goes so far as to connect Ps 7 explicitly to the incipit related to the Song of the Ark. He argues that these terms for arising and lifting are intrinsically related to the ark of the covenant. He writes:

> The oath of the innocent is obviously the presupposition for the appeal to Yahweh, the judge, which now follows. God is invoked in three imperatives קוּמָה, הִנָּשֵׂא, עוּרָה. The concepts and images of the expressed appeal suggest the thought of the ark of the covenant as the judicial throne of God.[13]

It is difficult to accept Kraus's conclusion that these verbs (קוּם in particular) must *always* be associated with the ark of the covenant. These verbs are quite common and there is no reason to think that in and of themselves they *must* evoke the ark and its attendant rituals and theology. What is interesting, however, is that while tying both the commands "arise" (קוּמָה) and "lift yourself up" (הִנָּשֵׂא) to the ark, Kraus does not see any significant connection in עוּרָה, dismissing it as residual evidence of a "lively mythological background," which has its roots in the Canaanite nature myth, which is "completely dead and gone" in the Psalter.[14] But this verb is situated in parallel with קוּם and נשׂא, and while עוּר by itself may not bear the same *overarching* connection to the ark of the covenant, in this setting it surely must be related.

The occurrence of the verb עוּר in Ps 80 (v. 2b [3b]) is of particular interest. This Psalm of Asaph is situated in the midst of a collection of psalms that calls to both corporate and individual commemoration the saving acts of God in Israel's past and urges God to stir up (עוֹרְרָה) the divine power.

> Give ear, O Shepherd of Israel, you who lead Joseph like a flock!
>   You who are seated upon the cherubim, shine forth
> before Ephraim and Benjamin and Manasseh.
>   Stir up [עוֹרְרָה] your might, and come to save us!
> Restore us, O God;

---

13. Hans-Joachim Kraus, *Psalms 1–59* (Minneapolis: Fortress, 1993), 171.

14. "In (v. 4b) and (v. 5), the appeal uses cultic 'reveille calls' of the Canaanite nature myth, by which a dying divinity is urged to reawaken and live…. To be sure, the mythological background of these calls is entirely absorbed in the OT Psalms. But the formulas summon YHWH to an effective intervention in the appeal of a persecuted innocent" (ibid., 541).

let your face shine, that we may be saved (vv. 1–3 [2–4]).

This stirring, this awakening of God's power, is connected explicitly in the psalm to the ark: The Divine Warrior is "seated (or enthroned) upon the cherubim," which is a not uncommon theophoric phrase.[15] What is not typical, however, is the way the imagery is employed. "ark theology" or "ark piety" is typically celebratory, as are the psalms that are dedicated in a more extensive way to describing the Divine Warrior; Ps 18 is a royal psalm of thanksgiving, Ps 24 an entrance liturgy inviting the earth and the fullness thereof to praise in worship, and Ps 68 is a praise psalm. This is not the case with Ps 80, nor with Pss 44 and 7. Each of these psalms are complaints, turning the motif of the Divine Warrior to a new purpose, calling upon the Divine Warrior to get up and get to business.[16]

If we take Pss 44 and 7 together, reading them in conversation, there are, in addition to their similarities, significant differences as well. Psalm 44 represents a situation in which actual physical conflict is in view. Enemies seek to do physical harm to the Israelites and to destroy the nation. Using similar language, Ps 7 addresses enemies who slander and falsely accuse the individual in a legal setting.[17] Psalm 7 essentially appropriates the national story—the deeds performed by the Divine Warrior in the con-

---

15. See Exod 25:22; Num 7:89; 10:35; 1 Sam 4:4; 2 Sam 6:2; 2 Kgs 19:15; and Ps 99:1, "YHWH is king; let the peoples tremble! He sits enthroned upon the cherubim; let the earth quake!" To quote Kraus once more, "The ark of the covenant (even after its reception in the Jerusalem temple at the time of Solomon) remained imbued with the traditions of the holy war, into which it was once carried as a palladium (Num 10:35–36; 1 Sam 4:3). The God-King enthroned above the ark is and remains the 'hero in battle' (Ps 24:8). Obviously Ps 7:6 must be interpreted in connection with these conceptions" (Kraus, *Psalms 1–59*, 171).

16. Num 10:35 and the lyric sung as the ark went out to battle; the word is קוּמָה (cf. Ps 132:8), not עוּרָה, although the two terms are used in parallel in Ps 7:7; and the same connection of *rîb* with a call to God to rise up (קוּמָה) occurs in Ps 74:22. As Miller has shown (*Divine Warrior*, 156, 159), there is a synergy of human and divine activity in Israel's wars. This shifted in later theological terms to an emphasis of "not by our strength." The expected synergy of action is lacking when the psalmist accuses God, and calls upon God to "get up, stand," wake up to the defense of the psalmist.

17. Ps 59 is an individual complaint, but the individual is most likely the king, who laments the national struggle: 59:4b–5[5b–6], "Rouse yourself, come to my help and see! You, YHWH God of hosts, are God of Israel. Awake to punish all the nations; spare none of those who treacherously plot evil." See also Ps 12, in which God arises [אָקוּם] to defend the poor.

quest (Ps 44:1–3)—for the individual. There is movement from the communal to the individual, from actual, physical danger, to real, nonphysical danger (psychological, emotional, social, relational). This suggests that in the appropriation of this language and imagery by the individual there is a shift in the theology of the Divine Warrior. The field of contest changes from the arena of physical combat to the realm of verbal contest.[18]

"Contend" in Psalms 74 and 43

The phrase רִיבָה רִיבִי occurs in a number of psalms,[19] and again for the sake of space I will focus on two: Pss 74 and 43. As with עוּרָה in Pss 44 and 7, Pss 74 and 43 are similar in that there is interplay between the communal and individual application of the concept of רִיב.

Psalm 74 pleads with God to take up the divine cause (רִיב) against the enemies of the nation. Psalm 43 is an individual example of the same phenomenon; but the enemies are the enemies of the psalmist. Psalm 74:22–23 reads:

> Rise up, O God, *plead your cause;* (קוּמָה אֱלֹהִים רִיבָה רִיבֶךָ)
> remember how the impious scoff at you all day long.
> Do not forget the clamor of your foes,
> the uproar of your adversaries that goes up continually.

Psalm 43:1 reads:

> Vindicate me, O God, and *defend my cause* [רִיבָה רִיבִי]
> against an ungodly people;
> from those who are deceitful and unjust deliver me!

---

18. In discussing Ps 94, William P. Brown draws a similar conclusion, "The epithet [of God as judge] transforms the battleground into a law court and casts the enemies' defeat as 'restitution' (94:23)" (*Seeing the Psalms: A Theology of Metaphor* [Louisville: Westminster John Knox, 2002], 190).

19. Ps 103 is a communal psalm which comforts the community with the promise that God will not always accuse them. Vv. 8–10 say, "YHWH is merciful and gracious, slow to anger and abounding in steadfast love. He will not always accuse, nor will he keep his anger forever. He does not deal with us according to our sins, nor repay us according to our iniquities." In Ps 119 the setting is individual, but the benefit, and the instruction, are for the many. V. 154 says, "Look on my misery and rescue me, for I do not forget your law. Plead my cause and redeem me; give me life according to your promise. Salvation is far from the wicked, for they do not seek your statutes."

Psalm 74 is a communal lament that begs the question why, if God has acted in Israel's past, which the Asaphite Psalms as a body aver, God does not seem to be acting in the present. God is called upon to contend for God's own cause, to protect the dwelling place of the divine name, and by extension to preserve the nation. In Ps 74, the enemies have devastated the places of God—the dwelling place of God's name, the meeting places of God—and the congregation of the nation. God's actions in the historical past are recalled in the face of this—the mnemohistorical material in which God is the Divine Warrior is recalled (vv. 12–17). Following this the psalmist presents his רִיב, which is based on these very terms. God has acted in the past and seems to be inactive in the present.

Psalm 43 is an individual psalm that calls upon God to defend the cause of the psalmist. Here, the psalmist is confronted by an almost faceless, generic enemy who is "deceitful" (v. 1) and "un-just" (עַוְלָה). The answer to this is the truth (and light) that comes from God.

As James Limburg has shown in regard to רִיב in the eighth-century prophets, the רִיב is always YHWH's.[20] But in the case of the psalms this is not true. The רִיב is essentially democratized. In Ps 74 God's cause is contended, but the psalmist (and his community) have a stake in the contention. The impious scoffing, clamor, and uproar of the foe must be answered. Psalm 43 marks a shift; the רִיב is the psalmist's. God is pictured as refuge, as dwelling on the holy hill, as "my God and my help," and the רִיב is lodged in reaction to the disoriented experience of the psalmist.

"Contend" and "Awake" in Psalm 35

The only case in which these two words occur in the same psalm is in an individual prayer for help. Psalm 35 is defined—at its beginning and end—by the plea to God to awaken and contend, or rather, to contend and awaken.[21] Psalm 35:1 begins:

---

20. James Limburg, "The Root רִיב and the Prophetic Lawsuit Speeches," *JBL* 88 (1969): 301.

21. The pattern of the psalm is a call to *rîb* [v. 1] / Divine Warrior [vv. 2–3, 10] / elements of the case [vv. 4–9, 11–21] / call to *ʿûrâ* [v. 23]. In Isa 51 these terms also form the beginning and end of the poem, but in reverse; God is first called to awake, and at the last called to arise: "Awake, awake (עוּרִי עוּרִי), put on strength, O arm of YHWH! Awake, as in days of old, the generations of long ago! Was it not you who cut Rahab in pieces, who pierced the dragon? Was it not you who dried up the sea, the waters of the

Contend, O YHWH, with those who contend with me (רִיבָה יְהוָה
אֶת־יְרִיבָי);
    fight against those who fight against me!

and toward its end we read:

Awake! Bestir yourself (הָעִירָה) for my defense,
    for my cause, my God and my Lord! (אֱלֹהַי וַאדֹנָי לְרִיבִי:) (v. 23).

God is called to fight on behalf of the psalmist, to contend, once again using the language of the Divine Warrior motif:

Take hold of shield and buckler,
    and rise up to help me!
Draw the spear and javelin against my pursuers;
    say to my soul, "I am your salvation." (vv. 2–3)

The one who elsewhere is enthroned upon the cherubim, riding the palladium to war, is invoked in the defense of the psalmist. As Goldingay notes:

It is an aspect of exodus faith that Yhwh is a warrior (Exod. 15); *Ps. 35 claims that theology for the individual as well as for the people as a whole.* "Contend" (v. 1) can be legal language (cf. v. 23) or military language (e.g., Ps 18:43[44]), "attacks"); it is thus a useful root here in light of the psalm's immediate use of military imagery and its subsequent use of legal imagery.[22]

---

great deep; who made the depths of the sea a way for the redeemed to cross over? So the ransomed of YHWH shall return, and come to Zion with singing; everlasting joy shall be upon their heads; they shall obtain joy and gladness, and sorrow and sighing shall flee away" (Isa 51:9-11). According to John Goldingay (*Psalms, Vol. 1: Psalms 42-89* [BCOTWP; Grand Rapids: Baker Academic, 2007], 489), the psalm as a whole has a pattern similar to that of Ps 42–43, with a threefold lamentation of attacks:

    35:1–10 || 42:1–4
    35:11–18 || 42:6b–10
    35:19–28 || 43:1–4

Ps 44, then, takes up the call to arms, calling God to rouse the divine self, to awake and answer these attacks, and Isa 51:22 says, "Thus says your Sovereign, YHWH, your God who pleads the cause (יָרִיב) of his people: See, I have taken from your hand the cup of staggering; you shall drink no more from the bowl of my wrath."

    22. Goldingay, *Psalms 1*, 491, emphasis added. See Peter C. Craigie and Marvin E. Tate (*Psalms 1-50* [WBC 19; Nashville: Thomas Nelson, 2004], 285–86), who take

The contending of the psalmist's enemies is characterized as being physical in nature ("fighting" [v. 1], nets and snares [v. 7]), but it is essentially verbal —

"malicious witnesses" (עֵדֵי חָמָס), v. 11
"slandered" / tore at me (קָרְעוּ),[23] v. 15
"mocked" (לְעֵגֵי), v. 16

The psalmist petitions God to act on her behalf, and in doing so characterizes God's actions in the language of the Divine Warrior, whose action—in the *Sitz im Leben* presented in the psalm—must also be verbal. God is called upon in verse 22 to "be not silent," and in verse 3 to "say to my soul, 'I am your salvation!'" Thus speech becomes the resolved function/weapon of the Divine Warrior, for which the actual accoutrements of war serve as metaphor.

Marc Brettler has shown in his study of the Divine Warrior imagery in the psalms that there are two ways in which the Divine Warrior answers: (1) in an oracle of salvation; and (2) in the performance of the deed itself. Once promised, it is then effected.[24] But, as Rolf Jacobson has observed, in addressing this request for divine declaration,

> The God quotation in Psalm 35 is not an oracle of salvation but a *request* for one. That is, in the context of Psalm 35, the request for [a] salvation oracle is a request for the effective power of God.[25]

---

the psalm's "military overtones" as the primary reason for identifying the psalm as a "royal psalm to be interpreted in an international context," a "royal or national lament … arising from some kind of human covenant relationship." While this may be true of Ps 59, I think this is exactly backwards in the case of Ps 35.

23. קרע typically means "rend" or "tear" (cf. Gen 37:29; Lev 13:56). In this case it may be that this tearing is figurative. In Ps 35:13-14 the psalmist has engaged in ritual actions relating to repentance or lamentation (cf. 2 Sam 3:31; Ezra 9:5) and it may be that in v. 15 those who gather to mock the psalmist do so by mocking his acts of repentance. So perhaps something like "tore their clothes at me." This translation would be a unique understanding of the verb in the Hebrew Bible, and is, perhaps, not necessary, but when paired with the actions of v. 16—mockery with/by the gnashing of teeth—make senses in parallel.

24. "Thus, the answer of YHWH in v. 5b may have two components that are mutually reinforcing: an oracle of deliverance, and the deliverance itself provided by YHWH's presence in the city" (Brettler, "Images of Yhwh," 141).

25. Rolf Jacobson, *Many Are Saying: The Function of Direct Discourse in the Hebrew Psalter* (JSOTSup 397; New York: T&T Clark, 2004), 123; emphasis original.

This effective power, couched in the imagery of the Divine Warrior, is verbal in nature. God must awaken to contend, to speak on behalf of the falsely accused. Notice also that God must, so it would seem, be awakened in order to speak on the psalmist's behalf. The accusation is that God is not aware, and must be made so. In describing the role of metaphors of divine anatomy, William P. Brown states that in the Psalter God's ability to see or sense are often challenged. But this challenge is "not by the psalmists. It is the wicked or unnamed enemies who proclaim that 'YH[WH] does not see' [94:7]."[26] For the most part this is certainly true. But here the psalmist takes up this challenge as his own. This unique function of the concept of רִיב puts the psalmist in contention with God, calling God to task because of God's perceived lack of seeing or even wakefulness; again, this takes place in a unique way.

CONCLUSION(S): YHWH COULD (SHOULD) HAVE BEEN A CONTENDER

There is something to be learned in a synchronic reading of these psalms in conversation with each other about the theology both of the Divine Warrior, and of the psalm of complaint.

The characterization of the Divine Warrior shifts as it is employed in individual psalms that lament God's apparent inaction in the face of the psalmist's need. In these applications the contest is oral. The psalmist is attacked in the court setting, and God is called upon to speak on behalf of the psalmist. This is not individual combat or national contest on the field of battle, but the arena of human relationships. God is seen to be sleeping through the trials of the psalmist and must be awoken to her defense.

Furthermore, in these psalms the idea of the רִיב is not the sole provenance of God, but is found in the mouths of the petitioner as well. Psalm 35, defined by the call to contend (רִיב) and to awake (עוּרָה), and against the backdrop of the earlier comparison of psalms such as 44 and 7, 74 and 43, may be read as a countercause.[27] Psalm 35 shifts the provenance of the

---

26. Brown, *Seeing the Psalms*, 171.

27. To borrow from Walter Brueggemann, this "shifts the calculus and redress of the distribution of power between the two parties, so that the petitionary party is taken seriously and the God who is addressed is newly engaged in the crisis in a way that puts God at risk" ("The Costly Loss of Lament," *JSOT* 36 [1986]: 59). In accusing God, both in the general sense of the רִיב, and in the specifics of accusing God of slothful slumber, the "lament form thus concerns a redistribution of power."

רִיב away from an exclusively divine provenance to a counter-רִיב spoken by the psalmist against God in complaint/lament/prayer for help.

This may be seen as a derivative of the "theology of defeat."[28] The plight of the psalmist is spoken against God, employed as evidence against God in a counterclaim. The psalmist is not faithless but falsely accused. The one praying is not sinful, but maligned. The misuse of discourse, the bearing of false witness, threatens the life of the faithful. And if the psalmist is not defended, protected, and finally acquitted through the agency of the Divine Warrior, then the proper speech of the faithful—praise and thanksgiving—cannot be uttered. As Walter Brueggemann points out (reflecting on Claus Westermann's "relational dynamics" in the psalms), laments typically follow a particular pattern, moving from articulation, to submission, to relinquishment vis-à-vis the complaint which drives the psalm.[29] In the case of Ps 35 this pattern is ruptured. There is only articulation and, far from submission or relinquishment, there is accusation—רִיב. God's inaction is out of keeping with Israel's covenant expectations, with ark piety and the motif of a vital, powerful, active Divine Warrior, who is challenged and called to rise to the challenge. Thus the countercase is conditional. Psalm 35 ends with a conditional vow of praise, but only after the case is tried and judgment delivered "my tongue shall tell of thy righteousness, all day (-long) of your praise."[30] This is the end to which the Divine Warrior motif is put in these psalms that demand that God awaken and contend.

Back, then, to the question of sleep. Does YHWH sleep? A common move in reading the psalms that wrestle with the problem of divine sleep is simply to dismiss the language of God's sleeping, or needing to be awakened, as a matter of "seeming," as Artur Weiser says, "the God who hides his face so that it *looks as if* he is asleep."[31] Konrad Schaefer characterizes these issues as a set of "bold metaphors, *implying* that God is inactive or asleep. The picture of a sleepy God does not agree with the description of

---

28. Millard Lind, *Yahweh Is a Warrior: The Theology of Warfare in Ancient Israel* (Scottsdale, Penn.: Herald, 1980), 111–12.

29. See Brueggemann, "Costly Loss of Lament," 58.

30. Goldingay (*Psalms 1*, 504), comments "That suppliant *withholds* praise now. Praise is an indication of recognition that Yhwh has acted. It would be meaningless to praise now. It would not be true to the actual situation. The present is a moment for protest, but moment for praise will come."

31. Artur Weiser, *The Psalms* (OTL; Philadelphia: Westminster, 1962), 359.

God's intense activity in the first two movements of the psalm."[32] At some point we must admit that we cannot know whether or not God sleeps. But there is more to these psalms, and to this question, I think, than mere seeming. The discontinuity between the parts of the psalm does not efface or overshadow the problem of divine sleep; in fact this serves to throw the tension into stark relief. This is the real lived experience of the psalmist. Not unlike when the people of Israel are languishing under the lash of Pharaoh (Exod 2:23–25), God must—these psalms argue—be made to hear the psalmist's groaning, made to remember the covenant; God must be made to take notice. If God does not sleep, then perhaps God is vacationing, or busy trimming the lawn, or otherwise detained. Regardless of the actuality behind the experience of God's absence, that experience gives rise to the psalmist's accusations.

In conclusion, let us return briefly to Wilson's critique of the "hymnbook" analogy for the Psalter. Wilson notes that he would choose another, "happier musical metaphor," that of the musical score:

> with its ability to bring together a diversity of instruments and patterns into proper timing and thus into a harmonious whole that exceeds the sum of its parts. Rather than a hymnbook, the Psalter is a symphony with many movements, or better yet an oratorio in which a multitude of voices—singly and in concert—rise in a crescendo of praise.[33]

This is, for me, the single greatest benefit of the shape and shaping movement, the advantage that it gives the interpreter in engaging not merely the solo voice of any given psalm, but the chorus of many psalms. Drawing themes, metaphors, imagery, and more together through the intentional intertextual reading of the psalms is, I believe, in harmony with attention to the shape of the Psalter. The Psalter as "score," as the musical framework in which the reader of the Psalms may find her own voice, is also made possible here.

Thus Ps 35, echoed, seconded, and harmonized by others (Pss 44, 7, 73), puts God in the defendant's chair, calling on God to bear witness to and for the psalmist's situation.[34] Perhaps in this sense, at least within the

---

32. Konrad Schaefer, *Psalms* (Berit Olam; Collegeville, Minn.: Liturgical Press, 2001), 112, cf. 145.

33. Wilson, "Shaping the Psalter," 82.

34. I have in mind here Elie Wiesel's *The Trial of God* (New York: Schocken,

purview of some of the psalms, the Divine Warrior has trained not our hands for war (Ps 144:1), but our lips for contention.

Bibliography

Ballard, H. Wayne Jr. *The Divine Warrior Motif in the Psalms*. BIBAL Dissertation Series. North Richland Hills, Tex.: D&F Scott, 1999.

Blumenthal, David. *Facing the Abusing God*. Louisville: Westminster John Knox, 1993.

Brettler, Marc. "Images of Yhwh the Warrior in Psalms." In *Women, War, and Metaphor: Language and Society in the Study of the Hebrew Bible*. Edited by Claudia V. Camp and Carole R. Fontaine. *Semeia* 61 (1993): 135–65.

Brown, William P. *Seeing the Psalms: A Theology of Metaphor*. Louisville: Westminster John Knox, 2002.

Brueggemann, Walter. "The Costly Loss of Lament." *JSOT* 36 (1986): 57–71.

Craigie, Peter C., and Melvin E. Tate. *Psalms 1–50*. WBC 19. Nashville: Thomas Nelson, 2004.

Goldingay, John. *Psalms, Vol. 1: Psalms 42–89*. BCOTWP. Grand Rapids: Baker Academic, 2007.

Jacobson, Karl. *Many Are Saying: The Function of Direct Discourse in the Hebrew Psalter*. JSOTSup 397. New York: T&T Clark, 2004.

Kraus, Hans. *Psalms 1–59*. Minneapolis: Fortress, 1993.

Limburg, James. "The Root רִיב and the Prophetic Lawsuit Speeches." *JBL* 88 (1969): 294–304.

Lind, Millard. *Yahweh Is a Warrior: The Theology of Warfare in Ancient Israel*. Scottsdale, Penn.: Herald, 1980.

McLaughlin, John L. *The Marzeah in the Prophetic Literature: References and Allusions in Light of the Extra-biblical Evidence*. VTSup 86. London: Brill, 2001.

Miller, Patrick, Jr. *The Divine Warrior in Early Israel*. Cambridge: Harvard University Press, 1973.

1986). As Robert McAfee Brown puts it, "If, as David Blumenthal argues in *Facing the Abusing God* (Louisville: Westminster John Knox, 1993), Wiesel's play 'is a modern rereading of the Book of Job,' it is also a rereading of the book of Jeremiah, many of the psalms, and much of the tradition, all of which are centrally expressing the cry, 'Why?'" Online: http://people.bu.edu/trialofg/brown1.html.

Schaefer, Konrad. *Psalms*. Berit Olam. Collegeville, Minn.: Liturgical, 2001.

Weiser, Artur. *The Psalms*. OTL. Philadelphia: Westminster, 1962.

Wiesel, Elie. *The Trial of God*. New York: Schocken, 1986.

Wilson, Gerald H. "Shaping the Psalter: A Consideration of Editorial Linkage in the Book of Psalms." Pages 72–82 in *Shape and Shaping of the Psalter*. Edited by J. Clinton McCann Jr. JSOT 159. Sheffield Academic, 1993.

Revisiting the Theocratic Agenda of Book 4 of the Psalter for Interpretive Premise

Sampson S. Ndoga

Introduction

Reading particular psalms as detached compositions conceivably fails to take into account the redactional principle for organizing the material in the five books of the Psalter. As such, a number of studies have in the past been undertaken to underscore the evidence of logical arrangement of the Psalter.[1] Most of such studies[2] are dependent on the groundbreaking work of Gerald H. Wilson, in which he argues for editorial intentionality in the placement of the psalms.[3] More recently, Koorevaar's examination of the subscripts and superscripts as a treatise to understanding the Psalter as a whole provides fertile ground on which such an approach

---

1. See Gerald H. Wilson, "The Qumran Psalms Manuscripts and the Consecutive Arrangement of Psalms in the Hebrew Psalter," *CBQ* 45 (1983): 377–88. See also Wilson, *Psalms, Volume 1* (NIVAC; Grand Rapids: Zondervan, 2002); David M. Howard Jr., "Editorial Activity in the Psalter: A State-of-the-Field Survey," *WW* 9 (1989): 274–85; Leslie McFall, "The Evidence for a Logical Arrangement of the Psalter," *WTJ* 62 (2000): 223–56.

2. See David M. Howard Jr., *The Structure of Psalms 93–100* (Winona Lake, Ind.: Eisenbrauns, 1997); Jerome Creach, "The Shape of Book Four of the Psalter and the Shape of Second Isaiah," *JSOT* 80 (1998): 63–76; and J. Clinton McCann Jr., "The Book of Psalms: Introduction, Commentary, and Reflections," in *The New Interpreter's Bible* (ed. Leander E. Keck; 12 vols.; Nashville: Abingdon, 1996), 4:641–1280.

3. Gerald H. Wilson, *The Editing of the Hebrew Psalter* (SBLDS 76; Chico, Calif.: Scholars Press, 1985).

could thrive.[4] In a similar vein are the works by Koh and Labuschagne.[5] Koh explores theories on the consciously labored organizing principles of the Masoretic Psalter, while Labuschagne focuses on the numerical features of the Psalter as the presumed organizing principle. The most comprehensive study, though, is David Howard's *The Structure of Psalms 93–100*.[6] He begins his study with the observation that questions related to a single, overriding organizing principle behind the book of Psalms, as well as connections between individual and neighboring psalms, or among group of psalms, have been ignored for the most part, in favor of seemingly more pressing matters.[7] His work is largely focused on the lexemic, and as such we will not repeat his findings. Gelston also attempts an analysis of the editorial arrangement of book 4, a task he treats as hypothetical, in view of the fact that there are no records of the editorial premise for the arrangement of the material in the Hebrew Bible.[8] Nevertheless, a deliberate arrangement of material in the Psalter is discernible which in our opinion is mostly thematic.

The present essay intends to posit book 4 of the Psalter as having been organized under a theocratic rubric. Theocracy refers to a form of government in which official policy is governed by immediate divine guidance or by officials who are regarded as (or who claim to be) divinely guided. The acclamation יהוה מָלָךְ (*yhwh mālak*), "YHWH reigns" in Ps 93:1 introduces the theocratic concept in book 4. The concept "theocracy," apparently coined by Josephus, seems to have been intended to contrast with the "monarchical, oligarchical[9] and democratic form of government," as Keil and Delitzsch surmise. They write:

---

4. Hendrik Koorevaar, "The Psalter as a Structured Theological Story with the Aid of Subscripts and Superscripts," in *The Composition of the Book of Psalms* (ed. Erich Zenger; Leuven: Peeters, 2010), 579–92.

5. Yee Von Koh and Gerald H. Wilson, "Theories on the Organizing of the Masoretic-Psalter," in *Genesis, Isaiah, and Psalms: A Festschrift to Honour Professor John Emerton for His Eightieth Birthday* (ed. Katharine J. Dell et al.; Leiden: Brill, 2010), 177–92; Casper J. Labuschagne, "Significant Compositional Techniques in the Psalms: Evidence for the Use of Numbers as an Organizing Principle," *VT* 59 (2009): 583–605.

6. Howard, *Structure of Psalms 93–100*.

7. Ibid., 1.

8. Anthony Gelston, "Editorial Arrangement in Book IV of the Psalter," *in Genesis, Isaiah, and Psalms: A Festschrift to Honour Professor John Emerton for His Eightieth Birthday* (ed. Katharine J. Dell et al; Leiden: Brill, 2010).

9. Oligarchy is a form of power structure in which power effectively rests with

The theocracy itself is a reciprocal relationship between God and men, exalted above these intermediary forms, which had its first manifest beginning when Jahve became Israel's King (Deut. 33:5, cf. Ex. 15:18), and which will be finally perfected by its breaking through this national self-limitation when the King of Israel becomes King of the whole world, that is overcome both outwardly and spiritually. Hence the theocracy is an object of prediction and of hope. And the word מָלַךְ is used with reference to Jahve not merely of the first beginning of His imperial dominion, and of the manifestation of the same in facts in the most prominent points of the redemptive history, but also of the commencement of the imperial dominion in its perfected glory.[10]

The prominence of the theocracy in book 4 of the Psalter obviously has some historical precedence. Some surmise a postexilic date wherein the group of theocratic psalms would function as a response to the sixth-century B.C.E. restoration after the Babylonian exile as proof to the psalmist of divine sovereignty. Howard states that there is no scholarly agreement pertaining to the date of composition of this material, particularly the dating method.[11] The exile provides an appropriate contextual occasion, but in the absence of editorial titles in the majority of the psalms in book 4 the task becomes, as Bullock says a "tenuous business."[12] As such, we cannot distinguish between the time of original writing and that of editorial arrangement. For example Ps 90, ascribed to Moses, is placed at the beginning of book 4, even though its superscription suggests that it is the oldest psalm in the Psalter. For this reason, the arrangement of the psalms was deliberate to serve a specific purpose. For book 4, the theocratic premise provides a reasonable interpretive ordering based on the following five determinants: (1) The way book 3 ends—Ps 89; (2) the way book 4 begins—Pss 90–92; (3) the focus on YHWH as king—Pss 93–99; (4) the way book 4 closes—Pss 100–106; and (5) the thematic links of book 5.

---

a small number of people. These people could be distinguished by royalty, wealth, family ties, education, corporate, or military control. Such states are often controlled by a few prominent families who pass their influence from one generation to the next.

10. C. F. Keil and Franz Delitzsch, *Commentary on the Old Testament* (10 vols.; Peabody, Mass.: Hendrickson, 2002), 5:610–11.

11. Howard, *Structure of Psalms 93–100*, 184–92.

12. C. Hassell Bullock, *Encountering the Book of Psalms: A Literary and Theological Introduction* (Grand Rapids: Baker Academic, 2001), 189. See also McFall, "Evidence for the Logical Arrangement of the Psalter," 223–56.

THE WAY BOOK 3 ENDS: PSALM 89

Book 3 closes by depicting the Davidic covenant as an unsuccessful venture, in contrast to Pss 2 and 72. Gelston suggests that in view of Pss 2 and 72, Ps 89 is pivotal in the organization of the Psalter.[13] Koh affirms a similar editorial organizing and extends it into book 5, which he regards as theocratic as well, as we will consider below.[14] The centrality of the Davidic covenant rests in the fact that it was a royal grant covenant (2 Sam 7:4–17; cf. Ps 89:3–4, 30–37) stipulating an unconditional commitment to the establishment of a Davidic dynasty. To read in Ps 89:38–45 the lament encapsulating the king's defeat and his inevitable removal in spite of the divine covenantal undertaking is rather exceptional. Wilson comments:

> But for Ps. 89 the Davidic covenant is not only an event of the distant past, neither is it simply the source for later kingly authority, rather it is now a covenant *failed*. YHWH is depicted as rejecting his anointed king and renouncing the Davidic covenant. "But now you have cast off and rejected / you are full of wrath against your anointed / you have renounced the covenant with your servant / you have defiled his crown in the dust" (89.38–39). As a result the king has suffered military defeat.[15]

But this is not the end. Despite the unavoidable punishment for disobedience (Ps 89:30–32), the lament holds out hope by pronouncing the Davidic covenant as inviolable (Ps 89:33–37). Carson's analysis of the Psalm is helpful:

> Three eight-line stanzas (38–41, 42–45, 46–49) and a four-line concluding prayer (51–52), match the opening section in shape. But contrast with it in theme: the fourteen affirmations of divine sovereignty (9–14) are balanced by fourteen verbs of personal divine destructive action contradicting the promises (38–45). The covenant has been renounced and national defenses have been shattered (38–41); enemies are in the ascendant and the throne lies on the ground (42–45); so where is all this

---

13. Gelston, "Editorial Arrangement," 168.

14. Koh and Wilson, "Theories on the Organization," 186.

15. Gerald H. Wilson, "The Use of the Royal Psalms at the 'Seams' of the Hebrew Psalter," *JSOT* 35 (1986): 90.

former … love that was pledged (46–49); Lord, *remember* your servants
and your anointed (50, 51).[16]

For the purposes of this essay, the actualization of divine sovereignty
in the psalm against the backdrop of a failed monarchy provides the literary amplification of the true and unchanging ruler. In fact the psalm commences with sentiments on the rule of YHWH (Ps 89:5–18) as the setting
for the remarks on the Davidic covenant that ensue (Ps 89:19–29). It seems
that the Psalter juxtaposes the failed monarchy and the thriving theocracy
to project reasonable future prospects for its readers/hearers. The Davidic
covenant thus seems to have theocratic overtones. Moreover, Howard
argues that book 3 emphasizes the problematic Davidic covenant.[17] Bullock states, "the compiler of Book Four answered the question raised in
Ps 89 in two ways: (1) an aggregate of psalms emphasizing the kingship
of Yahweh, the really important Monarch of Israel and the world; and (2)
a shift of attention away from the Davidic to the Mosaic and Abrahamic
covenants."[18] The shift here, though, must not be understood as a complete departure, but as intended to show the foundational basis that the
Abrahamic and Mosaic covenants provide for the Davidic covenant. For
this reason, book 4 opens appropriately with a Mosaic reminiscence that
predates the Davidic covenant, from which Israel's fortunes stem.

The Way Book 4 Begins: Psalms 90–92

As was already stated, book 4 commences with a composition ascribed
to Moses. The figures of Moses and the Torah are synonymous. Israel's
demise rested solely on the peoples' failure to observe the stipulations of
the Torah (see Exod 19:3–6; Deut 5:32–33). Therefore the words of Moses
at the beginning of book 4 serve, among other redactional purposes, to
remind the reader/hearer of the covenantal heritage through which Israel's
stability could be realized. The Mosaic theme is also retained in Pss 91 and
92. The Mosaic covenant was a suzerain-vassal treaty in which a conditional pledge for divine providence and protection was based on Israel's

---

16. Donald A. Carson, "Commentary on Psalm 89:38," in *New Bible Commentary:
Twenty-First Century Edition* (ed. Gordon Wenham et al.; Downers Grove, Ill.: Inter-
Varsity Press, 1994), 543.

17. Howard, *Structure of Psalms 93–100*, 167.

18. Bullock, "Encountering the Book of Psalms," 188.

total obedience to being made a treasured possession, a kingdom of priests and a holy nation.[19] Because the treaty was not between equal parties, the adoration of YHWH as the epitome of true security in Ps 91 and the individual declaration of his praise in Ps 92 are implicit retrospective recollections deliberately placed by the redactor for their topical aptness in the postexilic era. We will note superlative injunctions of divine acclamations in book 5 of the Psalter to underscore the climatic editorial agenda.

THE FOCUS ON YHWH AS KING: PSALMS 93–99

The veneration of YHWH's supremacy seen in Pss 91 and 92 is heightened in the *yhwh mālak* psalms found in Pss 93–99. Howard comments:

> This first section of book 4 begins to provide an "answer" of sorts to the questions and pessimistic outlooks found at the end of book 3 (and even signaled at its outset). It is an answer that begins slowly, but by the time a reader reaches Ps 92 great assurances of faith and trust in Yhwh are found in the expression of praise in that psalm for the Sabbath Day. Then the Psalter breaks forth into full-throated praise of Yhwh's kingship in 93, 95–99.[20]

With the exception of Ps 94, a fairly complex psalm comprised of an individual lament (1–7), a wisdom interlude (8–15), and a community lament (9–23),[21] Pss 93–99 feature the *mālak* designation decidedly. This raises questions related to the function of Ps 94 in its present position. We find Howard's study helpful as he writes:

> I argue here that Psalm 94 is indeed well suited to its present position. It serves as an appropriate hinge between the early part of book 4—which raised many questions about life's purpose and God's relationship with his people—and the middle part of the book, in which unfettered praise of *Yhwh* the king breaks forth.[22]

---

19. Sampson Ndoga, "Divine Covenant Faithfulness in the Face of Human Covenant Unfaithfulness," *Testamentum Imperium* 3 (2011): 1–17.

20. David M. Howard Jr., "Psalm 94 among the Kingship-of-Yhwh Psalms," *CBQ* 61 (1999): 667.

21. Ibid.

22. Ibid., 668.

He continues by showing that Ps 94 has numerous identifiable links—
not just random links—to the psalms surrounding it, with the strongest
occurring with the three psalms in closest proximity to it: Pss 92, 93, and
95.[23] One could also argue from the language and themes of Ps 94 that the
theocratic portrait is the common thread connecting the entire collection.
Howard is therefore correct in pointing out that "Psalm 94 functions to
remind the reader that YHWH's kingship is not yet fully experienced by
his people."[24]

Psalms 93 and 95–99 present a superlative manifestation of YHWH as
king (See also Pss 24:7–10; 45:5, 11, 15; 47:7, 26; 48:2). Tarazi maintains
that the "major difficulty facing the translator is how to render the Hebrew
perfect *mālak*,"[25] translated as "the Lord reigns" in most English translations.[26] The question of the correct translation raises the question of its
theological significance. Chinitz writes this about what he renders as "*Ha-
Shem melekh* (Ps 10:16); *Ha-Shem malakh* (Ps 93:1); and *Ha-Shem yimlokh
le-olam va'ed* (Exod 15:18): 'God reigns, God has reigned, God shall reign
for all eternity' ": "In combination, the three phrases express the eternity of
God's reign.... When Scripture uses past, present, and future with regard to
God, does the choice of tense have any particular theological meaning?"[27]
In a similar vein, Tarazi writes:

(1) Translating *malak* with the English past "reigned" (or perfect "has
reigned") suggests YHWH used to reign but does not anymore.
(2) Opting for "YHWH is king" in order to stress that He is king *now*
sounds like a general statement identifying YHWH that could have been
rendered in Hebrew with *yhwh melek*.
(3) Another possibility is to understand *malak* as referring to an action
that has just been consummated: "YHWH has become king." Although
this rendering quite correctly captures the notion that the perfect *malak*
reflects a specific action through which YHWH has established Himself

---

23. Ibid., 668–85.

24. Howard, *Structure of Psalms 93–100*, 174–75.

25. Paul N. Tarazi, "An Exegesis of Psalm 93," *SVTQ* (1991): 137.

26. A majority of translations go with the "the LORD reigns" rubric, and a few
attempt to capture the literal translation "God is King." See *The Message, New Century
Translation,* and *New Living Translation* for the latter.

27. Jacob Chinitz, "The Three Tenses in the Kingdom of God: God of Israel or of
the World," *JBQ* 38 (2010): 255.

as king, it unfortunately shifts the stress from the action itself of reigning to the abstract notion of being a king.[28]

The overall emphasis of the Psalter thus seems to be the kingship of YHWH. Jerome Creach argues that book 4 addresses the trauma of the exile.[29] His sentiments are echoed by Leuchter, who states that "a number of these psalms may arise from a pre-exilic context, but their current function is to affirm the sovereign authority of YHWH as king within the Psalter."[30] Leuchter suggests that even though a number of these psalms may have arisen from a preexilic context, their function serves to affirm YHWH as king within the Psalter and the liturgical universe of the Second Temple period.[31] Bullock concludes that "the acclamation is particularly powerful and effective in the context of the failed Davidic covenant, with its implications that the Lord had lost his sovereign rule over the world, how that a Davidic king no longer sat on Judah's throne, and his holy city and temple lay in ruins. What Israel needed was not a declaration that the Lord has become king, but that the Lord still reigned in his power and majestic glory."[32]

The Way Book 4 Closes: Psalms 100–106

Book 4 ends with a historical reflection on the exodus (Ps 106:7–33), the settlement (Ps 106:34–39), and the exile (Ps 106:40–46). The historical reflection is preceded in Ps 100 with an exhortation to worship YHWH on the basis of his goodness (Ps 100:1–2) and his deeds (Ps 100:3–5). This is followed by a Davidic psalm (Ps 101) that depicts ethical ideals associated with his throne. In Ps 102, an individual lament, the psalmist revisits the divine royalty motif (Ps 102:12) as a reminder of the themes in Pss 90–92 on the reliability of YHWH and in Pss 93–99 on his kingship. In the deliberate editorial arrangement here, Ps 103 is a hymn in praise of the irrefutable divine blessings (Ps 103:1–18) because of God's established throne (Ps 103:19; cf. Ps 102:12). Psalm 104 paints a portrait of God's

---

28. Tarazi, "Exegesis of Psalm 93," 137–38.

29. Creach, "Shape of Book Four," 65.

30. Mark Leuchter, "The Literary Strata and Narrative Sources of Psalm XCIX," *VT* 55 (2005): 20.

31. Ibid.

32. Bullock, *Encountering the Book of Psalms*, 188.

throne (104:1–4) through imagery that underscores his creative acts (vv. 5–23), his dominion over all creation (vv. 24–32); and his deserving praise (vv. 33–35). Psalm 105 presents Israel's history with what seems to be a deliberate intention to coincide with the Mosaic narration. Starting with Abraham and ending with the settlement in the land, history is interpreted from the viewpoint of what YHWH has done for the people of Israel. A large portion of this history is dedicated to the Mosaic annals and reiterates the message of Ps 90. Psalm 106, however, which closes book 4, ends with a broken covenant. This then seems to be a deliberate redactional pattern to end books 3 and 4 rather pessimistically and inconclusively as a literary device to project what ensues.

Creach states, "Psalms 90 and 106 provide a kind of envelope with close verbal parallels and general interest in Moses as mediator between God and Israel. The intervening psalms mention Moses three times (Pss 99:6; 103:7; 105:26) for a total of seven occurrences of the name in Book Four, with the only appearance elsewhere in the Psalter (Ps 77:21)."[33] The significance of Moses cannot be overstated, especially in view of the postexilic context occasioned by breaching the Mosaic covenant. Creach also points out that the *yhwh mālak* psalms that stand at the center of book 4 and enhance implicitly this Mosaic emphasis. Psalms 93–99 are bounded by references to the "decrees of Yahweh.... [This] offers good reason to view Psalms 90–106 ... as 'a Moses book.'"[34]

At the same time, Pss 100–105 provide subtle of reminders of the YHWH as king motif (Pss 102:12; 103:19; 104:1). Psalm 105 depicts YHWH as the maker of human (Israelite) history and is closely tied to Ps 106 in its historical portrayal. Both psalms show the significance of divine stipulations for national stability, endorsing Wilson's thesis that argues for the thematic link of the material in Pss 103–106 to the topic of God's kingship, thereby serving as a suitable closure to book 4.[35] I would argue further that Pss 101–106 provide a closure for book 4. Howard issues useful comments to view Pss 101–106 as a consecutive reading utilizing the principle of concatenation of terms.[36] Overall, while there seems to

---

33. Creach, "Shape of Book Four," 65–66.

34. Ibid., 66.

35. Lindsay Wilson, "On Psalms 103–106 as a Closure to Book IV of the Psalter," in *The Composition of the Psalter* (ed. Erich Zenger; Leuven: Peeters, 2010), 755–66.

36. Howard, *Structure of Psalms 93–100*, 181–92.

be a shift in book 4 from the Davidic covenant to the Mosaic, the two are complimentary.

Book 4 closes on a rather pessimistic note as does book 3. Psalm 89 recalls the Davidic covenant and expresses sorrow for the lost blessings; in book 4 the Mosaic covenant is similarly implicated. In both books, YHWH is featured as the only viable option for a reversal of the attendant misfortunes. While the Davidic and Mosaic covenants are prominent themes in the Psalter, in book 4 these would be incomplete without some consideration of the theocratic motif. The kingship of YHWH predates both the Mosaic and the Davidic covenants. Wilson is therefore correct when he states:

> [Book 4] reflects on the dismay expressed in Ps. 89 over the failure of the Davidic covenant which was experienced in the Exile, and responds to the positive hopes for the future restoration of the Davidic kingship.[37]

This inconclusive closure sets the stage for book 5.

THE THEMATIC LINKS OF BOOK 5

Observable links between books 4 and 5 of the Psalter appear to exhibit redactional intentionality. The first relates to the continuity on a number of fronts between Ps 106, which concludes book 4, and Ps 107, which commences book 5. Jinkyu Kim points out the following:

- Both Pss 106 and 107 are untitled.
- Many lexemic, phrasal, and thematic links are detectable between them.
- Except for the phrase "praise YHWH" in the first verse of Ps 106, both psalms begin with virtually the same sentence.
- The exodus motif appears in both psalms.
- The thematic key on the steadfast love appears in both (Pss 106:1, 7, 45; cf. 107:1, 8 , 15, 21, 31, 43).[38]

---

37. Wilson, "Use of the Royal Psalms," 92.

38. Jinkyu Kim, "The Strategic Arrangement of Royal Psalms in Books IV–V," *WTJ* 70 (2008): 144–45.

Kim maintains that the similarity between the two psalms demonstrates that there is no discernible break between books 4 and 5. I agree with Kim and maintain that the link is a significant editorial marker indicating that the unresolved issues raised in book 4 are addressed, if not settled, in book 5. Psalms 107–118, according to Dennis Tucker, are anti-imperial in ethos, as they seem bent on castigating one true king.[39] Without going deeper into book 5, we can safely deduce a theocratic agenda on the following bases:

- the strategic placement of the royal Pss 108–110 early in book 5 to echo the failed monarchy, followed by frequent "praise YHWH" phrase in Pss 111–118, extolling YHWH;
- the acrostic Ps 119, considered a wisdom psalm, as a celebration of the centrality of the Torah-oriented wisdom[40] to rekindle Mosaic universalism (cf. Ps 90);
- the presentation of the Temple motif in the Songs of the Ascents (Pss 120–134), in which YHWH's saving acts are explicitly epitomized and dependability implied;
- the predominance of the Davidic designation in Pss 135–145 that pay special tribute to YHWH in a variety of ways to underscore the true king;
- Psalms 146–150 as a doxology to the entire Psalter, in which the one and only king is understood.

Koh's sentiments are valid in view of the above when he writes that "the final redactors of the second segment saw it necessary to put together books 4 and 5 in such a way as to help direct the reader away from trust in human kings toward the kingship of Yahweh."[41]

I conclude this study with the following observations:

- Book 4 of the Psalter commences on the foreground of the failed Davidic covenant presented at the end of book 3.

---

39. W. Dennis Tucker Jr., "Empires and Enemies in Book V of the Psalter," in *The Composition of the Psalter* (ed. Erich Zenger; Leuven: Peeters, 2010), 723–31.

40. Kim, "Strategic Arrangement of Royal Psalms," 148.

41. Koh and Wilson, "Theories on the Organisation," 186.

- Book 4 opens and closes with an implicit recollection of the significance of the Mosaic covenant, and particularizes it as the rationale for Israel's historical demise.
- The documentation of these failures seems to be intentionally placed here by the redactor to heighten the successive portraiture of YHWH as *melek* in book 4.
- Book 5 thrives on the foundation laid in book 4.

In all this, editorial intentionality is discernible. For interpretational purposes, none of the psalms in book 4 can be read in isolation from their placement within the book and within the Psalter as a whole.

Bibliography

Bullock, C. Hassell. *Encountering the Book of Psalms: A Literary and Theological Introduction*. Grand Rapids: Baker Academic, 2001.

Carson, Donald A. "Commentary on Psalm 89:38." Page 543 in *New Bible Commentary: Twenty-First Century Edition*. Edited by Gordon Wenham, J. Alec Motyer, Donald A. Carson, and R. T. France. Downers Grove, Ill.: InterVarsity Press, 1994.

Creach, Jerome. "The Shape of Book Four of the Psalter and the Shape of Second Isaiah." JSOT 80 (1998): 63–76.

Chinitz, Jacob. "The Three Tenses in the Kingdom of God: God of Israel or of the World." *JBQ* 38 (2010): 255–60.

Gelston, Anthony. "Editorial Arrangement in Book IV of the Psalter." Pages 163–76 in *Genesis, Isaiah, and Psalms: A Festschrift to Honour Professor John Emerton for His Eightieth Birthday*. Edited by Katharine J. Dell, Graham Davies, and Yee Von Koh. Leiden: Brill, 2010.

Howard, David M. Jr. "Editorial Activity in the Psalter: A State-of-the-Field Survey." *WW* 9 (1989): 274–85.

———. "Psalm 94 among the Kingship-of-Yhwh Psalms." *CBQ* 61 (1999): 667–85.

———. *The Structure of Psalms 93–100*. Winona Lake, Ind.: Eisenbrauns, 1997.

Keil, C. F., and Franz Delitzsch. *Commentary on the Old Testament*. 10 vols. Peabody, Mass.: Hendrickson, 2002.

Kim, Jinkyu. "The Strategic Arrangement of Royal Psalms in Books IV–V." *WTJ* 70 (2008): 143–58.

Koh, Yee Von, and Gerald H. Wilson. "Theories on the Organizing of the Masoretic Psalter." Pages 177–92 in *Genesis, Isaiah, and Psalms: A Festchrift to Honour Professor John Emerton for His Eightieth Birthday*. Edited by Katharine J. Dell, Graham Davies, and Yee Von Koh. Leiden: Brill, 2010.

Koorevaar, Hendrik. "The Psalter as a Structured Theological Story with the Aid of Subscripts and Superscripts." Pages 579–92 in *The Composition of the Book of Psalms*. Edited by Erich Zenger. Leuven: Peeters, 2010.

Labuschagne, Casper J. "Significant Compositional Techniques in the Psalms: Evidence for the Use of Numbers as an Organizing Principle." *VT* 59 (2009): 583–605.

Leuchter, Mark. "The Literary Strata and Narrative Sources of Psalm XCIX." *VT* 55 (2005): 20–38.

McCann, J. Clinton Jr. "The Book of Psalms: Introduction, Commentary, and Reflections." Pages 641–1280 in vol. 4 of *The New Interpreter's Bible*. Edited by Leander E. Keck. Nashville: Abingdon, 1996.

McFall, Leslie. "The Evidence for a Logical Arrangement of the Psalter." *WTJ* 62 (2000): 223–56.

Ndoga, Sampson. "Divine Covenant Faithfulness in the Face of Human Covenant Unfaithfulness." *Testamentum Imperium* 3 (2011): 1–17.

Tarazi, Paul N. "An Exegesis of Psalm 93." SVTQ (1991): 137–48.

Tucker, W. Dennis, Jr. "Empires and Enemies in Book V of the Psalter." Pages 723–31 in *The Composition of the Psalter*. Edited by Erich Zenger. Leuven: Peeters, 2010.

Wenham, Gordon J., J. A. Motyer, D. A. Carson, and R. T. France, eds. *New Bible Commentary: Twenty-First Century Edition*. Downers Grove, Ill.: InterVarsity Press, 1994.

Wilson, Gerald H. *The Editing of the Hebrew Psalter*. SBLDS 76. Chico, Calif.: Scholars Press, 1985.

———. *Psalms, Volume 1*. NIVAC. Grand Rapids: Zondervan, 2002.

———. "The Qumran Psalms Manuscripts and the Consecutive Arrangement of Psalms in the Hebrew Psalter." *CBQ* 45 (1983): 377–88.

———. "The Use of the Royal Psalms at the 'Seams' of the Hebrew Psalter." JSOT 35 (1986): 85–94.

Wilson, Lindsay. "On Psalms 103–106 as a Closure to Book IV of the Psalter." Pages 755–66 in *The Composition of the Psalter*. Edited by Erich Zenger: Leuven: Peeters, 2010.

On Reading Psalms as Liturgy: Psalms 96–99

Jonathan Magonet

Introduction

Psalms 96–99 are familiar to synagogue goers from their liturgical use as part of the introduction to the Friday evening Shabbat service. This sequence, beginning with Ps 95 and concluding with Ps 29, was introduced by the kabbalistic circles in Safed in the middle of the sixteenth century. The custom is ascribed to Rabbi Moses Cordovero (1522–1570). The psalms are followed by the liturgical hymn *L'cha Dodi* ("Come my friend to greet the bride [the Sabbath]"), composed in the same circles. Immediately afterward come Pss 92 and 93, whose use can be traced back to temple times (m. Tamid 7:4), following which the formal evening service begins.

The familiarity of this group of psalms as a liturgical unit inevitably draws attention to a number of repetitions of words and phrases among some of them that suggest a more complex relationship among the individual psalms concerned. Most obvious is the fact that whereas both Pss 96 and 98 begin with the call to "sing to YHWH a new song!" Pss 97 and 99 begin with the assertion that "YHWH rules!" thus providing a set of alternating openings and suggesting a deliberate juxtaposition. A further connection links Ps 96 with Ps 93 through the exhortation to say to the nations the latter's opening words "YHWH rules" and the subsequent phrase "the world is set firm and cannot be shaken" (cf. Ps 93:1c and Ps 96:10). It is even possible that what is to be said to the nations is not only these two phrases from Ps 93 but the short psalm in its entirety.

Having viewed these four psalms from what is admittedly a much later liturgical usage, it is nevertheless interesting to ask whether and how they might have functioned as liturgy within the biblical period. This has been a matter of scholarly interest since the pioneering form-critical work of

Gunkel and theories about their function within a hypothetical New Year festival where Israel's God was enthroned, and its subsequent criticisms and revisions. Rather than address that broader issue, however, some more fundamental features still need to be examined about the nature and forms of liturgy itself and how we might determine whether an individual psalm or group of psalms fit into that genre. Having been engaged for a number of decades in the editing and composing of liturgies for the Jewish community, I thought it might be helpful to indicate some basic elements that commonly recur. The following points are fairly self-evident and not exhaustive but do provide a possible tool for analysis.

A preliminary note: The first broad assumption to be made is that liturgies express and reinforce the identity and value systems of the particular community of worshipers. Moreover, they serve to link them with past and future generations of members of that community, as well as with similar communities elsewhere. Conversely, the use of particular formulations may consciously exclude others from participation. Liturgies are adapted, altered, and manipulated in the face of changes in the circumstances of the particular community.

In viewing individual psalms or collections of psalms as liturgical pieces, the following elements should be considered:

1. the presence of a coherent or at least discernible narrative;
2. techniques for ensuring continuity between the various sections and "voices" so as to move the narrative forward; for instance, the use of linking words or phrases;
3. evidence of actions by the worshipers, such as a procession, bodily movements such as bowing or hand gestures;
4. overt liturgical features such as musical instructions, choral insertions, or antiphonal elements; and
5. indications of the specific occasion.[1]

---

1. This is not always clear, particularly because liturgies are built from a number of regularly employed common elements that will vary in their emphases or locations, allowing for some flexibility in adapting these elements to the specific event that is being evoked. Since the participants understand the nature of the occasion, little need be directly indicated in the text itself, because the specifics may be introduced outside the written text in the form of a ritual act, priestly intervention, or some kind of address.

To test the applicability of these five points, we can briefly examine the case of an obvious liturgical composition, Ps 118.[2]

EXCURSUS 1

Narrative

Within Ps 118 the "I-voice" expresses the narrative: "I was in distress; YHWH supported me; open the gates of justice that I may enter in and thank YHWH" (vv. 5–7, 10–14, 17–19, 21, 28). A second narrative belongs to the "master of ceremonies," who instructs the choir and "interprets" the liturgical process, saying: "A stone the builders rejected has become the chief cornerstone" (v. 22); "This is the day YHWH has made" (v. 24) (vv. 15, 20, 22–24, 26–27).

Linkages

When the individual says: "YHWH is with me, I shall not fear; what can אדם (humankind) do to me?" (v. 6), the choir responds: "It is better to take refuge in YHWH than to trust in אדם (v. 8). In verse 19 the individual asks, "Open the gates of *justice* that I may enter in," to which the "master of ceremonies" responds: "This is the gate of YHWH; the *just* may enter in" (v. 20).

Actions of the Worshipers

The liturgical nature is well indicated in this psalm by the "stage directions" in verse 27: "Form the procession with the branches up to the horns of the altar."

Liturgical Features

The antiphonal elements are particularly prominent (vv. 1–4, 29) in addition to the many repeated choral phrases: "His love is everlasting" (vv. 1–4, 29); "YHWH's right hand" (vv. 15c, 16); "YHWH we beseech you" (v. 25).

---

2. For a more detailed analysis of the structure of Ps 118, see Jonathan Magonet, *A Rabbi Reads the Psalms* (2nd ed.; London: SCM, 2004), 121–33.

The Occasion

Beyond the general possibilities that this is part of a regular festival occasion, or possibly that it marks the triumphant return of the army from a victory, there are no clear indications of the specific event.

PSALM 93

Given that Pss 93, 97, and 99 have the same opening phrase, "YHWH rules," and that Ps 93 is partly quoted in Ps 96, it is appropriate briefly to examine it.

Psalm 93 depicts God's ultimate control over the cosmos, enthroned as "king" in the past (v. 2) and secure in that role for all future time (v. 5). The outer verses, 1–2 and 5, reinforce the idea of stability through images of the firm establishment of the physical world and the trustworthy "proofs," the laws through which God underpins this stability. This power holds in check the turbulent waters, described at the center of the psalm (vv. 3–4) as being like a massive storm at sea, where each "wave" of words crashes down on the one before (v. 3). Yet above the mighty "rumbling" of the breakers of the sea, expressed by the onomatopoeic repetition of the letters *mem* and *resh*, "powerful on high is YHWH!" The climactic presence of YHWH as the last word of verse 4, literally located "above" the mighty seas, firmly establishes YHWH's rule even over these powerful waters. Thus these forces, whether understood literally or metaphorically, are allowed to storm, but still remain "held" within the stable structure that YHWH has created to contain them, conceptually and indeed literally, in the brief compass of the psalm itself, before, after, and above.[3]

If Ps 93 has established the controlling effect of YHWH's kingship, the next step might be to see how this theme is further explored in the two psalms (Pss 97 and 99) that begin with the same opening formulation. Assuming there is some kind of unifying structure to the four psalms we are studying (Pss 96–99), however, it might be helpful to begin instead with Ps 96, which opens the sequence.

---

3. The appendix offers a layout for the psalm that seeks to dramatize the contrast between the opening and closing "stability" and the dynamic movement of the central section. It is taken from Jonathan Magonet, ed., *Seder Ha-Tefillot, Forms of Prayer: Daily, Sabbath and Occasional Prayers* (8th ed.; London: Movement for Reform Judaism, 2008), 126.

Psalm 96

Psalm 96 presents itself as a hymn with the opening threefold exhortation to "sing to YHWH (a new song)" (vv. 1, 2a). This hymnlike quality is further reinforced by the similar threefold repetition of the phrase "give/ ascribe to YHWH" in verses 7 and 8, suggesting that this opens a second companion "verse." The likelihood of a formally structured musical composition made up of two "verses" (vv. 1–6, 7–10) is reinforced by the similarly located corresponding calls in each to "narrate among the nation" in verse 3, and "say among the nations" in verse 10. This leaves verses 11–13, which seem to be a separate unit, to introduce two new themes: how nature itself will rejoice (vv. 11–12), and how YHWH is coming to judge the earth and peoples (v. 13). These verses might serve as a kind of closing refrain, particularly since a very similar set of themes, with much of the same phraseology and vocabulary, occurs at the end of Ps 98 (vv. 8–10). In fact the existence of these two "refrains" offers strong evidence for a unified liturgical composition encompassing at least Pss 96 and 98.

This is to be a "new song," the reason presumably being to celebrate the "salvation" YHWH has wrought (v. 2b). No obvious information within the psalm indicates the particular event the psalmist might have had in mind, whether the exodus from Egypt, the return from exile, or any other cause for celebration in between. While it may be frustrating to try to pin down the historical moment of composition, it accords with the generalizing nature of liturgies that can be adapted to serve a number of different but relatively similar occasions. But whatever the event, it is not of significance to Israel alone, but something to be broadcast to the nations. The divine attributes to be conveyed are YHWH's כבוד (glory) and נפלאות (wondrous works) (v. 3). The conventional translation of כבוד as "glory" conceals the idea of the root meaning of "weight." In the particular context of these psalms, however, where קדוש (holy) features very prominently (especially in Ps 99), it may also have a more specialized meaning which requires a second brief excursus into Isa 6:3.

Excursus 2

Isaiah 6:3 is a depiction of perhaps the ultimate example of a biblical liturgy, one that is performed in praise of God in the heavenly court by the seraphim. The verse is dominated by the threefold repetition of קדוש with its basic sense of "separate," "apart," "other." This threefold repetition suggests that the divine "separateness" is infinitely extended, offering a biblical expression of what today we would term "transcendence." In contrast the earth is filled with God's כבוד, this "weightiness" suggesting God's presence in and indeed engagement with, the world, what we would term "immanence." This extraordinary sentence offers a biblical version of the paradox of God's simultaneous otherness and presence. Incidentally, this contrast is reinforced by the similar contrast in the surrounding verses. Using the key word מלא (full): in verse 1 God's throne is "on high," while God's train "fills" the temple; in verse 4 the outer walls shake but the building is "filled" with smoke.[4]

It is reasonable to assume that when both terms, קדוש and כבוד, appear together in a liturgical context they may carry this particular set of related meanings. So it is interesting to observe how they are utilized in the psalms under consideration. Thus כבוד is prominent in Pss 96 and 97, both of which explicitly refer to YHWH's saving acts for Israel witnessed by the peoples of the world. The term is, interestingly, absent in Pss 98 and 99. And while variations of the root קדש are found in all four psalms, they reach a significant threefold climax in Ps 99.[5]

YHWH's כבוד is a theme stressed in Ps 96, appearing three times (vv. 3, 7, 8). It is to be ascribed to YHWH by the "families of nations" and it is linked with עז (power) in verse 7. What is striking in verse 8 is that acknowledgement of YHWH's כבוד is directly linked to the invitations to bring an offering and to enter the temple courts. Indeed, visitors are to bow before YHWH in the "beauty of holiness." Is this invitation to the nations a purely rhetorical one, a liturgical formula expressing universal sentiments intended only for internal Israelite consumption, or does it actually reflect some kind of entry ceremony in which peoples of other nations who visit the temple, whether as individuals or formal delegations, are addressed and welcomed? There is no obvious reason to set aside such an explicit formulation as anything but literally intended. And incidentally, it coincides with the third point on our list of liturgical elements. These visi-

---

4. For a study of the chapter, see Jonathan Magonet, "On the Impossibility of Prophecy: A Study of Isaiah 6," in *Aspects of Liberal Judaism: Essays in Honour of John D. Rayner* (ed. David J. Goldberg and Edward Kessler; London: Vallentine Mitchell, 2004), 170–83.

5. The root *qdš* is briefly used in Ps 96 (v. 6b, the sanctuary; v. 9, the clothing of those in the sanctuary) and the "remembrance" of God's holiness is in Ps 97:12. The outstretched arm of YHWH's holiness appears in Ps 98:1.

tors are designated as "families of peoples," a phrase that evokes the call to Abraham (Gen 12:3) through whom all the families of the earth are to be blessed.[6] Solomon extended such an invitation to נכרי (foreigners) to worship at the temple (1 Kgs 8:41–43), and the references in obvious liturgical psalms to the participation of "those who fear YHWH" (Pss 115:11, 13; 118:4), outside the category of the "house of Israel," would seem to confirm their presence.[7]

The "admission price" to YHWH's sanctuary is presumably the rejection of other gods that has been emphasized in the previous verses of the psalm (vv. 4, 5), where YHWH's awesome power, greater than that of all other gods, is stressed. Indeed the other gods are considered to be mere אלילים (little gods), effectively in this context a diminutive term for אלהים (Elohim) that reinforces their insignificance, and which will recur in a key place in Ps 97:7. In contrast to the gods, YHWH made the heavens; "splendor and majesty" are before him; and power and beauty in his sanctuary. This latter term prepares the way for the instruction that follows to enter the courtyards of the sanctuary.

If the first "verse" of the song (vv. 1–6) hymns YHWH's power (vv. 3–6), the equivalent place in the second "verse" (vv. 7–10) reproduces the opening of Ps 93, as noted above. It concludes with a significant new dimension, however—God's role as righteous judge: "He will judge the peoples uprightly," thus establishing the theme that will subsequently become prominent.

To summarize, Ps 96 is expressed as a call to the "families of peoples" to recognize the uniqueness of Israel's God, in contrast to their אלילים, coupled with an invitation to enter the sanctuary with their offerings and celebrate YHWH's rule and the justice YHWH metes out. As noted above, there is no obvious reason to doubt that this invitation was literally intended and on occasion literally fulfilled.

PSALM 97

Psalm 97 begins with the earth and the distant isles rejoicing (v. 1) at YHWH's "rule," but the appearance becomes more and more threatening

---

6. The other variant on this phrase "families of nations" is found in Ps 22:28, where the context is again God's rule over all the nations.

7. The existence of such individuals, and the problem of participation in the liturgies of rival gods is nicely illustrated by the dilemma of Na'aman (2 Kgs 5:18).

as it resembles a powerful storm: fire strides before YHWH (v. 3); light-ning lights up the world so that the "earth" (either nature itself or YHWH's enemies) now trembles (v. 4); mountains melt like wax before the "master of all the earth." Yet concealed within these powerful forces is the founda-tion of YHWH's "throne" (v. 2). The term מכון כסאו (the foundation of his throne) echoes the assertion in Ps 93:2: נכון כסאך ("established is your throne from eternity"). But in Ps 97 the significance of that throne for the world is spelled out, for the bases of the establishment are צדך ומשפט (righteousness and justice), a theme and terms we have met already in Ps 96:13, which will recur throughout this set of psalms (Pss 97:2,6; 98:2, 9; 99:4). In terms of our interest in liturgical elements, this would constitute one of the underlying narratives, God's coming to establish "righteousness and justice" in the world.

A second theme emerges in verse 6, one already addressed in Ps 96:5. In comparison with YHWH, whose righteousness the very heavens pro-claim and all the nations have witnessed (v. 6), all who bow to an idol will be ashamed/disappointed, for what they worship are אלילים (little gods). In a further biting contrast, YHWH is מהלל (praised, 96:4), whereas the idolaters מתהללים באלילים (97:7), an effective alliteration that also plays on the "self-praise" implicit in the hithpael form of the verb הלל: "they vaunt themselves with vanities." Indeed, the verse continues, all the gods bow before YHWH. The theme of YHWH's elevation above the earth and all the gods is complemented by verse 9, which asserts that YHWH is "high" above all the earth, and much raised above "all the gods" that are defined as merely "earthbound," unlike YHWH, whose righteousness the very heav-ens proclaim. Between these two sets of assertions is verse 8, which for the first time evokes Zion and the "daughters of Judah," presumably the cities.[8] They are to rejoice precisely because of YHWH's judgments, even though, as in this location in the psalm, they are literally surrounded by idol worshipers.

Verses 10–12 add a new dimension, opening up the special protection and divine providence afforded to those who are not specifically desig-nated as "Israel" but are variously described as "loving YHWH," YHWH's "pious ones," the "righteous" and the "upright of heart." In light of the pos-sibility that Ps 96 reflects an actual invitation to people of other nations to visit the temple and worship YHWH, these more general terms for pious

---

8. See Marvin E. Tate, *Psalms 51–100* (WBC 20; Dallas: Word, 1990), 519.

adherents of YHWH would indicate the benefits that would accrue to any from the "families of peoples" who seriously accepted YHWH as their God. Unlike the dramatic lightning and fire that light the way before the Eternal's throne, there is a special light reserved for the צדיק (righteous). Just as the many isles are to rejoice at YHWH's rule at the beginning of the psalm, YHWH's loyal followers are to experience joy and rejoice when they give thanks as they remember YHWH's "holiness" (v. 12). We met this term in Ps 96:9 as it relates to the splendor of the worship in the sanctuary; now it is specifically expressed as an attribute of YHWH, suggesting that it is introducing the theme that will come to dominate Ps 99 (vv. 3, 5, 9).

To summarize, Ps 97 indicates the approach of YHWH, displaying the divine powers. All who serve other gods will be disappointed, and even their gods will come to bow before YHWH, just as the "visiting" nations have done (Ps 96:9). In contrast, those who worship YHWH, though not specifically named "Israel," will find light and joy. In the context of the sequence of psalms, Ps 97 makes concrete the closing "chorus" of Ps 96 that YHWH is coming to judge the earth and its people.

Psalm 98

Psalm 98 begins with the same call to sing to YHWH a new song. Two of the terms from 96:1, 3 reappear: נפלאות (wondrous deeds) (98:1, cf. 96:3); and ישועה (saving act) (Ps 98:1, 2; cf. Ps 96:2), though again with no specific event or events indicated. This latter term becomes the key one in verses 2 and 4, the awareness of YHWH's "saving act" being revealed to all the world, bracketing verse 3, where the specific nature of that salvation is spelled out, God's love and faithfulness to the house of Israel.

> YHWH has made known his "saving act";
>> In the eyes of the nations he has revealed his righteousness.
> He remembered his love[9] and faithfulness to the house of Israel.
>> All the ends of the earth have seen the "saving act" of our God (Ps
>> 98:2–3).

---

9. I understand the term חסד throughout these psalms to represent the "faithful love and loyalty" that are present between partners in a covenant, a loyalty that is over and above the simply legal and contractual elements in their relationship.

Whereas Ps 96 was universal, challenging the gods of the nations and inviting the peoples to enter the sanctuary, Ps 98 is specific about the special nature of YHWH's care for Israel. If these psalms are indeed to be understood as a sequence, then Ps 98 is picking up the reference to Israel ("Zion" and the "daughters of Judah") in Ps 97:8. Just as the term יְשׁוּעָה (salvation) served to open and close verses 2–3, similarly הָרִיעוּ (shout joyfully) opens and closes verses 4–6, presumably filling a musical function similar to the call to "sing" in verse 1. While הָרִיעוּ introduces the "orchestra" that is to play with harp, voices, trumpets, and shofar (6–7a), it also introduces once again the designation of YHWH as "the king." הָרִיעוּ לַיהוה ("shout joyfully to YHWH") in verse 4 becomes הָרִיעוּ לִפְנֵי הַמֶּלֶךְ יהוה ("shout joyfully before the king YHWH") in verse 6. Verses 1–3 and 4–6 become complementary: in the former YHWH proclaims his salvation to the nations and "all the ends of the earth" have seen it; in the latter "all the earth" are invited to celebrate YHWH, "the king." Whereas Ps 96 confines this celebration to those who had entered the temple, Ps 98 turns the whole world into a musical liturgical celebration of YHWH.[10]

As noted earlier, the concluding verses 8–10 of Ps 98 echo the conclusion of Ps 96 (vv. 11–13). Common to both is the phrase יִרְעַם הַיָּם וּמְלֹאוֹ ("let the sea and its fullness shout for joy," Pss 96:11c; 98:8a) as evidence of nature's rejoicing. Psalm 96 speaks of the fields and their produce and the trees of the forest (v. 12), whereas Ps 98 invokes the rivers and mountains.[11] Between them the two psalms cover all of nature, both cultivated and uncultivated, thus reinforcing the view that they belong together and mark a similar stage in the liturgical event, perhaps as a special choral intervention or congregational chant.

The cause for this celebration, as in Ps 96, is the imminent arrival of YHWH to judge the earth (Pss 96:13; 98:10c). The only difference is in the formulation of the second part of the sentence: God will judge the peoples with "faithfulness" in Ps 96:13, but with "uprightness" (a term introduced in Ps 96:10) in Ps 98:10. A possible link to the former term is the earlier appearance of אֱמוּנָה (faithfulness) in Ps 98:3, representing the faithful

---

10. I use the word "liturgical" because the instruments' names are specifically those used in temple worship, though they could equally belong to, for example, the royal court.

11. Possibly as an intentional reference, the "rivers" that expressed their power in Ps 93:3 are here dancing with joy.

care YHWH has displayed to the house of Israel (Ps 98:3), now extended to all the peoples of the world.

PSALM 99

In Ps 99 the divine journey (Pss 96:13; 97:8; 98:10), presumably to Zion, is complete. God is enthroned, seated above the cherubim (Ps 99:1), and is great in Zion and elevated above all the peoples who proclaim their thanks (Ps 99:3). Having established the awesome nature of God, now firmly enthroned and acknowledged by all peoples, the psalm turns from the universal to the particular, the special relationship with Israel, a relationship bound up with concepts of justice and righteousness that YHWH has given to them (v. 4). It is as if after all this public rejoicing and acknowledgement of God by nature itself and the peoples of the world, there is finally time for a private conversation with Israel.

This move from the universal to the particular may be regarded as a radical and disjunctive change, effectively isolating Ps 99 as a separate creation distinct from the other three. Nevertheless the "peoples" are still present (vv. 1, 2) and offer their thanksgiving (v. 3). The relationship between the universal and particular is already evident in the other psalms, Israel's fate and actions having consequences for the wider world. Again one might evoke the blessing given to Abraham, but also the opening phases of the covenant at Sinai where God indicates that Israel's task is to be a "kingdom of priests" (playing the role among the nations as the priest does who represents his people before YHWH) and at the same time a "holy nation" ("set apart" for a special exclusive relationship with YHWH, Exod 19:6). This change from universal to particular receives an interesting echo, however, in a rabbinic observation and teaching.

EXCURSUS 3

The rabbis noted the unusual practice that during the festival of Sukkot (Tabernacles) the Israelites would sacrifice a decreasing number of bulls daily, beginning with thirteen and ending on the seventh day with seven (Num 29:12–34). The total amounted to seventy, which the rabbis identified as referring to the seventy nations of the world for whom these sacrifices made atonement. Given the unusual nature of this sequence of sacrifices, it may well be that the rabbis had an authentic tradition about their universal intent. They noted that on the eighth day, the עצרת, only a single bull was offered (Num 29:35). What follows is a typical piece of rabbinic midrashic exegesis, which simply starts from the assumption that this tradition regarding the universal meaning of the seventy bulls is a given, so the challenge is to understand what it might mean. Hence the following comment attributed to Rabbi Eleazar:

> Rabbi Eleazar said: Seventy bulls for the seventy nations. But why a single bull? For the unique nation. This can be compared to a king of flesh and blood who said to his servants, "Make me a great feast." On the last day he said to his beloved, "Make me a little feast, that I may take pleasure in you." Rabbi Johanan said: Woe to those nations who sustained a loss, yet know not what they lost; for when the temple still stood, it used to atone for them, and now who will atone for them." (b. Sukkot 58b)

There is another factor here, however, that actually makes the move to particularism inevitable as an essential complement to the arrival of YHWH in the sanctuary, because Zion is also the home of YHWH's own particular people. Until now in these psalms, Israel has been seen indirectly, through the eyes of others, the peoples who are called upon to celebrate YHWH's saving acts with Israel (Pss 96:2; 98:3), or to bring an offering to the sanctuary, and through the anticipation felt by Zion and the "daughters of Judah" at YHWH's imminent arrival (Ps 97:8). With that arrival there is a logic to rehearsing the history of the relationship and something of its nature.

Nevertheless, the content of that conversation is puzzling. It seems to hinge on the meaning of Ps 99:4a, literally "the strength of a king (who) loves justice, you established uprightness." Since the only king mentioned so far throughout all the psalms we are discussing is YHWH, it seems most likely that the king referred to here is also YHWH. Alternatively, it could be a reference to the human king who sits on Israel's throne, and who is responsible for maintaining justice. But the subsequent verses make this unlikely. The figures from Israel's history singled out for mention as ideal leaders of the people and their intermediaries with YHWH are precisely the premonarchical leaders Moses, Aaron, and Samuel who share among themselves the roles of priest, prophet, and political leader. They are designated as recipients and guardians of the divine laws, whose calls to YHWH were answered (Ps 99:6b, 8a) by a God who was an אל נשא (forgiving God), as promised in Exod 34:6–7 and Ps 99:8b, but who also punished them for their wrongdoings (Ps 99:8c). It is consistent with the theme throughout the psalms we are considering that YHWH, who judges with uprightness, shows no favors, even to those special chosen ones. The absence of any reference to a human king in this list may reflect the historical situation at the time of its composition, but given the context it may simply be intended to emphasize that YHWH alone is Israel's true king.

Psalm 99:7 seems to conflate the cloud that led the Israelites in the wilderness with the cloud that descended on Mount Sinai at the revelation. Yet, again assuming some kind of internal connection within these Psalms, it echoes the use of עָנָן (cloud) in Ps 97:2, the cloud and darkness that surround YHWH. A word play between עָנָן and the verb עָנָה (answer, 99: 6, 8), twice links the cloud to God's "answering" the three representative figures, thus indicating YHWH's continuing communication with Israel even after the wilderness period.

CONCLUSION

Is there sufficient evidence here to assume that Pss 96–99 (possibly introduced by Ps 93) form a single, coherent liturgical unit, made up of alternating hymns and "kingship" psalms? Certainly there is considerable common terminology that links the two kinds of psalms, so that something referred to in one is echoed in the psalm that follows.

Though the two "kingship" psalms are introduced by the statement that YHWH rules, the theme of YHWH as king is present in both of the "hymns" as well, most obviously in the "quote" from Ps 93 in Ps 96:10 and in the way that YHWH is emphatically acclaimed as *the* king in Ps 98:7.

The call to worship and bow before YHWH (Ps 96:9) is even applied to the אֱלִילִים in 97:7, and builds to the climax in Ps 99 (vv. 5, 9) when all are invited to elevate YHWH and bow before his footstool and his holy mountain. The insignificance of the "other gods," specifically the אֱלִילִים (little gods), links Pss 96:5 and 97:7. Once they are effectively dismissed, they make no further appearance in Pss 98 and 99.

The use of variations on קָדוֹשׁ (holy) is found in all four psalms. The garments of holiness associated with temple worship (Ps 96:9) and the temple itself (Ps 96:6); the remembrance of YHWH's holiness for which the righteous give thanks (Ps 97:12); YHWH's "holy arm" with which YHWH saved Israel (Ps 98:1), all these variations come together in the threefold celebration of YHWH's holiness in Ps 99 (vv. 3, 5, 9).[12] We have noted

---

12. It is tempting to see in the threefold use of קָדוֹשׁ (holy) a conscious echo of Isa 6:3.

above the appearance of כבוד in Pss 96 and 97, referring to the tangible evidence in the world of YHWH's readiness to intervene in human affairs, the divine immanence. If we take קדש (holy) to emphasize YHWH's "otherness" or "transcendence," then this becomes the climactic expression of God's divine kingship that the four/five psalms celebrate.

YHWH's special relationship to Israel is also marked throughout—the "salvation" YHWH wrought for them (Pss 96:2; 98:1, 2, 4); the joy of Zion and the "daughters of Judah" (Ps 97:8); YHWH's engagement with Israel (Ps 99:6–8). But this salvation is significant mostly because of its effect on the other peoples, who will one day benefit from YHWH's arrival to bring justice to the entire world (Pss 96:13; 98:10).

The emphasis throughout on צדק ומשפט (righteousness and justice) helps define the special concern of Israel's God. Indeed, it takes us back again to the figure of Abraham, who was chosen to exemplify these characteristics and pass them on to his children (Gen 18:18–19).[13] YHWH has placed these values within Jacob (Ps 99:4). YHWH is now coming to bring true justice to the world (Pss 96:13; 98:10), because צדק ומשפט are the foundations of YHWH's throne (Ps 97:2).[14]

Interestingly, nature provides the dramatic background against which the events within the psalms take place: Pss 93, 96:11–12; 97:1–5; 98:8–9.

To return to our five elements of liturgy, they are certainly present in these psalms, both individually and collectively.

1. *Narrative.* The main "narrative" is about YHWH's journey to his place between the cherubim in Zion. Secondary narratives, however, include YHWH's saving acts for Israel (expressions of YHWH's כבוד [immanence]) and their effect on the families of peoples who observe them, cast off their idols, and turn to Israel's God, even participating in worship in the sanctuary.

---

13. We have already noted above another possible connection to Abraham, linking the use of the term "the families of peoples" in Ps 96:7 with the promise to Abraham at his initial call that through him the "families of the earth" would find blessing (Gen 12:3).

14. The other references to these two terms include צדק (righteousness) alone: the heavens proclaim YHWH's צדק (Ps 97:6) and YHWH's special care for the צדיק (righteous, Ps 97:11, 12); while Zion rejoices in YHWH's משפט (judgment, Ps 97:8). The related term to the theme of righteousness, מישרים (uprightness) appears in 96:10; 98:10 and 99:4, while the reference to YHWH's אמונה (faithfulness, Pss 96:13; 98:3) serve to reinforce this emphasis.

2. *Linkages.* We have indicated a number of linkages between the psalms that establish thematic continuity throughout them, building to the climactic celebration of God's "holiness." For example אלילים (little gods) linking Pss 96:5 and 97:7; מישרים (equity) linking Pss 96:10, 98:10 and 99:4; variations on ישׁוע (salvation) linking Pss 96:2 and Ps 98:1, 2, 4; and אמונה (faithfulness) linking Pss 96:13 and 98:3.

3. *Actions of the worshipers.* There is evidence throughout of actions to be performed by the worshipers, bringing their offerings and prostrating (Pss 96:9; 97:7; 99:5, 9).

4. *Liturgical Features.* Liturgical features include instructions for musical performance (Ps 98:6–7) and the invocation to the congregation to "sing" (Pss 96:1–2; 98:1) and to bless (Ps 96:2). The "refrain" in Pss 96:11–13 and 98:8–10 suggests an overarching and unifying passage, perhaps requiring choral or community performance.

5. *The Occasion.* Finally, in the absence of any concrete evidence, it is not possible to pin down the specific occasion, or regularly recurring event, where these psalms might have been utilized together. The scholarly view that would link the "enthronement" psalms to the autumn festivals, together with the opening universalistic aspect of the first two psalms, fits in well with the rabbinic observation about the universalistic aspect of the festival of Sukkot.

Despite this analysis, there can be no conclusive presumption of an overarching unity, because we have no knowledge of how the psalms were actually performed so as to highlight or emphasize particular themes or elements. Just to illustrate the point, one need only visit a variety of synagogues to see how differently the identical liturgical texts may be read, sung, chanted, or read silently; while standing, sitting, or parading; interrupted by liturgical actions (opening or closing the ark); supplemented by the insertion of improvised clarifications, by instructions, or addresses. Even the music can vary enormously, encouraging awed solemnity or cheerful participation. In short, the texts themselves are merely the raw material around which the liturgical event is staged.

Between them, this collection of Psalms present a number of contrasting polarities: between כבוד (glory) and קדושׁ (holiness); between the אלילים (little gods) and YHWH; between the other peoples and Israel. It is certainly possible to construct a "narrative" linking the four passages as part of a temple liturgy, with the two distinctive elements, "hymns" and "kingship psalms," alternating. Together they celebrate the journey of God to Zion and the temple, recounting along the way YHWH's saving acts

(כבוד, glory), acknowledged by all peoples, and climaxing in the celebration of YHWH's enthronement in holiness, presumably within the holy of holies. In its favor are the many linkages across the psalms that we have noted. Against it is the possibility that each of these independent psalms simply utilizes a range of conventional liturgical language. Nevertheless, on balance, I would argue for a coherent sequence, one that celebrates and sets out to define the implications of YHWH's kingship, for Israel and for the peoples of the world, with righteousness and justice being the principal feature. Nevertheless, what can be said is that this particular set of psalms offers enough coherence, continuity, and grandeur to make for a powerful liturgical experience.

Appendix: Psalm 93

1. The Creator reigns
   robed in pride,
   God is robed in power,
   clothed in strength.
   So the world was set firm
   and cannot be shaken,
2. Your throne was set firm long ago,
   from eternity You are.

3. Almighty, the floods may storm,
   the floods may storm aloud,
   the floods may storm and thunder.

4. Even above the roar of great waves,
   mighty breakers of the ocean,
   supreme is the might of the Creator.

5. The proofs You give are very sure,
   holiness is the mark of Your house,
   God, as long as time endures.

BIBLIOGRAPHY

Magonet, Jonathan. "On the Impossibility of Prophecy: A Study of Isaiah 6." Pages 170–83 in *Aspects of Liberal Judaism: Essays in Honour of John D. Rayner*. Edited by David J. Goldberg and Edward Kessler. London: Vallentine Mitchell, 2004.

——. *A Rabbi Reads the Psalms*. 2nd ed. London: SCM, 2004.

——, ed. *Seder Ha-Tefillot, Forms of Prayer: Daily, Sabbath and Occasional Prayers*. 8th ed. London: Movement for Reform Judaism, 2008.

Tate, Marvin E. *Psalms 51–100*. WBC 20. Dallas: Word, 1990.

THE ROLE OF THE FOE IN BOOK 5:
REFLECTIONS ON THE FINAL COMPOSITION
OF THE PSALTER

W. Dennis Tucker Jr.

INTRODUCTION

In celebration of the twenty-fifth anniversary of *The Editing of the Hebrew Psalter*, the 2011 Book of Psalms Section of the Society of Biblical Literature paid homage to the contributions of Gerald Wilson's work and recognized his influence methodologically upon subsequent work in the discipline. The present article, however, is more modest in scope, limiting its comments to Wilson's understanding of book 5 alone. Admittedly, this proves challenging due to the untimely death of Wilson and, consequently, the limited number of works he was able to complete on book 5.[1] Nevertheless, a few comments are in order.

In response to Wilson's treatment of book 5, I would like to suggest that the role of the enemies in this portion of the Psalter, and more particularly, the role of imperial power vis-à-vis the surrounding nations, represents an important strand throughout the collection, one that Wilson seemingly overlooked, or at least failed to stress, in his initial analysis of Pss 107–145. Attention to power in book 5 also supports the assertion by another Psalms scholar who departed too quickly from us. Erich Zenger suggested that the Psalter in its final form represented an "anti-imperial

---

1. In his Psalms commentary (*Psalms, Volume 1* [NIVAC; Grand Rapids: Zondervan, 2002]), Wilson deferred full treatment of the shape of the Psalter for vol. 2. Unfortunately, he did not complete the second volume before his death.

book," a *Kampfbuch* against imperial power.[2] Such an understanding of book 5 may in the end provide insight into the final composition, both structurally and socially.

Gerald Wilson and Book 5 of the Psalter

In the final chapter of *The Editing of the Hebrew Psalter*, Wilson addresses the final shape of the Psalter and the editorial activity evidenced within. When considering Pss 107–145, however, Wilson surmises that a "detailed analysis of the editorial organization of the fifth book" proves difficult due to its unwieldy size (44 psalms) and the appearance of previous collections within book 5 that, he suggests, would appear to limit "the amount of editorial manipulation possible."[3] Despite these initial disclaimers, Wilson does proffer a number of points that relate to the editorial structure of book 5, but only one can be considered here.

Wilson notes that there are two groups of Davidic psalms preserved in book 5 (Pss 108–110, 138–145), and that their placement at the beginning and end of the collection suggests editorial intention. Strikingly, however, Wilson concludes, "While it is difficult to trace any clear strategy of editorial juxtaposition threading its way through the individual pss … the groups as a whole seem to intend to set up David as a model in response to the concerns of the pss which precede them."[4] Wilson was surely correct in his assertion that book 5 was meant to generate an attitude of trust and reliance upon YHWH, as modeled in the life of David. Yet generally absent from his discussion are the threats posed by the political foes.[5] A brief sketch of the nature of such threats appears below.

---

2. Erich Zenger, "Der jüdische Psalter—Ein anti-imperiales Buch?" in *Religion und Gesellschaft: Studien zu ihrer Wechselbeziehung in den Kulturen des Antiken Vorderen Orients* (ed. R. Albertz; Münster: Ugarit, 1997), 97.

3. Gerald H. Wilson, *The Editing of the Hebrew Psalter* (SBLDS 76; Chico, Calif.: Scholars, 1985), 220. Wilson notes that the large number of consecutive untitled psalms within books 4 and 5 also present challenges in identifying an editorial strategy (177).

4. Ibid., 221.

5. Ibid., 227.

The Presence of Enemy Powers in Book 5

Psalm 107

The opening psalm of book 5, Ps 107, connects the identity of the people with their experience at the hands of foreign powers. Verse 2 begins by announcing that גְּאוּלֵי יהוה (the redeemed of YHWH) have been delivered מִיַּד־צָר (from the hand of the oppressor). The latter phrase, מִיַּד־צָר, has been rendered as "trouble" in the NRSV, thereby stripping the term of the political connotations so often associated with it.[6] Walter Beyerlin contends that the phrase "the hand of the צָר" refers instead to historical-political enemies.[7] When צָר appears in the Hebrew Bible, it is frequently a clear reference to the political or military enemies of Israel or Judah.[8] In such instances, the term צָר is best understood as coming from the root צרר II, "to be hostile," and not from צרר I, "to be in distress."[9] Further evidence for rendering צָר as a political term can be garnered from Ps 106.[10] In Ps 106:10, speaking of Israel's deliverance from Egypt, the psalmist announces:

He delivered them from the hand of the foe (מִיַּד שׂוֹנֵא);
And he redeemed (גאל) them from the hand of enemy (מִיַּד אוֹיֵב).

Later, in Ps 106:41, the psalmist explains that YHWH "gave them into the hand of the nations" (בְּיַד־גּוֹיִם) and they were "subdued under their hand"

---

6. W. Dennis Tucker Jr., "Empires and Enemies in Book Five of the Psalter," in *The Composition of the Book of Psalms* (ed. Erich Zenger; Leuven: Peeters, 2010), 723–32.

7. Walter Beyerlin, *Werden und Wesen des 107 Psalms* (BZAW 153; Berlin: de Gruyter, 1970).

8. Num 10:9; 24:8; Deut 32:27; 33:7; Josh 5:13; 2 Sam 24:13 = 1 Chr 21:12; Isa 63:18; Jer 30:16; 50:7; Ezek 30:16; 39:23; Amos 3:11; Mic 5:8; Zech 8:10; Pss 44:6, 8, 11; 60:13–14 = 108:13–14; 74:10; 78:42, 61; 81:15; 105:24; 106:11; 107:2; 136:24; Lam 1:5, 7, 10, 17; 2:17; Esth 7:6; Ezra 4:1; Neh 4:5.

9. See Ernst Jenni, "צרר," in *Theological Lexicon of the Old Testament* (3 vols.; ed. Claus Westermann and Ernst Jenni; trans. Mark E. Biddle; Peabody, Mass.: Hendrickson, 1997), 3:1098. See also Bruce Baloian, "צרר II," in *New International Dictionary of Old Testament Theology and Exegesis* (ed. W. A. VanGemeren; Grand Rapids: Zondervan, 1997), 3:859.

10. Frank-Lothar Hossfeld and Erich Zenger not only note that Pss 106 and 107 are semantically and conceptually bound together but, more importantly, provide an exhaustive list of words and images shared between them (*Psalmen 101–150* [HTKAT; Freiburg: Herder, 2008], 145).

(יָדָם). While the term צָר has been replaced with synonymous terms, the use of the phrase "the hand of X" clearly links such language with sociopolitical realities that proved hostile to the people of God.

The nuanced language used in the opening lines of Ps 107 does more than simply connect Ps 107 to the historical reviews found in the two preceding psalms. On the contrary, such language serves to construct an image of Israel and the nations, highlighting the role of empire within her storied past. Israel's identity is bound up with the acknowledgement that the יַד־צָר (hand of the oppressor) has been (and continues to be) a threat to its existence. Although the psalmist calls the community to give thanks for having been gathered from the lands, suspicion of empire and power appears to linger in the poetry found in the rest of the collection.

A similar concern about threats to existence appears in verses 4–32. The four extended stanzas in the psalm are meant to rehearse deliverance from the places that threatened the lives of God's people. Although a number of the images recall deliverance from exile, Hossfeld and Zenger have noted that the "topographical indicator for their trouble is not a concrete region but the description of a situation that evokes the diminishment of life and destruction of vitality through metaphors of imprisonment (Gefangenseins)."[11] Repeated in each strophe is the cry

> Then they cried to YHWH in their trouble (צָר),
> and he delivered them from their distress (vv. 6, 13, 19, 28).

The NRSV, like most translations, employs the term "trouble" or a similar term presumably because it comes from a different root, yet such a rendering fails to capture the association with verse 2. The repeated refrain throughout each of the four scenes alludes back to the claim made in verse 2 that Israel was under "the hand of the foe."[12] If the term is rendered as "trouble," the connection between verse 2 and the refrain in verses 6, 13, 19, and 28 is minimized, if not altogether lost, as is the thematic thread

---

11. Ibid., 101.

12. Beyerlin (Werden und Wesen des 107 Psalms, 13) contends that verses 2–3 were added in the final stage of the psalm's compilation, with the primary intent to announce the triumphant warring of YHWH with the historical-political enemies in order to bring about the final restitution of his people. Whether Beyerlin's reconstruction is plausible or not, his claim that verses 2–3 significantly influence the reading of the remainder of the psalm remains valid.

alluding to Israel's historic threat from those in power. In an effort to capture the play on imagery, Hossfeld and Zenger translate the phrase in verse 2 as "out of the hand of the oppressors (*Bedrängers*)," and in the repeated refrain, "They cried to the Lord in their oppression (*Bedrängnis*)."[13] Unfortunately, their play on words is lost in the English translation of their work.

In short, while Ps 107 is a song of thanksgiving, celebrating deliverance, the psalmist carefully constructs the identity of the returned exiles in light of their experience at the hands of oppressive powers. Allusions to foes, enemy nations, and imperial power appear repeatedly in the remainder of the book.

Psalms 108–110

Egbert Ballhorn has suggested that the primary theme that binds Pss 108–110 together is the threat of the foreign nations (*Fremdvölkerbedrängnis*).[14] Psalms 108 and 110, in particular, give evidence to his claim. The threat of the foreign nations unfolds throughout Ps 108. The second half of the psalm offers a more explicit mention of the nations and peoples that appear to threaten the people of God. Frank van der Velden understands the language in verses 8–11 to be a metaphorical use of the *Feindvölkersummarium*.[15] The point of the metaphor, however, is not the identification of particular enemies, so to speak, but the construction of "an utopian concept of history."[16] Following the psalmist's plea that "the beloved ones" be delivered, an oracle of God is cited in verses 8–10.[17]

> With exultation, I will divide up Shechem
>   and portion out the Vale of Succoth.
> Gilead is mine; Manasseh is mine;
>   Ephraim is my helmet;
> Judah my scepter.
>   Moab is my washbasin;

---

13. Hossfeld and Zenger, *Psalmen 101–150*, 139.

14. Egbert Ballhorn, *Zum Telos des Psalters: Der Textzusammenhang des Vierten und Fünften Psalmenbuches (Psalms 90–150)* (BBB 138; Berlin: Philo, 2004), 377.

15. Frank van der Velden, *Psalm 109 und die Aussagen zur Feindschädigung in den Psalmen* (Stuttgart: Katholisches, 1997), 145–52.

16. Ibid., 149.

17. See Rolf Jacobson, *"Many Are Saying": The Function of Direct Discourse in the Hebrew Psalter* (JSOTSup 397; London: T&T Clark, 2004).

upon Edom I cast my shoe;
over Philistia, I shout in triumph.

The oracle is pregnant with metaphorical language and imagery, particularly that of a great king dividing up his spoil following a victory, with helmet in place and scepter in hand.[18] While the neighboring people groups of Moab, Edom, and Philistia may have had a different function in Ps 60, the text from which this section is drawn, they appear in Ps 108 as ciphers for the "nations" and the "peoples" (v. 4), the imperial powers that threaten the people of God.[19] As Tournay explains, "the perspectives have been universalized. Edom has become the symbol of all the enemies of God and God's people."[20] Although the geographical regions identified mark out a territory reminiscent of the Davidic empire following the fall of Samaria, the focus of the oracle remains upon YHWH as a warrior, the *Kreigsmann*, in overcoming the powers that threaten the people of God.[21] The oracle, then, is not primarily a "map" referring to the boundaries of a restored community, but instead an affirmation that hostile forces can and will be overcome by the Divine Warrior with the goal of a new political order.[22]

Following the summary of the enemy nations, the community pleads in verse 13 for God to help against "the foe" (צָר) and concludes the psalm with an affirmation that "it is he who will tread down our foes" (צָר). As in Ps 107:2, the term צָר in Ps 108 surely alludes to geopolitical powers capable of continuing to oppress the people of God.[23]

---

18. Hossfeld and Zenger, *Psalmen 101–150*, 171.

19. See Stephen L. Cook, "Apocalypticism and the Psalter," *ZAW* 104 (1992): 92. Cook avers, "Place names understood literally in Psalm 60 are understood as symbolic aggressors in Psalm 108. Because in Psalm 108 we now read these geographical names in the light of verses 3 and 5 in the first part of the psalm, they are given a more 'universal' connotation." See also Joachim Becker, *Israel deutet seine Psalmen* (Stuttgart: Katholisches, 1966), 66–67. The use of Edom in particular as a cipher for an enemy people can be found extending to the Psalms Targum, where both the "wicked city of Rome" and "Constantinople" are mentioned as Edom.

20. Raymond Jacques Tournay, *Seeing and Hearing God with the Psalms: The Prophetic Liturgy of the Second Temple in Jerusalem* (trans. J. Edward Crowley; JSOTSup 118; Sheffield: Sheffield Academic, 1991), 181.

21. Hossfeld and Zenger, *Psalmen 101–150*, 170.

22. Ibid., 172.

23. Jerome Creach, *The Destiny of the Righteous in the Psalms* (St. Louis: Chalice, 2008), 80–81.

Psalm 110 confirms the political nature of such foes. In the first stro-phe, the psalmist mentions the enemies, preferring in this instance the plural form of אֹיֵב. In the second strophe of the psalm, the psalmist unfolds more fully the identity of the enemies, announcing:

> YHWH is at your right hand,
>> he will shatter kings on the day of his wrath.
> He will execute judgment among the nations, filling them with corpses;
>> he will shatter the heads over the wide earth.[24]

The theme of Ps 110, then, is the help of God against the foreign nations.[25] Or as Zenger avers, the psalm is above all a "political text," one that is "a counterproposal to the foreign powers that oppress Israel."[26] In short, Ps 110 concludes the first collection in book 5 with the claim that YHWH will thwart the oppressive nations that threaten the people of God.

The frequency of language associated with oppressive enemies in Ps 107 and also in Pss 108–110 continues in the other collections found in the remaining portions of the book 5. Although book 5 is often lauded for the dominance of hymnic language, over against the more lament satu-rated collections in books 1 through 3, such hymnic language holds the language of praise in tension with the reality of empire. Put differently, the celebration of the kingship of YHWH in book 5 appears to be juxtaposed with the reality of other kings and powers that are attempting to lay claim to what is rightly YHWH's and YHWH's alone.

The Appearance of the Foes in Other Collections in Book 5

Gerald Wilson and Reinhard Gregor Kratz observed three collections within book 5 based upon the הודו (give thanks) introductions and the הללו (praise) conclusions (Pss 107–117, 118–135, and 136–145).[27] In my

---

24. Following the note in BHS, preferring ראשׁי to ראשׁ.

25. Ballhorn, *Zum Telos des Psalters*, 156. The identity of the "king" in Ps 110 remains a matter of considerable debate. Ballhorn contends that the poor (אֶבְיוֹן) men-tioned in Ps 109:31 (as well as Ps 107:41) are those "enthroned" in Ps 110. Hossfeld and Zenger, however, suggest that Ps 110 refers to a "renewed Davidic kingship" (*Psalms 101–150*, 154).

26. Frank Lothar Hossfeld and Erich Zenger, *Psalms 3* (Hermeneia; Minneapolis: Fortress, 2011), 154.

27. Gerald Wilson, "Shaping the Psalter," 78–79; Reinhard Gregor Kratz, "Die

opinion, however, Zenger's earlier challenge that both Wilson and Kratz have overly interpreted the use of הודו and הללו terms is probably merited.[28] Chief among the problems is that it separates psalms that appear logically connected (e.g., Ps 135 from Ps 136; Ps 117 from Ps 118). More recently, Hossfeld and Zenger have suggested that book 5 has three major collections in addition to the opening Davidic collection: the Pesach Hallel (113–118), the Pilgrimage Psalter (Pss 120–134, with the addition of Pss 135–136), and the Fifth Davidic Psalter (Pss 138–145, understanding Ps 137 as connecting).[29] As explained below, the concluding psalm in each collection recapitulates the theme found running through Ps 107 and the opening Davidic collection, namely that while there are kings and nations who threaten the people of God, these imperial powers will be undone by the God who delivers the oppressed (Ps 107:6, 13, 19, 28).

Psalm 118 concludes the Pesach Hallel and Ps 136 concludes the extended Pilgrimage Psalter. Both psalms, however, open with the same command:

> Give thanks to YHWH
>> for he is good,
> His steadfast love endures forever.

These verses not only are identical to Ps 107:1 but, as Hossfeld and Zenger contend, they are linked together to create a compositional arc (Pss 107–136), one that gives thanks for the renewal of Israel in the postexilic period.[30]

In Pss 118 and 136, as in Ps 107, the nations and foes play a central role. In Ps 118:5, the psalmist announces:

> Out of my oppression (הַמֵּצַר), I called to YHWH,
>> YH answered me in a wide open place.[31]

Tora Davids: Psalm 1 und die doxologische Fünfteilung des Psalters," *ZTK* 93 (1995): 23–28.

28. Erich Zenger, "The Composition and Theology of the Fifth Book of Psalms, Psalms 107–145," *JSOT* 80 (1998): 87–88.

29. Hossfeld and Zenger, *Psalms 3*, 2–6.

30. Ibid., 5.

31. The Hebrew appears somewhat puzzling, leading most translators to render the colon, "The Lord answered me and set me in a broad place" (RSV) or "Yh heard me and led me into a broad place" (Hossfeld and Zenger, *Psalms 3*). In both trans-

With YHWH on my side, I do not fear.
What can humans do to me?

And then a few verses later, the psalmist remembers the threat of the nations all around them.

All nations surrounded me;
  in the name of YHWH, indeed, I cast them off.
They surrounded me, they surrounded me;
  in the name of YHWH, indeed, I cast them off.

In Pss 108 and 110, the metaphor of the right hand is employed in order to signal the routing of the enemies by YHWH. In Ps 118, the psalmist returns to such language not once, but three times (vv. 15b, 16a, 16b), confirming that the locus of power rests with YHWH and YHWH alone.[32]

The struggle against foes can also be found in Pss 135 and 136. These two psalms follow the Pilgrimage Psalter, adjoining to the creation and Zion theologies of the Pilgrimage Psalter the historical and theological confessions rooted in Israel's past.[33] The initial command in Ps 136 to "Give thanks to YHWH for he is good, for his steadfast love endures forever," is a repeat of Pss 107:1 and 118:1, as mentioned above. The psalmist then provides a rehearsal of the creative power of YHWH in Ps 136:4–9. Yet the bulk of Ps 136 (vv. 10–24) rehearses YHWH's deliverance of the people of God from the powerful foes that oppressed them, beginning first with Pharaoh (vv. 10–15), then the mention of "great kings" (v. 17) and "famous kings" (v. 18), and concluding with named kings such as Sihon, the king of the Amorites and Og, king of Bashan (vv. 19–20). In verse 24 the psalmist announces that YHWH "rescued us from our foes (צָר)," once again, returning the rhetoric back to the language employed in Ps 107. As Erhard Gerstenberger has suggested, these "legendary, even mythological

---

lations, the second verb is absent in the Hebrew, requiring it to be supplied by the translator. The MT can be retained if one understands the parallelism at work in the verse. In colon A, the psalmist is depicted as a captive, while in colon B, the deliverer, YHWH, is depicted as one who is entirely free in a "wide open place." The deliverance for the psalmist is to be where YHWH is, to be taken to a "wide open place," set free from captivity. The only plausible answer for the psalmist in verse 5a is to be joined with YHWH in the wide open places.

32. See Creach, *Destiny of the Righteous*, 70–83.
33. Hossfeld and Zenger, *Psalms 3*, 500.

figures, have been made into exemplary prototypes of enemies, no doubt with an eye to the great kings of Babylonia and Persia."[34] The one who overcame the chaos of creation likewise thwarted the imperial powers of Pharaoh, Sihon, and Og, put down the other "great kings," and rescued the people of God from their foes. And because of this, the repeated refrain, "for his steadfast love endures forever," takes on added weight, signaling the solidarity of YHWH with his oppressed people against the regimes, both past and present, that dot their storied history.[35]

Finally, within the Fifth Davidic Psalter, Pss 138–145, the threat against the poor servants of YHWH remains a persistent theme throughout a collection that both starts and concludes with the acknowledgement of the kingship of YHWH. Hossfeld and Zenger have suggested that Ps 144, however, functions in some sense as the conclusion to the last Davidic Psalter. In addition to its being a royal psalm, it contains the only speech by the community in this last portion of the Psalter, while also providing the closing beatitudes for the people (v. 15).[36] To this argument, we might add that Ps 145 appears to function as a conclusion to the entirety of book 5.

The enemy in Ps 144 is identified by the phrase מִיַּד בְּנֵי־נֵכָר found in verses 7 and 11. This phrase recalls the opening psalm of book 5. In Ps 107:2, the psalmist praises YHWH for having redeemed the people מִיַּד־צָר. As noted above, in 107:2 the threat appears to be a political or perhaps military enemy. Likewise, the similar phrase מִיַּד בְּנֵי־נֵכָר, used in Ps 144:7 and 11, appears to suggest a political or military threat. In the psalms considered in book 5, both Pss 118 and 136 speak of the enemies as vanquished nations, kings, and peoples but, as Gerstenberger suggests, these figures function as prototypes of the threats now experienced by the people of God. In Ps 144, however, the threats against the people of God are not veiled in historical recollection, but instead are posited as real and

---

34. Erhard Gerstenberger, *Psalms, Part 2, and Lamentations* (FOTL 15; Grand Rapids: Eerdmans, 2001), 387. The concluding predicate, "God of heaven" in v. 26, appears regularly in literature from the Persian period (Ezra 1:2; 5:11; 6:9; 7:12; Neh 1:2; 2:4; Jon 1:9; 2 Chr 36:23 as well as Dan 2:18), perhaps buttressing Gerstenberger's suggestion concerning the prototypical function of the enemies in Ps 136 (Hossfeld and Zenger, *Psalms 3*, 505).

35. On the notion of solidarity, see Gerstenberger, *Psalms, Part 2, and Lamentations*, 384–89.

36. Hossfeld and Zenger, *Psalms 3*, 590.

present threats, threats capable of undoing the future of God's people were it not for the kingship of YHWH. The acknowledgement of this persistent threat in Ps 144 leads into the acrostic poem of Ps 145, one that celebrates the kingship of YHWH, a rule marked by deliverance for the downcast (v. 14) and destruction for the wicked (v. 20).

Conclusion

To conclude, we return to the original claim by Wilson, namely that two Davidic collections in book 5 did not appear to have any editorial intention, but instead were meant to establish David as a faithful paradigm. The brief review above was not meant to unseat Wilson's view of David in book 5, though the depiction of David as a nonmessianic figure with a didactic function alone in book 5 has been challenged repeatedly in the works of David Mitchell, Jerome Creach, Jamie Grant, and David Howard, among many others.[37] The purpose of this paper has been to suggest that the role of the foe, vis-à-vis the enemy nations or people groups, plays a more significant function in book 5 than Wilson first suggested.

The above analysis leads to additional observations worth considering. First, the concluding psalm in each collection in book 5 makes reference to enemy kings and nations. These are not the only references to kings and nations in book 5 (see Pss 119 and 120–129 in particular), but the appearance of these themes in the closing psalm of each collection is suggestive. Second, Hossfeld and Zenger have contended that Pss 107–136 creates a compositional arc forming what they term "a grand literary-fictional 'liturgy of thanksgiving.'"[38] Within the arc, the language of empire present in Ps 107 and in the concluding psalms in the first three collections (Pss 110, 118, 136) shapes the language of thanksgiving and, I would contend, helps to create an anti-imperial ethos. Third, the use of different language

---

37. David C. Mitchell, *The Message of the Psalter: An Eschatological Programme in the Book of Psalms* (JSOTSup 252; Sheffield: Sheffield, 1997), 78–81; Mitchell, "Lord Remember David: G. H. Wilson and the Message of the Psalter," *VT* (2006): 526–48; Creach, *Destiny of the Righteous in the Psalms*; Jamie A. Grant, *The King as Exemplar: The Function of Deuteronomy's Kingship Law in the Shape and Shaping of the Book of Psalms* (SBLAcBib 17; Society of Biblical Literature: Atlanta, 2004), 33–39; David M. Howard, *The Structure of Psalms 93–100* (Winona Lake, Ill.: Eisenbrauns, 1997), 201–2.

38. Hossfeld and Zenger, *Psalms 3*, 2.

in Ps 144, but language with an anti-imperial thrust nonetheless, may suggest that the final Davidic Psalter was a subsequent addition, one meant to reinforce more strenuously the kingship of YHWH in the face of persistent imperial powers. Finally, the frequent allusion to such a threat only makes sense if the social situation of the editors necessitated the reiteration of an anti-imperial theme.

In all four collections in book 5, imperial power can be overcome, but only by YHWH. In short, we may conclude that book 5 operates with an anti-imperial bias, seeking to build a world absent of power, save that of YHWH alone.

Bibliography

Ballhorn, Egbert. *Zum Telos des Psalters: Der Textzusammenhang des Vierten und Fünften Psalmenbuches (Psalms 90–150)*. BBB 138. Berlin: Philo, 2004.
Baloian, Bruce. "צרר II." Page 859 in vol. 3 of *New International Dictionary of Old Testament Theology and Exegesis*. 5 vols. Edited by W. A. VanGemeren. Grand Rapids: Zondervan, 1997.
Becker, Joachim. *Israel deutet seine Psalmen*. Stuttgart: Katholisches, 1966.
Beyerlin, Walter. *Werden und Wesen des 107. Psalms*. BZAW 153. Berlin: de Gruyter, 1970.
Cook, Stephen L. "Apocalypticism and the Psalter." *ZAW* 104 (1992): 82–99.
Creach, Jerome. *The Destiny of the Righteous in the Psalms*. St. Louis: Chalice, 2008.
Gerstenberger, Erhard. *Psalms, Part 2, and Lamentations*. FOTL 15. Grand Rapids: Eerdmans, 2001.
Grant, Jamie A. *The King as Exemplar: The Function of Deuteronomy's Kingship Law in the Shape and Shaping of the Book of Psalms*. SBLAcBib 17. Atlanta: Society of Biblical Literature, 2004.
Hossfeld, Frank-Lothar, and Erich Zenger. *Psalmen 101–150*. HTKAT. Freiburg: Herder, 2008.
Howard, David M. *The Structure of Psalms 93–100*. Winona Lake, Ill.: Eisenbrauns, 1997.
Jacobson, Rolf. *Many are Saying: The Function of Direct Discourse in the Hebrew Psalter*. JSOTSup 397. London: T&T Clark, 2004.
Jenni, Ernst. "צרר." Page 1098 in vol. 3 of *Theological Lexicon of the Old*

Testament. 3 vols. Edited by Claus Westermann and Ernst Jenni. Translated by Mark E. Biddle. Peabody, Mass.: Hendrickson, 1997.

Kratz, Reinhard Gregor. "Die Tora Davids: Psalm 1 und die doxologische Fünfteilung des Psalters." *ZTK* 93 (1996): 1–34.

Mitchell, David C. "Lord, Remember David: G. H. Wilson and the Message of the Psalter." *VT* 56 (2006): 526–48.

———. *The Message of the Psalter: An Eschatological Programme in the Book of Psalms.* JSOTSup 252. Sheffield: Sheffield Academic, 1997.

Tournay, Raymond Jacques. *Seeing and Hearing God with the Psalms: The Prophetic Liturgy of the Second Temple in Jerusalem.* Translated by J. Edward Crowley. JSOTSup 118. Sheffield: Sheffield Academic, 1991.

Tucker, W. Dennis, Jr. "Empires and Enemies in Book Five of the Psalter." Pages 723–31 in *The Composition of the Book of Psalms.* Edited by Erich Zenger. Leuven: Peeters, 2010.

Velden, Frank van der. *Psalm 109 und die Aussagen zur Feindschädigung in den Psalmen.* Stuttgart: Katholisches, 1997.

Wilson, Gerald H. *The Editing of the Hebrew Psalter.* SBLDS 76. Chico, Calif.: Scholars, 1985.

———. *Psalms, Volume 1.* NIVAC. Grand Rapids: Zondervan, 2002.

Zenger, Erich. "The Composition and Theology of the Fifth Book of Psalms: Psalms 107–145." *JSOT* 80 (1998): 77–102.

———. "Der jüdische Psalter—Ein anti-imperiales Buch?" Pages 95–108 in *Religion und Gesellschaft: Studien zu ihrer Wechselbeziehung in den Kulturen des Antiken Vorderen Orients.* Edited by R. Albertz. Münster: Ugarit, 1997.

Gerald Wilson and the Characterization of David in Book 5 of the Psalter

Robert E. Wallace

Introduction

I first encountered *The Editing of the Hebrew Psalter* and Wilson's follow-up research while in preparation for my preliminary exams. His research has shaped mine, though likely not in the way he might have expected. It struck me that even though Wilson was speaking of the early redaction of the Psalter, a sense of story, plot, and characterization began to emerge when Wilson looked at the Psalter. Though perhaps not purposely, Wilson was noting that although the Psalter is not narrative material, as Robert Alter noted, a narrative impulse exists in biblical poetry. That narrative impulse began to emerge across the whole Psalter for me, and I had what every graduate student wants—a dissertation topic.

My first work focused on book 4, and later, the ending of book 3. In each case, Wilson's conclusions were supported by my readings.[1] That resonance likely led to my willingness to accept Wilson's reading of the characterization of David in book 5. In the work that followed the *Editing of the Hebrew Psalter*, Wilson fully developed the thesis that an overarching sapiential framework governs the interpretation of the Psalter, and the royal frame (which is contained by the wisdom frame) is therefore relegated to a secondary interpretation.[2]

---

1. Robert E. Wallace, *The Narrative Effect of Book IV of the Hebrew Psalter* (StBL 112; New York: Peter Lang, 2007); Wallace, "The Narrative Effect of Psalms 84–89," *JHS* 11 (2011). Online: http://www.jhsonline.org/Articles/article_157.pdf.

2. Gerald H. Wilson, "Shaping the Psalter: A Consideration of Editorial Linkage in the Book of Psalms," in *The Shape and Shaping of the Psalter* (ed. J. Clinton McCann Jr.; JSOTSup 20; Sheffield: JSOT, 1993), 72–82.

That proposed editing of the Psalter was governed by, or at the very minimum reflected, the role of the character of David. In Wilson's reading, Davidic covenant and David's role changes in the story and editing of the Psalter. For Wilson, books 1 and 2 promote the Davidic monarchy. Book 3 deals with the reality of exile and asks the hard questions of the seeming failure of the Davidic covenant. Book 4 provides the climax and turning point in the story as the exilic community finds an answer that predates the Davidic covenant, the Sinaitic covenant. Rather than David as king, enthroned forever, the community is challenged to remember that YHWH is king, enthroned forever, and Moses is the appropriate mediator of that covenant.[3]

Wilson reads book 5 as emerging from this exilic question with adjusted priorities. There, YHWH is celebrated as an unchallenged king, and David is relegated to a secondary, perhaps even priestly, role.[4] The last Davidic psalm in the Psalter, Ps 145, opens with a celebration of YHWH as God and king forever. The first psalm of Wilson's concluding doxological frame (Pss 146–150) ends with the remembrance that YHWH will reign forever. For Wilson, by the end of the Psalter, David's role clearly has been subjugated. The Psalter has moved from David as king to YHWH as king.[5]

Though methodologically Wilson was focusing on redactional concerns when speaking of the Psalter, he was often speaking in narrative categories when speaking about the "character" of David. The broad narrative impulse throughout the entire Psalter, when combined with the settings of the individual psalms and the semantic and thematic connections the Psalter shares with other portions of the Hebrew Bible, contributed to a sense of "plot." This "plot" for Wilson generally paralleled Israel's historical experience.

The psalms also demonstrate a number of lexical and thematic connections with other psalms and with important narrative texts of the Hebrew Scriptures. Those connections allow the reader to "narrativize"

---

3. Ibid., 75–78.

4. Gerald Wilson, "King, Messiah, and the Reign of God: Revisiting the Royal Psalms and the Shape of the Psalter," in *The Book of Psalms: Composition and Reception* (ed. Peter W. Flint and Patrick D. Miller Jr.; Leiden: Brill, 2005), 396–400.

5. This idea is reflected throughout Wilson's research. It is probably best seen in Wilson, "King, Messiah, and the Reign of God," 391–406, and Wilson, "The Structure of the Psalter," in *Interpreting the Psalms: Issues and Approaches* (ed. David G. Firth and Philip S. Johnston; Downers Grove, Ill.: InterVarsity Press, 2005), 229–46.

the poetic text. Wilson did not read the Psalter in a narrative, ahistorical setting, but attempted to set the Psalter in a historical framework of its first redaction. Even so, his discussion of David easily could have used the terms "characterization" and "plot development."

CHALLENGES TO WILSON

Perhaps the most appealing thing about Wilson's argument is that it makes sense. Conceptually, one can easily connect Wilson's interpretive framework to a particular construction of Israel's history. Certainly, Israel celebrated the monarchy during the period of the monarchy. One would imagine that the monarchy would insist on it. Certainly, Israel would need to answer hard questions when the enduring and everlasting promises of YHWH came to an end in 586 B.C.E. Certainly, Israel would need to turn to an ancient authority to speak when David's authority was compromised. Moses and Mosaic covenant are sensible choices. Certainly, Israel would look at David differently and talk about David differently after their "dark night of the soul." It makes sense.

It also makes sense, however, that a heavier object falls to earth faster than a lighter one, and yet Galileo established that was incorrect—whether it makes sense or not. In the same way, Wilson's reading of the Psalter has not been met with universal acceptance. Wilson's reading only works if everyone agrees on a late date for the redaction of the Psalter and only speaks of the interpretation of the Psalter at that time.[6] It also only works if the character "David" in the Psalter is really referring to the character David from the Deuteronomistic history, and if, therefore, the royal psalms that celebrate David and Davidic monarchy are really celebrating David and Davidic monarchy. "David" could be a metonym for YHWH's reign. Wilson would likely not accept a devalued YHWH in the text. "David" could represent an exilic Israel throughout the centuries or, more basically, Wilson could simply be reading the character of "David" wrongly. Perhaps, instead of David as YHWH's "priest," David remains "king."

One alternative reading which predates Wilson comes from Samson Raphael Hirsch. For Hirsch, David is the key to the Psalter in the way that Moses is the key to Torah. Even in psalms which are not explicitly

---

6. David Mitchell, "Lord, Remember David: G. H. Wilson and the Message of the Psalter," *VT* 56 (2006): 540–47.

connected to David, Hirsch notes that, "The spirit of David pervades all [non-Davidic] Psalms whose content is primarily of import to the nation as a whole."[7] Hirsch extrapolates each psalm from the life of David to the ancient and, relevant to his time, the nineteenth-century, exilic state of Israel. The "David" of the psalms for Hirsch is really a metonym for the Jewish struggle throughout the centuries.

Providing another challenge to Wilson's position, Clint McCann argues compellingly that perhaps the royal psalms might not have to be exclusively associated with the Davidic monarchy. If the entire Psalter is about how to live the "happy/blessed" life and this life derives fundamentally from the conviction that YHWH rules the earth, then the kind of character progression that Wilson sees in the Psalter is not necessarily the primary sense of the text.[8] If the psalms are Torah, then each of the royal psalms can be read as relating primarily to the kingship of God, rather than to any one earthly king.[9] In that sense, as James Mays asserts, "Yahweh reigns" throughout the Psalter, not as a new discovery or renewed focus in book 4 and a new reality in book 5.[10]

David Mitchell offers further criticism. Building on the work of Brevard Childs and Joseph P. Brennan and others,[11] Mitchell suggests that the strategic placement of the Davidic psalms throughout the Psalter represents an eschatological program at work. Since the Psalter was redacted at a time when the Davidic monarch did not exist, for Mitchell the inclusion of Davidic psalms does not look backward at failed Davidic monarchy, but most naturally refers to a descendant of David who is to come.[12] Childs noted that even when the psalmist's perspective looks to the past in praise

---

7. Samson Raphael Hirsch, *The Psalms* (trans. Gertrude Hirschler; 2 vols; New York: Feldheim, 1960), 1:xx.

8. J. Clinton McCann Jr., "The Shape of Book I of the Psalter and the Shape of Human Happiness," in *The Book of Psalms: Composition and Reception* (ed. Peter W. Flint and Patrick D. Miller Jr.; Leiden: Brill, 2005), 340–48.

9. J. Clinton McCann Jr., *A Theological Introduction to the Book of Psalms: The Psalms as Torah* (Nashville: Abingdon, 1993), 43–45.

10. James Mays, *The Lord Reigns: A Theological Handbook to the Psalms* (Louisville: Westminster John Knox, 1994), 245.

11. Franz Delitzsch, *Biblical Commentary of the Psalms* (trans. D. Eaton; London, 1887), 88–95; Brevard S. Childs, *Introduction to the Old Testament as Scripture* (Philadelphia: Fortress, 1979), 516–17; Joseph P. Brennan, "Psalms 1–8: Some Hidden Harmonies," *BTB* 10 (1980): 25–29.

12. Mitchell, "Lord, Remember David," 527–48.

of the great works YHWH has worked for the people, the psalmist quickly moves to the future in hopes those works will be done again (as in Ps 126:6).[13] For Childs and Mitchell, the final form of the Psalter was "highly eschatological."[14]

David Howard notes that the position of Ps 2 as an introduction to the Psalter (when it is rightly read as part of a composition which includes Ps 1) undermines Wilson's belief that Davidic kingship is mitigated in the text. If a Torah psalm (Ps 1) and a royal psalm (Ps 2) introduce the Psalter, it would seem to be an affirmation of both traditions. One could argue, therefore, that these psalms shape the reader's experience of the text. Howard suggests that "the introduction to the Psalter (Pss 1–2) states that what follows is indeed Torah, to be studied (Ps 1), that YHWH is king (Ps 2), and that he has vested a human king with kingly authority (Ps 2)."[15] Howard further argues that the joining of a Davidic psalm at the end of the Psalter (Ps 144) with a psalm that celebrates the divine kingship of YHWH (Ps 145) further conflates the reigns in the minds of the reader and would mitigate any distinction Wilson would want to make.[16]

With these cautions in mind, how should one read the character of David in book 5? Is there a case to be made for Wilson's subjugation of David to YHWH's kingship? Could David and YHWH be considered coregents? With the conflation of the thrones of YHWH and David in Ps 2, and the kingship of God celebrated in the last psalm of David in the Psalter, Ps 145, when one speaks of the reign of David and the reign of YHWH, is it textual to speak of their kingships interchangeably?

This reading takes a step away from the Wilson's redactional concerns. Instead, the process of reading the Hebrew Psalter is important. Microcanonical issues, including poetic vocabulary and syntax, within individual psalms are considered. Form-critical questions and historical questions regarding the editorial process of the Hebrew Psalter are noted; however, they are only important to this study as they inform the reading of the text—*Sitz im Leben* will be replaced by *Sitz im Buch*.

---

13. Childs, *Introduction to the Old Testament*, 518.

14. Ibid.

15. David Howard, *The Structure of Psalms 93–100* (Winona Lake, Ind.: Eisenbrauns, 1997), 204.

16. David Howard, "The Psalms in Current Study," in *Interpreting the Psalms: Issues and Approaches* (ed. David G. Firth and Philip S. Johnston; Downers Grove, Ill.: InterVarsity Press, 2005), 27.

As an analysis based on the canonical shape of the text of the Psalter, this reading takes the superscriptions of the psalms seriously, perhaps too seriously for some. While the majority of scholars might not go as far as von Rad and say the superscriptions have "have no authoritative value,"[17] many would also not allow the superscription to influence the context of the reading of the text to the degree this project does. If the reader is going to take seriously the canonical form of this text, however, the superscriptions have to be more than an interesting canonical note. The superscriptions should find a place within the interpretation of the psalm. When the text makes an association to a historical setting or with an individual, a canonical reader of the psalms needs to wrestle with the implications of that association. In this analysis, the superscriptions provide an interpretive setting through which a reader encounters the text.

Wilson appears to be uneven in his use of the superscriptions. In Ps 145:1, the superscription provides important support for Wilson's reading. The last Davidic psalm in the Psalter opens with a confession of YHWH as king and does not demand restoration or long for an earthly reign. In that context, Wilson seems happy to use the superscription to provide a hermeneutic lens through which to view the psalm.

In the five Davidic superscriptions that occur in the Ascent Psalms, however, Wilson notes that "the appearance of these psalms in the fifth book may owe more to their prior inclusion in the Ascent collection than any specific editorial purpose."[18] It is interesting that Wilson's dismissal of the superscriptions and editorial purpose corresponds to a collection of psalms that celebrate Jerusalem and Zion, and therefore give tacit support to the Davidic covenant.

David's Reappearance

While the "prayers of David, the son of Jesse" are ended in Ps 72, this has not prevented David from some guest appearances in books 3 and 4. Book 3 has one Davidic psalm; book 4 has two. In book 5, however, David's presence is hard to ignore. Fifteen of forty-four psalms bear a Davidic superscription. Additionally, though it lacks a Davidic superscription, Ps 132 focuses on David and the Davidic monarchy throughout the psalm.

---

17. Gerhard von Rad, "Psalm 90," in *God at Work in Israel* (trans. John H. Marks; Nashville: Abingdon, 1980), 212.

18. Wilson, "King, Messiah, and the Reign of God," 396.

On the surface, Wilson's belief in a priestly David or a David with some type of reduced role or influence would certainly seem plausible. While מלך (king) frequently refers to the king of Israel and to YHWH in books 1–3, the word is only used to reference the divine (and kings of other nations) in books 4 and 5.[19] The kings of Judah and Israel can be called "servants" or "anointed," but never מלך. Wilson maintains this leads the reader to long for a king who is an "anointed servant" and not seek the kind of "kingly rulership" associated with מלך.[20] In fact, Howard argues that in some of Wilson later works, he made a little more room for an eschatological reading of the psalter, though Wilson still clearly saw a subjugation of the Davidic monarchy in book 5.[21]

PSALMS 108–138

David's first appearances in book 5 seems to put Wilson's reading on solid footing. David in Ps 108 longs for happier times. In this communal lament, David sings "You have rejected us, O God; God, you do not march with our armies. Grant us your aid against the foe" (Ps 108:12). Psalm 109 does not find David in any better mood. This imprecatory psalm contains some of the most vivid cursing language in the Psalter and shows some connections to other ancient cursing texts.[22] It reveals a David desperately seeking vengeance on his enemies. In the midst of the strong language, David four times uses the word חסד,[23] the first two times imploring that God not show his enemy חסד (ḥesed) since his enemy had not shown mercy. The third occurrence of the word defines the character of the divine (Ps 109:21). The final occurrence implores the divine to rescue the singer according to the divine חסד.[24]

If we understand חסד as more than simple kindness, but rather carrying the sense of covenantal loyalty, one could easily read the cry at the end of Ps 109 to be a plea for YHWH to remember the Davidic covenant that

---

19. Ibid., 402; Wilson, "Structure of the Psalter," 236.

20. Wilson, "King, Messiah, and the Reign of God," 402–3.

21. Howard, "The Psalms in Current Study," 27.

22. Anne Marie Kitz, "An Oath, Its Curse and Anointing Ritual," *JAOS* 124 (2004): 315–21.

23. Ps 109:12, 16, 21, 26.

24. Walter Brueggemann, "Psalm 109: Steadfast Love as Social Solidarity," in *The Psalms and the Life of Faith* (ed. Patrick D. Miller Jr.; Minneapolis: Fortress, 1995), 275.

lies in ruins, due in part to the enemies surrounding the psalmist. The use of the word חסד takes the reader back to Ps 89, which asserts that David has been forever entrusted with the divine חסד,[25] but also questions where that חסד has gone in the face of the present distress.[26]

It seems that at the beginning of book 5, Wilson's reading finds a great deal of support. In Ps 108, David longs for happier times when the Almighty fought on behalf of Israel, and in Ps 109, David prays that YHWH will "help me … save me in accord with your חסד" (Ps 109:26). David does not seem to be the victorious king whose reign is synonymous with the Almighty.

The demands made of YHWH in Ps 108 and 109, however, are made using words from Dennis Tucker's shame semantic word field, which might imply a patron-client expectation in these psalms.[27] YHWH, as the faithful patron, has a responsibility, therefore, to take up the case of the victims (in this case David) for relationships to be restored.[28] Tucker's shame words occur with greater frequency in the first three books of the Psalter than in the last two. In Pss 108 and 109, however, it seems that David's prayers of lament are not appreciably different from David's prayers in the early part of the Psalter. Things are not good for David in these two psalms, but things have been bad for David before. In form, these laments of David in book 5 (where Wilson suggests that monarchy is deemphasized) look very much like laments from the beginning of the Psalter, where Wilson suggests the Davidic monarchy has its stronger emphasis.

Further calling Wilson's reading into question, the reader encounters Ps 110. Rather than a meek supplicant approaching the divine, desperate for his enemies to be destroyed and for himself to be restored, Ps 110 shows a strong David whose enemies are a footstool (Ps 110:1). Though the word מלך (king) is never explicitly used, David is portrayed as a righteous, military, conquering king, and he is called a priest forever in the order of Melchizedek. Wilson supports his argument for a "priestly" David in book 5 by emphasizing this connection to Melchizedek (Ps 110:4). While he concedes the strong military imagery associated with this kingship, he maintains the priestly order of Melchizedek mitigates any coregency with

---

25. Ps 89:2–4, 25, 29, 34 [Eng. 1–3, 24, 28, 33].

26. Ps 89:50 [Eng. 49].

27. Dennis Tucker Jr., "Is Shame a Matter of Patronage in the Communal Laments?" *JSOT* 31 (2007): 467–48.

28. Ibid., 474–79.

YHWH to a role of priest.[29] While the nebulous character of Melchizedek is difficult to define, his name is not. Melchizedek is not the "my priest is righteous," but "my king is righteous."

David's coregency with YHWH, however, is not an idea with which many would be comfortable. Through most of the Hebrew Bible, YHWH is a jealous god, and YHWH does not like to share the divine throne. An exception might be made, however, for David. In Ps 110:1, God gives David a seat at the right hand of the divine. David Hay believes that this psalm is referenced in the vision of the divine throne room in Dan 7:9–14 with its plural use of the word "thrones." Hay notes that this is the "only scriptural text which explicitly speaks of someone enthroned beside God."[30] Hay's reading finds some support in Jewish tradition. While Rabbi Akiba's opinion is not universally accepted, in the Talmud he is said to have taught that two thrones sat in the divine throne room: one for the divine and one for David (or Davidic messiah).[31]

There are times in the Psalter where it seems that the reigns of David and YHWH are deliberately conflated. In Ps 110:1, the reader would assume that אדני (my Lord) is the king. While אדני in verse 5 may refer to YHWH, that אדני drinks from the river like a human being.[32] This conflation is consistent with other sections of the Psalter. Robert Cole argues that the reigns of YHWH and David are combined in book 3.[33] Additionally, Mitchell makes the case that Ps 45:7 uses אלהים (God) in the vocative as an address to the king, not simply a repetition of the word to indicate which divine or to provide emphasis.[34]

While this analysis focuses on the MT of the Psalms, the LXX text might strengthen an argument for later comfort with the idea of coregency. Psalms that are untitled in the MT are labeled "psalms of David" in the LXX. The majority of these untitled psalms in book 4 are psalms that celebrate YHWH's reign over Israel and all the earth. This close association of YHWH's kingship and Davidic superscription might suggest to a reader

29. Wilson, "King, Messiah, and the Reign of God," 403–4.

30. David Hay, *Glory at the Right Hand: Ps 110 in Early Christianity* (SBLMS 18; Nashville: Abingdon, 1973), 26.

31. b. Sanh 38b.

32. Mitchell, "Message of the Psalter," 538.

33. Robert L. Cole, *The Shape and Message of Book III* (JSOTSup 307; Sheffield: Sheffield Academic, 2000), 120–21.

34. Mitchell, *Message of the Psalter*, 246–47.

of the LXX that the two kingships are not separate. It certainly does seem that by the time the LXX Psalter is redacted, any subjugation which Wilson suggests existed in the original redaction of the MT no longer exists, and at the very minimum, Davidic monarchy has returned to the reading Wilson suggests for books 1 and 2, that is, the celebration of YHWH as King and David as his representative and adopted son.

Additionally, Wilson's analysis of the Dead Sea Psalms scrolls seems to suggest a far higher place for David than the Masoretic Psalter. Marvin Tate called the Masoretic text of book 4 a "Moses book."[35] This idea has been lost at Qumran and replaced with psalms that promote David and the Davidic monarchy, likely reflecting an eschatological reading.[36]

On the heels of being asked to sit at the divine's right hand in Ps 110, David sings again in Pss 122, 124, and 131. These psalms show a David who exhibits confidence in YHWH's ability to deliver. As part of the "Psalms of Ascent" collection (Pss 120–134), these individual and communal psalms of thanksgiving celebrate pilgrimage to Jerusalem. The throne of David seems sure. The city of David is well established and protected by the divine. The David of the early part of book 5, then, seems to be the King-Messiah who is able to presume upon the divine, conquer his enemies, and enter Jerusalem to worship in the city of David and at the city's established thrones of David.[37]

Psalm 132 interrupts this happy celebration and progression of David. While Ps 132 lacks a Davidic superscription, the psalm cries out on behalf of David and in support of the Davidic monarchy. The psalm is a reminder to God of the Davidic covenant and a desire to support David. Wilson notes the that conditional nature of the covenant revealed in Ps 132:12 provides an explanation for why David's sons are not on the throne. In his reading, although David is celebrated, the focus of the psalm is YHWH's kingship, which is celebrated after David's conditional covenant.[38]

In Ps 132, the reader finds echoes of Ps 89, reminding God of the divine oath that was promised: "One of the sons of your body I will set on your throne" (Ps 132:11). The end of Ps 132, however, reminds the reader that God is certainly within the divine right to void this royal warranty. In

---

35. Marvin Tate, *Psalm 51–100* (WBC 20; Dallas: Word, 1990), xxvi.

36. Gerald Wilson, "The Qumran Psalms Scroll Reconsidered: Analysis of the Debate," *CBQ* 47 (1985): 626–28.

37. Mitchell, *Message of the Psalter*, 537.

38. Wilson, "King, Messiah, and the Reign of God," 397.

verse 12 the psalmist notes that this offer is only valid "if your sons keep my covenant."

Wilson, however, may push the argument too far in defense of his position in this psalm. He does concede that the ending of the psalm is an anticipated exaltation of an eschatological David, but he is unwilling to read that figure as "king, " arguing instead that the "crown" of verse 18 is more commonly used to refer to honor bestowed upon priests; and therefore, in spite of the word's occurrence in a royal psalm that recalls David and the Davidic covenant and promises future honor to David line, it should not be read as royal celebration, but a priestly one.[39]

Certainly, from a form-critical perspective, things seem to go very well for David early in the psalms of book 5. After the imprecation of Ps 109, the next five psalms with Davidic superscriptions are generally classified as individual or communal hymns that celebrate David.[40] David is sitting at the right hand of God, entering Jerusalem with confidence. In Ps 138:7, David celebrates that "though I walk in the midst of trouble, [YHWH] preserves my life."

PSALMS 139–146

Wilson's reading of book 5, though called into question early in the text, is better supported at the end of the book. In Ps 139, David apparently feels so secure in his position that he implores YHWH to "search and know my thoughts, try and know my mind." Ironically, however, after this close analysis, things go rather badly for the character David in the Psalter. Psalm 139 may be read as a proclamation of innocence in the face of external troubles; and indeed, the next four psalms, which follow the request of the Almighty's close scrutiny, Pss 140–143, are classified form-critically as laments.

Each of these psalms depicts a David in desperate need of divine help against the enemies that surround him. In Ps 140:1, David implores YHWH to deliver him from violent evildoers. David establishes his innocence in Ps 141 and his need for YHWH to protect him from the traps laid for him. In Ps 142:6, David's persecutors have brought him low, and he cannot function without divine help. David prays in Ps 143:3, "For the

---

39. Ibid., 397–98.

40. Nancy L. deClaissé-Walford, *Introduction to the Psalms: A Song from Ancient Israel* (St. Louis: Chalice, 2004), 149–50.

enemy has pursued me, crushing my life to the ground, making me sit in darkness like those long dead." In Ps 144:11 David implores God, "rescue me from the cruel sword and deliver me from the hand of aliens, whose mouths speak lies."

These five consecutive psalms of desperation culminate in Ps 145 wherein David exclaims in verse 1, "I will extoll you, my God and my King." Leading up to Wilson's Royal Framework which ends in Ps 145, the psalmist portrays a David faced with the problems of exile. Ps 145 lacks any request to restore the kingship of David. It lacks any concern for earthly kingdom at all. Instead the last word of David in the Psalter clearly establishes YHWH as the monarch and David as one who is simply committed to him.

Wilson calls attention to the fact that Pss 144 and 146 both contain the word אשרי (happy, blessed) and the psalm between them celebrates YHWH's kingship.[41] Wilson's implication would seem to be that much as אשרי forms an inclusio for Pss 1 and 2 and those two psalms provide an interpretive agenda for the rest of the Psalter, the word אשרי in Ps 144:15 and Ps 146:5 provides a kind of inclusio around Ps 145. Wilson believes this editorial move highlights the Davidic acrostic psalm, which celebrates YHWH's kingship.[42] At the very minimum, Wilson would argue that this acknowledgement of YHWH's kingship is the secret to the "happy/blessed" life.

At the end of book 5, Wilson's reading seems to be on solid ground. Davidic monarchy is deemphasized and there is a strong concern for YHWH's kingship. David is a humble supplicant interceding on his own behalf and, by extension, interceding on behalf of his people.

CONCLUSIONS

Book 5's portrayal of David seems to be mixed. While David is referred to differently in book 5 that he is in the remainder of the Psalter, he is also referred to in the same way. It does not seem that a self-evidently eschatological program is at work; though it is equally unconvincing to read a priestly David whose role has been diminished by exile. It is true that Wilson is overstating the relegation of David to secondary status in

---

41. Wilson, "Structure of the Psalter," 240.
42. Ibid.

book 5, but it is also not fair to say that there is a fully developed and realized eschatological messiah reflected in the characterization of David in book 5.

In this rare case a canonical reading might allow a reader to say that everyone is right—at least in part. David Clines sees the theme of the Pentateuch as partial fulfillment, and therefore partial nonfulfillment, of the patriarchal promise of Genesis 12.[43] Perhaps his argument concerning the Pentateuch provides some language for making sense of these competing characterizations of David in book 5 of the Psalter.

There is an "already but not yet" quality to book 5. In the first half of the book, the reader glimpses what the community desires: a strong David who serves as coregent with the Almighty. That Davidic monarch is able to call on the divine with a sense of expectation, much like the David in books 1 and 2. One can easily understand how this might reflect the community's desire for an eschatological or, at least, a utopian or ideal vision that is not yet fulfilled. Once the divine takes a close look at David in Ps 139, however, the reader gets a glimpse of what the community is experiencing, a "David" surrounded by enemies, a kingship that has failed, and a community in need of YHWH as king. These characterizations leave the reader with a sense of expectation—the same sense of expectation or partial fulfillment found elsewhere in scripture.

Perhaps the reader finds in book 5 a move toward and desire for, but not yet a fully realized, Davidic coregency with God. It would be in keeping with other the great cliffhanger endings of the Bible: Genesis, with Abraham's promise of nation and land not yet realized; Deuteronomy, with Moses final commission to the people to take the land; Malachi, with the prophet Elijah's return to prepare for the great and terrible day of YHWH; and even 2 Chronicles, with the edict of Cyrus and its charge to rebuild the temple.

Perhaps the Psalter finishes with a sense of expectation as well. Book 5 begins with the David the Psalter remembers and wants—ruler and anointed. Book 5 ends with the David the Psalter sees—present enemies and empty throne. Through it all, however, there is one fact with which everyone, including David, agrees—YHWH reigns.

---

43. David J. A. Clines, *The Theme of the Pentateuch* (Sheffield: Sheffield Academic, 1997), 30.

BIBLIOGRAPHY

Brennan, Joseph P. "Psalms 1–8: Some Hidden Harmonies." *BTB* 10 (1980): 25–29.

Brueggemann, Walter. "Psalm 109: Steadfast Love as Social Solidarity." Pages 268–82 in *The Psalms and the Life of Faith*. Edited by Patrick D. Miller Jr. Minneapolis: Fortress, 1995.

Childs, Brevard S. *Introduction to the Old Testament as Scripture*. Philadelphia: Fortress, 1979.

Clines, David J. A. *The Theme of the Pentateuch*. Sheffield: Sheffield Academic, 1997.

Cole, Robert L. *The Shape and Message of Book III*. JSOTSup 307. Sheffield: Sheffield Academic, 2000.

deClaissé-Walford, Nancy L. *Introduction to the Psalms: A Song from Ancient Israel*. St. Louis: Chalice, 2004.

Delitzsch, Franz. *Biblical Commentary of the Psalms*. Translated by D. Eaton. London, 1887.

Hay, David. *Glory at the Right Hand: Ps 110 in Early Christianity*. SBLMS 18. Nashville: Abingdon, 1973.

Hirsch, Samson Raphael. *The Psalms*. Translated by Gertrude Hirschler. 2 vols. New York: Feldheim, 1960.

Howard, David. "The Psalms in Current Study." Pages 23–40 in *Interpreting the Psalms: Issues and Approaches*. Edited by David G. Firth and Philip S. Johnston. Downers Grove, Ill.: InterVarsity Press, 2005.

———. *The Structure of Psalms 93–100*. Winona Lake, Ind.: Eisenbrauns, 1997.

Kitz, Anne Marie. "An Oath, Its Curse and Anointing Ritual." *JAOS* 124 (2004): 315–21.

Mays, James. *The Lord Reigns: A Theological Handbook to the Psalms*. Louisville: Westminster John Knox, 1994.

McCann, J. Clinton Jr. "The Shape of Book I of the Psalter and the Shape of Human Happiness." Pages 340–48 in *The Book of Psalms: Composition and Reception*. Edited by Peter W. Flint and Patrick D. Miller Jr. Leiden: Brill, 2005.

———. *A Theological Introduction to the Book of Psalms: The Psalms as Torah*. Nashville: Abingdon, 1993.

Mitchell, David. "Lord, Remember David: G. H. Wilson and the Message of the Psalter." *VT* 56 (2006): 527–48.

Rad, Gerhard von. "Psalm 90." In *God at Work in Israel*. Translated by John H. Marks. Nashville: Abingdon, 1980.

Tate, Marvin. *Psalm 51–100*. WBC 20. Dallas: Word, 1990.

Tucker, Dennis, Jr. "Is Shame a Matter of Patronage in the Communal Laments?" *JSOT* 31 (2007): 465–80.

Wallace, Robert E. *The Narrative Effect of Book IV of the Hebrew Psalter*. StBL 112. New York: Peter Lang, 2007.

———. "The Narrative Effect of Psalms 84–89." *JHS* 11 (2011): 2–15. Online: http://www.jhsonline.org/Articles/article_157.pdf.

Wilson, Gerald H. "King, Messiah, and the Reign of God: Revisiting the Royal Psalms and the Shape of the Psalter." Pages 391–406 in *The Book of Psalms: Composition and Reception*. Edited by Peter W. Flint and Patrick D. Miller Jr. Leiden: Brill, 2005.

———. "The Qumran Psalms Scroll Reconsidered: Analysis of the Debate." CBQ 47 (1985): 624–42.

———. "Shaping the Psalter: A Consideration of Editorial Linkage in the Book of Psalms." Pages 72–82 in *The Shape and Shaping of the Psalter*. Edited by J. Clinton McCann Jr. JSOTSup 20. Sheffield: JSOT, 1993.

———. "The Structure of the Psalter." Pages 229–46 in *Interpreting the Psalms: Issues and Approaches*. Edited by David G. Firth and Philip S. Johnston. Downers Grove, Ill.: InterVarsity Press, 2005.

The Contribution of Gerald Wilson toward Understanding the Book of Psalms in Light of the Psalms Scrolls

Peter W. Flint

Introduction

As of late 2013, forty-five psalms manuscripts or ones that incorporate psalms had been found (forty-one near Qumran, one at Nahal Hever, and two at Masada). The only book represented by a comparable number of copies is Deuteronomy, with forty-two scrolls (thirty-nine found near Qumran). As our earliest extant witnesses to the scriptural text of the psalms, these scrolls are important for understanding the psalms in the later Second Temple period and their finalization as a collection. Moreover, the prominence of the psalms scrolls at Qumran highlights the importance of the psalms among the *Yahad* or Essene movement, whose most prominent center was at the site.

Although the psalms scrolls were discovered over a relatively short period of time (from 1949 to 1965), their impact upon scholars and their relevance for the book of Psalms has taken many decades to unfold. Gerald H. Wilson played an important role toward a fuller understanding of the book of Psalms in light of the psalms scrolls.

This article begins by surveying the discovery of the psalms scrolls and the caves that contained them. It then presents four periods of research on the psalms scrolls, and concludes by evaluating the evidence from all the psalms scrolls for understanding the book of Psalms, and the role played by Gerald Wilson toward this realization. An up-to-date bibliography is provided, in two parts: (a) Editions, Translations, and Reference Lists on the Psalms Scrolls; and (b) Some Key Books and Articles on the Psalms Scrolls, including those by Gerald Wilson.

Cave 1 at Qumran

The first archaeological excavation of Cave 1 took place from February 15 to March 5, 1949, led by G. Lankester Harding, Director of Antiquities in Jordan, and Pére Roland de Vaux, Director of the École Biblique et Archéologique Française (the French Archaeological School). In addition to many jars and other objects, about six hundred fragments from numerous scrolls were found, including three psalms scrolls (1QPs^a, 1QPs^b, and 1QPs^c).

Caves 2–11

Between 1952 and 1956, ten more caves were discovered in the vicinity of Qumran. Harding and de Vaux discovered seven minor ones (3–5, 7–10), none of which contained extensive manuscript remains. The Bedouin, with their intimate knowledge of the terrain, however, discovered the three richest caves (1, 4, 11) and two minor ones (2 and 6). The manuscript remains include four psalms scrolls from the Minor Caves (3QPs, 5QPs, pap6QPs, and 8QS), twenty-five from Cave 4 (of which two are other works incorporating psalms), and six from Cave 11. The most extensive of these is the Great Psalms Scroll from Cave 11 (11QPs^a).

Other Sites in the Judean Desert

Two sites, Wadi Murabba'at and Nahal Hever, feature manuscripts mostly dating to the Bar Kokhba period (132–135 C.E.). Wadi Murabba'at, discovered by Bedouin in 1951, contained about 170 documents, most notably a scroll of the Twelve Minor Prophets. Nahal Hever was found by Bedouin in 1952, and excavated by Yigael Yadin in 1960–1961. A large number of scroll fragments were discovered in Cave 5/6 (the Cave of Letters), and some in Cave 8 (the Cave of Horrors). A few are biblical, including one psalms scroll from the Cave of Letters (5/6HevPs).

Masada, the last rebel stronghold in the First Jewish Revolt (68–73), was also excavated by Yadin in 1963–1965. The site yielded more than seven hundred ostraca, mostly inscribed in Hebrew or Aramaic. Fragments of fifteen manuscripts were also found, seven of them biblical, including two psalms scrolls (MasPs[a] and MasPs[b]).

Period 1: Publication and Implications of the Psalms Scrolls from Cave 1 and the Minor Caves at Qumran (1947–1962)

This period begins with the excavation of Cave 1 in 1947, includes the publication of the three Cave 1 psalms scrolls in DJD 1 (1955),[1] and culminates with the five psalms scrolls from the "Minor Caves" published in DJD 3 (1962).[2]

Note on the Tables: "Variant Order" means a sequence of psalms different from the one found in the Masoretic Text. "Different Content" denotes apocryphal psalms or other compositions in the same manuscript. "Range of Contents" denotes the earliest and latest verse in the Masoretic order of Pss 1–150. This does not necessarily imply that all the intervening text is preserved in a particular scroll, nor even that it even contained psalms in that order.

Scroll by Siglum/Number	Variant Order	Different Content	Range of Contents (Using MT Order)	Date or Period when Copied
1QPs[a]/1Q10			86:5 to 119:80	ca. 50 B.C.E.
1QPs[b]/1Q11			126:6 to 128:3	first century C.E.
1QPs[c]/1Q12			44:3–25	Herodian
2QPs/2Q14			103:2 to 104:11	Herodian
3QPs/3Q2			2:6–7	first century C.E.
5QPs/5Q5			119:99 to 119:142	first century C.E.

---

1. Dominique Barthélemy and Józef T. Milik, "Psautier (i)" and "Psautier (ii)," in *Qumran Cave I* (DJD 1; Oxford: Clarendon, 1955), 69–72 + plate xiii.

2. Maurice Baillet, J. T. Milik, and Roland de Vaux, *Les "Petites Grottes" de Qumran: Exploration de la falaise, Les grottes 2Q, 3Q, 5Q, 6Q, 7Q, à 10Q, Le rouleau de cuivre* (2 vols.; DJDJ 3; Oxford: Clarendon, 1962), 1:69–71, 94, 112, 148–49, 174; 2:plates xiii, xviii, xxiii, xxxi, xxxvii.

pap6QPs/6Q5	78:36–37	?
8QPs/8Q2	17:5 to 18:13	first century C.E.

Only sixteen psalms are represented in these eight manuscripts, all of them very fragmentary. Scholars noted a few variant readings against the Masoretic Psalter in three scrolls (1QPs^a, 1QPs^a and 8QPs), but found no variations in the order of psalms, and no differences in content (i.e., apocryphal psalms or other compositions). It seemed that for both the copyists of these psalms scrolls and their readers, the book of Psalms was very much like the collection of 150 psalms found in the Masoretic Text.

Period 2: Publication and Implications of the Great Psalms Scroll from Cave 11 (1965–1985)

This period begins with the edition of 11QPs^a in by James A. Sanders in DJD 4 (1965),[3] continues with the publication of another section of this scroll (1966 and 1967), and extends up to 1985 (the first extensive use of the Cave 4 psalms scrolls by Gerald Wilson).[4] The Great Psalms Scroll preserves text from thirty-two psalms not counted so far, as well as eleven apocryphal psalms (or other compositions).

Scroll by Siglum/Number	Variant Order	Different Content	Range of Contents (Using MT Order)	Date or Period When Copied
11QPs^a/11Q5	X	X	93:1 to 150:6	30–50 C.E.

In 1961, James Sanders unrolled the Great Psalm Scroll (11QPs^a), which was published years as *The Psalms Scroll of Qumrân Cave 11 (11QPsa)* in DJD 4 (1965). The edition featured four loose pieces (Fragments A–D) and twenty-eight adjoining columns (1–28) of the manuscript. Two years later, he published *The Dead Sea Psalms Scroll*, a more popular edition with facing Hebrew text and English translation.[5] This "Cornell Edition" incor-

---

3. James A. Sanders, *The Psalms Scroll of Qumrân Cave 11 (11QPsa)* (DJDJ 4; Oxford: Clarendon, 1965).

4. See under period 3 below.

5. James A. Sanders, *The Dead Sea Psalms Scroll* (Ithaca, N.Y.: Cornell University Press, 1967), 155–65 + plate.

porated an additional part of the manuscript (Fragment E), which Yigael Yadin had published a year earlier.[6]

The Great Psalm Scroll diverges radically from the MT-150 Psalter, both in the ordering of contents and in the presence of eleven additional compositions. Forty-nine pieces are preserved—with at least one more (Ps 120) now missing—in the following order (→ indicates that a composition follows directly, not by reconstruction):

Psalm 101 → 102 → 103; 109; 118 → 104 → 147 → 105 → 146 → 148 [+ 120] → 121 → 122 → 123 → 124 → 125 → 126 → 127 → 128 → 129 → 130 → 131 → 132 → 119 → 135 → 136 → *Catena* → 145(with postscript) → *154* → *Plea for Deliverance* → 139 → 137 → 138 → Sirach 51 → *Apostrophe to Zion* → Ps 93 → 141 → 133 → 144 → *155* → 142 → 143 → 149 → 150 → *Hymn to the Creator* → David's Last Words → *David's Compositions* → Ps 140 → 134 → *151A* → *151B* → blank column [*end*]

IMPLICATIONS FOR UNDERSTANDING THE BOOK OF PSALMS

Scholars who believed that early Jews used only one edition of the Psalter—the 150 Psalms found in the MT, in that order—offered a ready explanation for the different arrangement in 11QPs[a]. They viewed it a liturgical collection of psalms from the MT-150 Psalter and other compositions, rearranged in its own order. Yet as he analyzed the scroll and prepared the DJD edition, Sanders was coming to a very different conclusion. In a series of articles commencing in 1966,[7] he developed arguments that challenged traditional views on the text and canonization of the book of Psalms.[8] Most notably, this "Qumran Psalms Hypothesis" maintained that:

---

6. Yigael Yadin, "Another Fragment (E) of the Psalms Scroll from Qumran Cave 11 (11QPsa)," *Textus* 5 (1966): 1–10 + plates i–v.

7. James A. Sanders, "Variorum in the Psalms Scroll (11QPsa)," *HTR* 59 (1966): 83–94.

8. James A. Sanders, "Cave 11 Surprises and the Question of Canon," *McCQ* 21 (1968): 1–15; repr. in *New Directions in Biblical Archaeology* (Garden City, N.Y.: Doubleday, 1969); repr. in *The Canon and Masorah of the Hebrew Bible: An Introductory Reader* (New York: KTAV, 1974); Sanders, "The Qumran Psalms Scroll (11QPsa) Reviewed," in *On Language, Culture, and Religion: In Honor of Eugene A. Nida* (ed. M. Black and W. A. Smalley; The Hague: Mouton, 1974), 79–99; Shemaryahu Talmon, "The Textual Study of the Bible—A New Outlook," in *Qumran and the History of the*

- The Great Psalms Scroll contains the latter part of an edition of the book of Psalms, and is part of a true Davidic Psalter, at least for the community associated with Qumran.
- 11QPs[a] and other psalms scrolls bear witness to a Psalter that was stabilized over time in two distinct stages: first Pss 1–89 or so, and then Pss 90 (or Ps 93) onward. (The precise cutoff point is unclear, since Ps 93 is the earliest one preserved by this scroll in terms of the Masoretic order).

The decade following the publication of 11QPs[a] saw a heated debate over the shape and development of the book of Psalms. The majority of scholars agreed with formidable names such as Shemaryahu Talmon, Moshe H. Goshen-Gottstein, and Patrick W. Skehan that the MT-150 Psalter had already been finalized (or virtually so) centuries before the common era and that 11QPs[a] is a liturgical collection derived from, and secondary to, the MT.[9] On the other side, and almost alone, was Sanders, who defended and refined his view that 11QPs[a] contains the latter part of an authentic edition of the book of Psalms, which I have termed the "11QPs[a]-Psalter."[10]

The notion that 11QPs[a] contains the latter part of an edition of the book of Psalms was likewise viewed with skepticism. For example, Patrick Skehan argued[11] that 11QPs[a] is almost fully extant, that it originally began with Ps 101 in Fragment A, and that it never contained text from Pss 1–89 (or Pss 1–92). Reconstruction confirms that Skehan was correct that 11QPs[a] began with Ps 101—but not necessarily correct about the Psalter it

Biblical Text (ed. F. M. Cross and S. Talmon; Cambridge, Mass.: Harvard University Press, 1975), 321–400.

9. Shemaryahu Talmon, "Pisqah Be'emsa' Pasuq and 11QPs[a]," *Textus* 5 (1966): 11–21; Talmon, "Review of James A. Sanders, *The Psalms Scroll From Qumran*," *Tarbiz* 37 (1967): 99–104, esp. 100–101; Moshe H. Goshen-Gottstein, "The Psalms Scroll (11QPsa): A Problem of Canon and Text," *Textus* 5 (1967): 22–33; Patrick W. Skehan, "A Liturgical Complex in 11QPsa," *CBQ* 34 (1973): 195–205; Skehan, "Qumran and Old Testament Criticism," in *Qumrân: Sa piété, sa théologie et son milieu* (ed. M. Delcor; BETL 46; Paris: Éditions Duculot, 1978), 163–82.

10. For example, Peter Flint, *The Dead Sea Psalms Scrolls and the Book of Psalms* (STDJ 17; Leiden: Brill, 1997); Flint, "Psalms and Psalters in the Dead Sea Scrolls," *Scripture and the Scrolls* (vol. 1 of *The Bible and the Dead Sea Scrolls*; ed. James H. Charlesworth; Waco, Tex.: Baylor University Press, 2006), 233–72.

11. Patrick W. Skehan, "Qumran and Old Testament Criticism," 170.

represents. The issue could only be resolved with additional evidence from other scrolls.

As George Brooke observed,[12] the debate between Sanders and his formidable opponents was centered on a single manuscript. Two main questions stood out. First, is there evidence for the 11QPsª-Psalter in manuscripts other than the Great Psalms Scroll? Second, do any manuscripts indicate that this Psalter originally contained psalms from its earlier section (Pss 1–89 or thereabouts)? An impasse had been reached—one that called for further evidence and additional data.

The first additional evidence appeared in three psalms scrolls from sites other than Qumran, published by Yigael Yadin in very preliminary and incomplete editions: the Nahal Hever psalms scroll[13] and the two Masada psalms scrolls.[14] These scrolls lent some impetus to the view that the MT-150 Psalter had already been finalized before the common era, and that 11QPsª was a secondary liturgical collection. Since the final and far more extensive editions were published many years later, however, these three psalms scrolls will thus be discussed under period 4 below.

PERIOD 3: PUBLICATION AND IMPLICATIONS OF THE PSALMS SCROLLS
(OR TEXTS INCORPORATING PSALMS) FROM CAVE 4 (1985–2000)

This period begins with the first book to make extensive use of the Cave 4 psalms scrolls, Gerald Wilson's *The Editing of the Hebrew Psalter* (1985),[15] and culminates with the publication of all these manuscripts in DJD 16 (2000).[16] Among them, these twenty-five scrolls preserve text from fifty-one

---

12. George Brooke, "Psalms 105 and 106 at Qumran," *RevQ* 54 (1989): 267–92, here 269.

13. Yigael Yadin, "Expedition D," *IEJ* 11 (1961): 36–52 + plates, esp. 40 + plate 20D.

14. Yigael Yadin, "The Excavation of Masada—1963/64. Preliminary Report," *IEJ* 15 (1965): 1–120 + plates, esp. 81, 103–104 + plate 19A; Yadin, *Masada: Herod's Fortress and the Zealots' Last Stand* (New York: Random House, 1966).

15. Gerald H. Wilson, *The Editing of the Hebrew Psalter* (SBLDS 76; Chico, Calif.: Scholars Press, 1985).

16. Patrick W. Skehan, Eugene Ulrich, and Peter W. Flint, "Psalms," in *Qumran Cave 4.XI: Psalms to Chronicles* (ed. E. Ulrich; DJD 16; Oxford: Clarendon 2000), 7–160, 163–68 + plates i–xx. Note: *The Prophecy* (or *Apocryphon*) *of Joshua* (4Q522) was published earlier by Émile Puech as "4Q522. 4QProphétie de Josué = Prophecy of Joshua" in *Qumran Cave 4.XVIII: Textes hébreux (4Q521–4Q528, 4Q576–4Q579)*

psalms not counted so far, as well as four apocryphal psalms (or other compositions).

Scroll by Siglum/ Number	Variant Order	Different Content	Range of Contents (Using MT Order)	Date or Period When Copied
4QPs^a/4Q83	X		5:9 to 71:14	mid-second century B.C.E.
4QPs^b/4Q84	X		91:5 to 118:29	Herodian
4QPs^c/4Q85			16:7 to 53:1	ca. 50–68 C.E.
4QPs^d/4Q86	X		104:1 to 147:20	mid-first century B.C.E.
4QPs^e/4Q87	X		76:10 to 146:1(?)	mid-first century B.C.E.
4QPs^f/4Q88	X	X	22:15 to 109:28	ca. 50 B.C.E.
4QPs^g/4Q89			119:37 to 119:92	ca. 50 C.E.
4QPs^h/4Q90			119:10–21	Herodian
4QPs^j/4Q91			48:1 to 53:5	ca. 50 C.E.
4QPs^k/4Q92	X		(?)99:1 to 135:16	first century B.C.E.
4QPs^l/4Q93			104:3 to 104:12	second half first century B.C.E.

(ed. Émile Puech; DJD 25; Oxford: Clarendon, 1998), 39–74 + plates iv–v. Only the portion containing Ps 122:1–9 (67–70 + plate iv) was republished in DJD 16 (169–70). Also, one of the Cave 4 scrolls listed in the Table (*Apocryphal Psalm and Prayer* = 4Q448) was published separately by Esti Eshel, Hanan Eshel, and Ada Yardeni as "4Q448: Apocryphal Psalm and Prayer" in *Qumran Cave 4: VI, Poetical and Liturgical Texts, Part 1* (ed. Esti Eshel; DJD 11; Oxford: Clarendon, 1998), 403–25 + plate xxxii.

4QPs^m/4Q94		93:3 to 98:8	Herodian
4QPs^n/4Q95	X	135:6 to 136:23	Herodian
4QPs^o/4Q96		114:7 to 116:10	late first century B.C.E.
4QPs^p/4Q97		143:3 to 143:8	Herodian
4QPs^q/4Q98	X	31:24 to 35:20	mid-first century C.E.
4QPs^r/4Q98a		26:7 to 30:13	Herodian
4QPs^s/4Q98b		5:8 to 6:1	50–68 C.E.
4QPs^t/4Q98c		88:15–17	50 C.E. or later
4QPs^u/4Q98d		42:5 only	ca. 50 C.E.
4QPs^v/4Q98e		99:1 only	late first century C.E.
4QPs^w/4Q98f		112:1–9	Hasmonean
4QPs^x/4Q236		89:20–31	175–125 B.C.E.
4QProphecy of Joshua/4Q522	X	122:1–9	mid-first century B.C.E.
4QApocryphal Psalm and Prayer/4Q448	X	154:17–20 (Apocryphal Ps)	103–76 B.C.E.

GERALD WILSON'S ROLE IN MOVING THE
PSALMS SCROLLS DEBATE FORWARD

The impasse reached at the end of period 2 set an ideal stage set for Wilson's work on the psalms scrolls. Do any manuscripts other than the Great

Psalms Scroll contain evidence for the 11QPs[a]-Psalter? And do any manuscripts indicate that this Psalter originally contained psalms from its earlier section (Pss 1–89 or thereabouts)?

Wilson's early findings appeared in articles such as "The Qumran Psalms Manuscripts and the Consecutive Arrangement of Psalms in the Hebrew Psalter"[17] and "The Qumran Psalms Scroll Reconsidered: Analysis of the Debate."[18] His most important work—a slightly edited version of his Yale dissertation—is *The Editing of the Hebrew Psalter*. With respect to the biblical scrolls and the book of Psalms, this is a landmark volume for two reasons. First, it was the first book to make extensive use of the Cave 4 psalms scrolls, since Patrick Skehan (who was preparing the Cave 4 psalms scrolls for the DJD series) had given Wilson access to his unpublished notes and transcriptions.

Second, by taking into consideration 11QPs[a] and most of the Cave 4 scrolls, Wilson's research expanded the psalms debate and contributed significantly to the discussion. His conclusions support several elements of the Qumran Psalms Hypothesis, especially that many psalms scrolls point to stabilization the book of Psalms over time, and that 11QPs[a] was regarded by at least some early Jews as a true scriptural Psalter, not as a secondary collection.

Wilson's analysis shows that the 11QPs[a] Psalter is organized in accordance with principles similar to those found in books 4 and 5 in the MT-150 Psalter. Such organization is most evident in the juxtaposition of superscripts and postscripts[19] that highlight different kinds of groupings in 11QPs[a]. One example is found in fragment E plus Columns 1–2:

Psalm	Superscript	Postscript
118	[הודוליהוהכיטוב][20]	_____
104	לדויד	הללויה
147	[_____]	[הללו יה]

---

17. Gerald H. Wilson, "The Qumran Psalms Manuscripts and the Consecutive Arrangement of Psalms in the Hebrew Psalter," *CBQ* 45 (1983): 377–88.

18. Gerald H. Wilson, "The Qumran Psalms Scroll Reconsidered: Analysis of the Debate," *CBQ* 47 (1985): 624–42.

19. Here Wilson's use of the term "postscripts" is loosely defined, since the *hallelujahs* and doxologies that he cites do not strictly qualify.

20. This doxology is not preserved in frg. E of 11QPsa, but supplied by Wilson on the basis of its appearance in the MT and in the *Catena* in col. 16.

105	הודוליהוהכיטוב	[?]
146	[?]	הללויה
148	_____	[הללו יה]

Wilson noted the regularity of this structure but also its variation from
the MT-150 Psalter. He also regarded the alternation between הודו and
הללו-יה psalms as systematic, since the הודו phrase in Ps 105 is an "addition" when compared to the received Psalter. Wilson concluded that this
addition was intentionally made in order to fill out the symmetry of the
grouping in 11QPsᵃ.[21] The similarity in organization to the MT-150 Psalter
is apparent. In that collection, for example, the principle of juxtaposing
הללו-יה psalms occurs in the grouping of Pss 104–106, which concludes
book 4, and in the grouping of Pss 146–150, which concludes book 5:

Psalm	Superscript	Postscript
104		הללויה
105		הללויה
106	הודו—הללויה	הללויה—Doxology
146	הללויה	הללויה
147	הללויה	הללויה
148	הללויה	הללויה
149	הללויה	הללויה
150	הללויה	הללויה

ADDITIONAL COMMENTS ON PERIOD 3
AND THE PSALMS SCROLLS DEBATE

With respect to earlier psalms in the traditional sequence, my own analysis shows that 4QPsᵃ is an important witness to the stabilization of the
first part of the Psalter.[22] This is the oldest of the psalms scrolls (dated to
about 150 B.C.E.), and second only to 11QPsᵃ with respect to the number
of verses represented. Among the twenty-two identified fragments (some
quite substantial), text from nineteen psalms is found, and three more (Pss
64, 65, and 68) may be included on the basis of reconstruction. Among all

21. Wilson, *The Editing of the Hebrew Psalter*, 126.
22. Flint, *Dead Sea Psalms Scrolls and the Book of Psalms*, 141–46, 168–69.

the psalms scrolls found in the Judean Desert, 4QPs^a alone contains material from Pss 34, 38, 47, 54, 56, 62–63, 66–67, and 69.

Since some fragments preserve portions of more than one psalm,
and others are contiguous, several psalms directly followed others, usually physically (denoted →), and in some cases by reconstruction (denoted
[→]). The overall contents are as follows (verse numbers not included):

> Psalms 5→ 6; 25; 31→ 33; 34→ 35→ 36; 38→ 71; 47; 53→ 54; 56; 62 → 63 [→
> 64 → 65 →] 66 → 67 [→ 68 →] 69

4QPs^a generally reflects stabilization of the first part of the Psalter (at least
from Pss 5 through 69). Two striking deviations are evident. Psalm 31 is
directly followed by Ps 33 (a sequence also found in 4QPs^q), and Ps 38 is
directly followed by Ps 71.

The Cave 4 Psalms Scrolls and the Psalms Scrolls Debate

To sum up phase 3, the Cave 4 psalms scrolls speak to the Qumran Psalms
Hypothesis in two ways:

- They indicate that the 11QPs^a-Psalter is organized in accordance with principles similar to the ones used for books 4 and
  5 in the MT-150 Psalter. This supports the view that the Great
  Psalms Scroll contains the latter part of an edition of the book
  of Psalms and is part of a true Davidic Psalter.
- 4QPs^a (and a few other, less preserved, psalms scrolls) point
  to stabilization of the first part of the Psalter (at least from Pss
  5 through 69, the cutoff point being uncertain). This supports
  the view that 11QPs^a bears witness to a Psalter that was stabilized over time in two distinct stages.

At the close of period 3, three problems remained, however. The first is
surprising to many scholars: none of the Cave 4 psalms scrolls *unambiguously* confirms the overall order of the received Masoretic Text (1–150)
as opposed to the 11QPs^a-Psalter. Appealing to arrangements such as Pss
125–130 in 4QPs^e in support of the MT-150 Psalter is inconclusive, since
this sequence is also found in 11QPs^a.

Second, do any of the Cave 4 scrolls represent the 11QPs^a-Psalter? The
only possible candidate is 4QPs^e, which possibly has a distinctive arrange-

ment also found in 11QPsᵃ: Psalms 118 → 104 [→ 147 →] 105 → 146(?). (If so, 4QPsᵉ may be considered the only exemplar of the 11QPsᵃ-Psalter from Cave 4.) This sequence is not assured, however, since much of the text is no longer preserved, and Ps 147 has to be reconstructed. 4QPsᵉ will be revisited in the discussion of another psalms scroll from Cave 11 (11QPsᵇ) in phase 4 below.

Third, is there any evidence among the Cave 4 scrolls that the Psalter represented by 11QPsᵃ (as the second half of the "11QPsᵃ-Psalter") originally contained any psalms prior to 93? Again, only 4QPsᵉ may qualify. If it indeed has the distinctive arrangement mentioned above, then 4QPsᵉ also provides evidence for the earlier part of this Psalter, since it preserves text from Pss 76–78, 81, 86, and 88–89.

PERIOD 4: PUBLICATION AND IMPLICATIONS OF ADDITIONAL PSALMS
SCROLLS FROM CAVE 11 AND PSALMS SCROLLS FROM OTHER SITES IN
THE JUDEAN DESERT (1998–2000)

This period overlaps with period 3, since it extends from the publication of four more psalms scrolls from Cave 11 in DJD 23 (1998),[23] includes the full editions of the two psalms scrolls found at Masada (1999),[24] and ends with the Nahal Hever psalms scroll in DJD 38 (2000).[25] Among them, these scrolls preserve text from twenty-four psalms not counted so far, as well as three apocryphal psalms (or other compositions).

---

23. Florentino García Martínez, Eibert J. C. Tigchelaar, and A. S. van der Woude, "11QPsᵃ, Fragments E, F, 11QPsᵇ, 11QPsᶜ, and 11QPsᵉ?" in *Qumran Cave 11.II: 11Q2–11Q18, 11Q20–11Q30* (DJD 23; Oxford: Clarendon, 1998), 29–78 + plates iii–vii.

24. Shemaryahu Talmon, "Hebrew Fragments from Masada: 1(f) MasPsᵃ and (g) MasPsᵇ," in *Masada VI: Yigael Yadin Excavations from 1963–1965: Final Reports* (ed. S. Talmon and Y. Yadin; Jerusalem: Israel Exploration Society and the Hebrew University of Jerusalem, 1999), 76–97 (including two plates).

25. Peter W. Flint, "Biblical Scrolls from Nahal Hever and 'Wadi Seiyal': 1b. 5/6HevPsalms," in *Miscellaneous Texts from the Judaean Desert* (consulting eds. J. C. VanderKam and M. Brady; DJD 38; Oxford: Clarendon, 2000), 141–166 + plates xxv–xxvii.

Scroll by Siglum/Number	Variant Order	Different Content	Range of Contents (Using MT Order)	Date or Period When Copied
11QPs^b/11Q6	X	X	77:18 to 144:2	first half of first century C.E.
11QPs^c/11Q7			2:1 to 25:27	Herodian
11QPs^d/11Q8			6:2 to 116:1	Herodian
11QPs^e/11Q9			50:5–7	Herodian
11QapocrPs/11Q11	X	X	91:1 to 91:16	mid-first century C.E.
5/6HevPs/5/6Hev 1b			7:13 to 31:22	second half of first century C.E.
MasPs^a/ M1039–160			81:2 to 85:6	first half of first century C.E.
MasPs^b/ M1103–1742			150:1–6	second half of first century B.C.E.

These psalms scrolls are important for understanding the finalization of the book of Psalms in four respects:

Stabilization of the first part of the Psalter: Like 4QPs^a, the Nahal Hever psalms scroll (with text from Pss 7 to 31) and the first Masada scroll (MasPs^a, with portions of Pss 81 to 85) speak to the stabilization of the first part of the Psalter (up to Ps 89 or so).

Ending of the mt-150 Psalter: The second Masada scroll (MasPs^b) provides the first evidence of a book of Psalms ending with Ps 150 (since a blank column follows). Although the manuscript preserves only Pss 147:18–19 and 150:1–6, for many scholars the Psalter that it represents originally contained all or some of the precursor to the MT-150 Psalter.

Confirmation of the 11QPsa-Psalter: The second psalms scroll from Cave 11 (11QPs[b]) is a true exemplar of the 11QPs[a]-Psalter. It features a distinctive arrangement (Pss 141 → 133 → 144) and distinctive contents (the *Catena, Plea for Deliverance,* and *Apostrophe to Zion*) also found in 11QPs[a].[26]

The full 11QPsa-Psalter includes a first half not found in the Great Psalms Scroll: 11QPs[b] preserves material from both the earlier and later sections of the 11QPs[a]-Psalter. In the preliminary editions (1967 and 1992),[27] the first preserved fragment contained text from Ps 119, which lent no support for the existence of earlier material in the 11QPs[a] Psalter. In the critical edition in DJD 23 (1998), however, the editors include Pss 77:18–78:1 in 11QPs[b] as frg. 1[28]—whereas van der Ploeg had previously placed it in 11QPs[c].[29] The new placement confirms that this Psalter included material preceding the psalms found in 11QPs[a]. Moreover, if 4QPs[e] indeed preserves a distinctive arrangement found in the 11QPs[a]-Psalter, it also preserves text from this Psalter (portions of Pss 76–78, 81, 86, and 88–89).

---

26. See Peter W. Flint, "Five Surprises in the Psalms Scrolls," in *Flores Florentino: Dead Sea Scrolls and Other Early Jewish Studies in Honour of Florentino García Martínez* (ed. Anthony Hilhorst et al.; JSJSup 122; Leiden: Brill, 2007), 183–95; Flint, "11QPsb and the 11QPsa–Psalter," in *Diachronic and Synchronic: Proceedings of the Baylor Symposium on the Book of Psalms, May 18–20, 2006* (ed. Joel S. Burnett et al.; London: T&T Clark, 2007), 157–66.

27. J. P. M. van der Ploeg, "Fragments d'un manuscrit de Psaumes de Qumran (11QPs[b])," *RB* 74 (1967): 408–12 + plate xviii; Ploeg, "Fragments de Psaumes de Qumrân," in *Intertestamental Essays in Honour of Józef Tadeusz Milik* (ed. Z. J. Kapera; Qumranica Mogilanensia 6; Kraków: Enigma, 1992), 233–37.

28. Page 40, based on the scribal hand and length of lines. They write: "Van der Ploeg included this fragment with 11QPsc on the basis of a superficial similarity between it and 11QPs[c] frg. 8. The scribal hand of frg. 1, however, bears a marked affinity with that of 11QPs[b] and is dissimilar to that of 11QPs[c].... In addition, the line length of frg. 1 matches that of 11QPs[b], and not that of 11QPs[c]" (DJD 23: 40).

29. J. P. M. van der Ploeg, "Fragments d'un Psautier de Qumrân," in *Symbolae biblicae et Mesopotamicae Francisco Mario Theodoro de Liagre Böhl dedicatae* (ed. M. A. Beek et al.; Leiden: Brill, 1973), 308–9 + plate ii; Ploeg, "Fragments de Psaumes," 234.

Recent Developments and Concluding Comments:
Two Additional Psalms Scrolls and the Number of
Psalms Preserved in the Scrolls

By 2000, forty psalms scrolls (or scrolls incorporating psalms) had been published in the series Discoveries in the Judaean Desert, from DJD 1 (1955) to the Cave 4 psalms scrolls in DJD 16 (2000) and the Nahal Hever psalm scroll in DJD 38 (2000). The two scrolls found at Masada were published in *Masada* VI (1999). More recently, several additional scrolls, most containing biblical texts, have been purchased by collectors and institutions in Europe and the United States. All were very likely found in the caves near Qumran.

Between 2000 and 2005, Norwegian collector Martin Schøyen purchased about forty fragments, including one psalms scroll with text from Ps 9:8–13. In 2010, Southwestern Baptist Theological Seminary (Fort Worth, Texas) bought an ancient pen and fragments of six biblical scrolls, among them one psalms scroll (Ps 22:4–13). In 2011, the Green Collection (Oklahoma City, Okla.) purchased twelve scrolls, including one psalms scroll (Ps 11:1–4). No additional psalms to those featured in periods 1–4 above are found in these three psalms scrolls.

Between them, the forty-five psalms scrolls or scrolls incorporating psalms contain text from 123 psalms and eighteen apocryphal compositions. Of the 150 in the traditional MT-Psalter, no text has been found so far from twenty-seven psalms (Pss 1, 3–4, 20–21, 32, 41, 46?, 55, 57–58, 61, 64–65, 70, 72–75, 79–80, and 87, 90, 108?, 110, 111, 117). One reason for this imbalance is that the beginnings of rolled scrolls are usually on the outside, and are thus far more prone to deterioration.

Most or possibly all the "missing" twenty-seven psalms were likely represented in the psalms scrolls, but are now lost due of their fragmentary condition. Furthermore, many psalms are alluded to, or sometimes quoted, in various nonbiblical scrolls. This topic requires further research, however, since several allusions involve only a few words or merely an echo of a particular psalm.[30]

There are no missing compositions among the apocryphal psalms. Since some psalms scrolls include Pss 151, 154, and 155, and some editions

---

30. See the extensive list in Armin Lange and Matthias Weigold, *Biblical Quotations and Allusions in Second Temple Jewish Literature* (JAJSup 5; Göttingen: Vandenhoeck & Ruprecht, 2011), 163–78.

of the Syriac Bible contain Pss 151–155, we may note that Pss 152 and 153 have not been found among the scrolls.

Conclusions on the Psalms Scrolls and the Development of the Book of Psalms

The evidence from all the psalms scrolls attests to diversity concerning the shape of the Psalter, not to uniformity in accordance with the MT-150 arrangement. In his forthcoming article for *The New Cambridge History of the Bible*,[31] Eugene Ulrich writes: "Variant editions for half or more of the twenty-four books of the Hebrew Bible existed in Jewish circles at the birth of Christianity and Rabbinic Judaism." We may conclude that three editions of the psalms were in circulation in the late Second Temple period:

- *Edition I:* An early edition of the Psalter that was mostly stabilized, beginning with Pss 1 or 2 and ending with Ps 89 or so (or at least from Ps 5 to Ps 69 as in 4QPs^a, the earliest and most complete example).
- *Edition IIa:* The 11QPs^a-Psalter, consisting of Edition I plus Pss 101 to 151 as in the Great Psalms Scroll and including Ps 93. It is attested by three manuscripts (11QPs^a, 11QPs^b, possibly 4QPs^e) with common arrangements of key compositions (*Catena, Plea for Deliverance,* and *Apostrophe to Zion*) and sequences (Pss 141 → 133 → 144 in 11QPs^a and 11QPs^b; and perhaps Pss 118 → 104 →[147 →] 105 → 146 in 4QPs^e).
- *Edition IIb:* The MT-150 Psalter, comprising Edition I plus Pss 90 to 150 as found in the Masoretic Text. This arrangement is not *unambiguously* confirmed by any Qumran scroll, but partial confirmation is provided by MasPs^b (second half of the 1st century B.C.E.), which ends with Ps 150. The MT-150 Psalter, or parts of it, was possibly found in some Qumran psalms scrolls before they were so damaged, but most are too fragmentary for any real conclusions to be reached.

---

31. Eugene Ulrich, "The Old Testament Text and Its Transmission," in *The New Cambridge History of the Bible* (Cambridge: Cambridge University Press) [in press].

ADDITIONAL COLLECTIONS OF PSALMS

Further arrangements of psalms appear in several scrolls from Qumran. These are not editions of the book of Psalms, but arrangements of material from *Edition IIa* or *Edition IIb* and other poems. Three examples: 4QPs[b] (includes Pss 103 → 112, with 104–111 lacking); 4QPs[d] (Pss 106 → 147 → 104); 4QPs[f] (Pss 107 [+ 108?] +109 and apocryphal psalms); and 11QapocPs (three apocryphal psalms followed by Ps 91).

GERALD WILSON'S CONTRIBUTION TO UNDERSTANDING THE BOOK OF PSALMS IN LIGHT OF THE PSALMS SCROLLS

The shape of the various psalms scrolls has led to a reassessment of the development of the Psalter in the Second Temple period. It has taken several decades for many scholars to accept that the manuscript evidence shows that the book of Psalms was put together in several stages. At a very vulnerable time, when debate concerning the textual value of the psalms scrolls had reached an impasse, and further evidence was urgently called for, Gerald Wilson came to the rescue.

He published the first book to make extensive use of the Cave 4 psalms scrolls and, by taking into consideration 11QPs[a] and most of the Cave 4 scrolls, expanded the psalms debate and contributed significantly to the discussion. (For example, Wilson showed that the 11QPs[a]-Psalter is organized in accordance with principles similar to those found in books 4 and 5 in the MT-150 Psalter.) His conclusions support several elements of the Qumran Psalms Hypothesis, especially that many psalms scrolls point to stabilization of the book of Psalms over time, and that 11QPs[a] was regarded by at least some early Jews as a true scriptural Psalter, not as a secondary collection.

BIBLIOGRAPHY

Editions, Translations, and Reference Lists on the Psalms Scrolls

Baillet, Maurice, Józef T. Milik, and Roland de Vaux. *Les "Petites Grottes" de Qumran: Exploration de la falaise. Les grottes 2Q, 3Q, 5Q, 6Q, 7Q, à 10Q. Le rouleau de cuivre.* 2 vols. DJDJ 3. Oxford: Clarendon, 1962.

Barthélemy, Dominique, and Józef T. Milik. "Psautier (i)" and "Psautier (ii)." Pages 69–72 + plate xiii in *Qumran Cave I.* DJD 1. Oxford: Clarendon, 1955.

Eshel, Esti, Hanan Eshel, and Ada Yardeni. "4Q448: Apocryphal Psalm and Prayer." Pages 403–25 + plate xxxii in *Qumran Cave 4: VI, Poetical and Liturgical Texts, Part 1.* Edited by Esti Eshel. DJD 11. Oxford: Clarendon, 1998.

Flint, Peter. W. "Psalms." Pages 505–89 in Martin Abegg, Peter W. Flint and Eugene Ulrich, *The Dead Sea Scrolls Bible.* San Francisco: HarperCollins, 1999.

———. "Biblical Scrolls from Nahal Hever and 'Wadi Seiyal': 1b. 5/6HevPsalms." Pages 141–66 + plates xxv–xxvii in *Miscellaneous Texts from the Judaean Desert.* Consulting Editors James C. VanderKam and Monica Brady. DJD 38; Oxford: Clarendon, 2000.

———. *The Great Psalms Scroll from Cave 11 (11QPsa).* Dead Sea Scrolls Editions; Leiden: Brill. [in preparation]

García Martínez, Florentino, Eibert J. C. Tigchelaar, and Adam S. van der Woude. "11QPsª, Fragments E, F, 11QPsᵇ, 11QPsᶜ, and 11QPsᵉ?" Pages 29–78 + plates iii–viii in *Qumran Cave 11.II: 11Q2–11Q18, 11Q20–11Q30.* DJD 23. Oxford: Clarendon, 1998.

Lange, Armin, and Matthias Weigold. *Biblical Quotations and Allusions in Second Temple Jewish Literature.* JAJSup 5. Göttingen: Vandenhoeck & Ruprecht, 2011.

Ploeg, Johannes P. M. van der. "Fragments d'un manuscrit de Psaumes de Qumran (11QPsᵇ)," *RB* 74 (1967): 408–12 + plate xviii.

———. "Fragments d'un Psautier de Qumrân." Pages 308–9 + plate ii in *Symbolae biblicae et Mesopotamicae Francisco Mario Theodoro de Liagre Böhl dedicatae.* Edited by M. A. Beek, A. A. Kampman, C. Nijland, and J. Ryckmans. Leiden: Brill, 1973.

———. "Fragments de Psaumes de Qumrân." Pages 233–37 in *Intertestamental Essays in Honour of Józef Tadeusz Milik.* Edited by Z. J. Kapera. Qumranica Mogilanensia 6; Kraków: Enigma, 1992.

Puech, Émile. "4Q522. 4QProphétie de Josué = Prophecy of Joshua." Pages 39–74 + plates iv–v in *Qumran Cave 4.XVIII: Textes hébreux (4Q521–4Q528, 4Q576–4Q579).* Edited by Émile Puech. DJD 25. Oxford: Clarendon, 1998.

Sanders, James A. *The Psalms Scroll of Qumrân Cave 11 (11QPsa).* DJDJ 4; Oxford: Clarendon, 1965.

——. *The Dead Sea Psalms Scroll*. Ithaca, N. Y.: Cornell University Press, 1967.

Skehan, Patrick W., Eugene Ulrich, and Peter W. Flint. "Psalms." Pages 7–160, 163–68 + plates i–xx in *Qumran Cave 4.XI: Psalms to Chronicles*. Edited by E. Ulrich. DJD 16. Oxford: Clarendon, 2000.

——. "Psalms: Fragments." Pages 627–93 in *The Biblical Qumran Scrolls: Transcriptions and Textual Variants*. Edited by Eugene Ulrich. VTSup 134. Leiden: Brill, 2010.

Talmon, Shemaryahu. "Hebrew Fragments from Masada: 1(f) MasPs[a] and (g) MasPs[b]." Pages 76–97 (including two plates) in *Masada VI: Yigael Yadin Excavations from 1963–1965: Final Reports*. Edited by Shemaryahu Talmon and Yigael Yadin. Jerusalem: Israel Exploration Society and the Hebrew University of Jerusalem, 1999.

Yadin, Yigael. "Another Fragment (E) of the Psalms Scroll from Qumran Cave 11 (11QPs[a])" *Textus* 5 (1966): 1–10 + plates i–v.

——. "The Excavation of Masada—1963/64. Preliminary Report." *IEJ* 15 (1965): 1–120 + plates.

——. "Expedition D." *IEJ* 11 (1961): 36–52 + plates.

——. *Masada: Herod's Fortress and the Zealots' Last Stand*. New York: Random House, 1966.

Some Key Books and Articles on the Psalms Scrolls (Including Those by Gerald Wilson)

Brooke, George J. "Psalms 105 and 106 at Qumran." *RevQ* 54 (1989): 267–92.

Dahmen, Ulrich. *Psalmen- und Psalter-Rezeption im Frühjudentum. Rekonstruktion, Textbestand, Struktur und Pragmatik der Psalmenrolle 11QPsa aus Qumran*. STDJ 49. Leiden: Brill, 2003.

Flint, Peter W. *The Dead Sea Psalms Scrolls and the Book of Psalms*. STDJ 17. Leiden: Brill, 1997.

——. "Psalms and Psalters in the Dead Sea Scrolls." Pages 233–72 in *Scripture and the Scrolls*. Vol. 1 of *The Bible and the Dead Sea Scrolls*. Edited by James H. Charlesworth. Waco, Tex.: Baylor University Press, 2006.

——. "Five Surprises in the Psalms Scrolls." Pages 183–95 in *Flores Florentino: Dead Sea Scrolls and Other Early Jewish Studies in Honour of Florentino García Martínez*. Edited by Anthony Hilhorst, Émile Puech, and Eibert Tigchelaar. JSJSup 122. Leiden: Brill, 2007.

———. "11QPs^b and the 11QPs^a–Psalter." Pages 157–66 in *Diachronic and Synchronic: Proceedings of the Baylor Symposium on the Book of Psalms, May 18–20, 2006.* Edited by Joel S. Burnett, William H. Bellinger, Jr., and W. Dennis Tucker. London: T&T Clark, 2007.

———. "The Dead Sea Psalms Scrolls. Psalms Manuscripts, Editions, and the *Oxford Hebrew Bible.*" Pages 11–34 in *Jewish and Christian Approaches to the Psalms: Conflict and Convergence.* Edited by Susan Gillingham. Oxford: Oxford University Press, 2012.

Goshen-Gottstein, Moshe H. "The Psalms Scroll (11QPs^a): A Problem of Canon and Text." *Textus* 5 (1966): 22–33.

Sanders, James A. "Cave 11 Surprises and the Question of Canon." *McCQ* 21 (1968): 1–15. Repr. pages 101–116 in *New Directions in Biblical Archaeology.* Edited by David N. Freedman and Jonas C. Greenfield. Garden City, N.Y.: Doubleday, 1969; repr. pages 37–51 in *The Canon and Masorah of the Hebrew Bible: An Introductory Reader.* Edited by Sid Z. Leiman. New York: KTAV, 1974.

———. "The Qumran Psalms Scroll (11QPs^a) Reviewed." Pages 79–99 in *On Language, Culture, and Religion: In Honor of Eugene A. Nida.* Edited by Matthew Black and William A. Smalley. The Hague: Mouton, 1974.

———. "Variorum in the Psalms Scroll (11QPs^a)." *HTR* 59 (1966): 83–94.

Skehan, Patrick W. "A Liturgical Complex in 11QPs^a." *CBQ* 34 (1973): 195–205.

———. "Qumran and Old Testament Criticism." Pages 163–82 in *Qumrân: Sa piété, sa théologie et son milieu.* Edited by M. Delcor. BETL 46. Paris: Éditions Duculot, 1978.

Talmon, Shemaryahu. "Pisqah Be'emsa' Pasuq and 11QPs^a." *Textus* 5 (1966): 11–21.

———. Review of "James A. Sanders, *The Psalms Scroll from Qumran.*" *Tarbiz* 37 (1967): 99–104.

———. "The Textual Study of the Bible—A New Outlook." Pages 321–400 in *Qumran and the History of the Biblical Text.* Edited by Frank M. Cross and Shemaryahu Talmon. Cambridge, Mass.: Harvard University Press, 1975.

Tov, Emanuel. "Special Layout of Poetical Units in the Texts from the Judean Desert." Pages 105–28 in *Give Ear to My Words: Psalms and Other Poetry in and around the Hebrew Bible.* Edited by Janet W. Dyk. Amsterdam: Societas Hebraica Amstelodamensis, 1996.

Ulrich, Eugene. "The Old Testament Text and Its Transmission." In *The

New Cambridge History of the Bible. Cambridge: Cambridge University Press. [in press]

Wilson, Gerald. H. *The Editing of the Hebrew Psalter*. SBLDS 76; Chico, Calif.: Scholars Press, 1985.

———. "The Qumran Psalms Manuscripts and the Consecutive Arrangement of Psalms in the Hebrew Psalter." *CBQ* 45 (1983): 377–88.

———. "The Qumran Psalms Scroll Reconsidered: Analysis of the Debate." *CBQ* 47 (1985): 624–42.

Imagining the Future of Psalms Studies[*]

Rolf A. Jacobson

"It Is Difficult to Make Predictions, Especially about the Future"—Yogi Berra

I wish to thank the Book of Psalms Section steering committee for the invitation to contribute an essay to this volume on a look at the state of the study of the Psalter twenty-five years after Gerald Wilson's groundbreaking *The Editing of the Hebrew Psalter*. I was mulling over the fact that many others have much more wisdom to share on this subject that I do. Then it occurred to me that, precisely because they have more wisdom than I, they all declined to give a paper on the future of psalms study. As the great baseball player Yogi Berra is reputed to have said, "It is difficult to make predictions, especially about the future." If I could predict the future, I would not be writing this paper—I would be working in a building that somebody is occupying or sitting on one of the beaches on my private island. So let me begin with an obvious statement. Nobody can predict the future—certainly not I.

Yet in spite of the impossibility of projecting the future, I have found the exercise of writing this essay to be a generative experience in imagination. When Gerald Wilson published *The Editing of the Hebrew Psalter*, it reshaped scholarly imagination about how to interpret the psalms. In this spirit of Wilson's contributions and on the twenty-fifth anniversary of

---

[*] This essay is a revised and expanded version of a paper that I was invited to deliver in November 2011 at a special session of the Book of Psalms Section of the Society of Biblical Literature, which was dedicated to considering the impact of the work of Gerald Wilson on the shape and shaping of the Hebrew Psalter. It was an honor to know Wilson, who in my experience truly was the model of what a gentleman and scholar should be. I thank God for his life and work.

the publication of his seminal volume, it is fitting that the Book of Psalms Section should pause again to imagine together what the next twenty-five years of psalms study might look like. So, in the spirit of scholarly imagination, I have two points, each of which I will in turn introduce with a quotation from Professor Berra.

"This Is Like Déjà Vu All Over Again"—Yogi Berra

When I think about the near future in psalms studies, I think of Yogi Berra's great line, "This is like déjà vu all over again." Or, as a friend of mine says: "The most reliable predictor of future behavior is past behavior," which is another way of saying that the more things change, they more they stay the same.

In other words, my first point is that the methods and approaches to the interpretation of the Hebrew Psalter that have been most productive in recent years will continue. Broadly speaking, these approaches that have been helpful and will continue are:

- form-critical approaches to the interpretation of the psalms;
- canonical or "shape and shaping" approaches to the Psalter;
- poetic approaches, which build on recent research into the nature of Hebrew poetry; and
- theological approaches, which explore the implicit and explicit theological nature of the psalms.

All four of these approaches will continue, precisely because all four have been fruitful approaches for both scholarly research into understanding of the psalms and for the wide range of ecumenical communities that continue to worship the God whom the book of Psalms confesses as Lord. Because of limitations of space, I am only able comment on the first two, form-critical and canonical-critical approaches to the psalms.

Form Criticism

The twentieth century was dominated, most broadly speaking, by form-critical approaches to the psalms, as introduced by Hermann Gunkel and then worked in numerous ways by smaller schools of thought such as the cult-functional school (Mowinckel, Kaiser, Johnson, Kraus, and others), the canonical school (Wilson, deClaissé-Walford, Zenger, Hossfeld, Millard, and others), the theological school (Westermann, Brueggemann, Miller, and others), the juridical school (Schmidt and others), the clan-based school (Gerstenberger), poetic approaches to psalms (Berlin, Kugel, Alter, and others), and so on. As Patrick Miller wrote toward the end of the twentieth century, "Form-critical study of the psalms has dominated, if not controlled, the way in which this part of scripture has been handled during this century—a fact that is as evident in popular treatments of the psalms and in commentaries as it is in the scholarly literature."[1] As one looks into the future in a mirror dimly, there is no reason to imagine this will change. As Bill Brown writes, "Delineating [psalms according to common forms] has been a staple of psalms study for more than a century, *and it always will be.*"[2] The reason for the success of this approach is rather obvious. In order to understand any one instance of a phenomenon, a student compares and contrasts it with other examples of the same phenomenon in order to identify common patterns and distinctive features and to wonder what they mean. In the case of psalms, the student compares and contrasts a given psalm with other psalms and poems in the wider Old Testament, with non-canonical Israelite and early Jewish psalms, with other Semitic poems, and with poems from the broader ancient Near East.

To borrow the language of the enthronement psalms (a form-critical category), "form criticism is king"—or perhaps should I should say, "form criticism has become king; let the earth rejoice." And form criticism shall continue to reign, but it shall do so in a dynamic fashion. It is not as if there is nothing new to say. Form-critical approaches to the psalms are poised, I believe, to go much deeper, to bring us to richer and more meaningful understandings of the psalms. As the insights and conclusions of form criticism are questioned, as the data that it surfaces are interpreted and debated, I believe the result of this work will be cumulative and enriching, without necessarily producing consensus.

Here are two examples of what I mean. First, form-critical approaches have long lingered over and commented on the sudden shift of mood that occurs in the so-called individual lament psalms. Earlier, more positivistic approaches to this datum of research proposed specific historical, behind-the-text solutions to this datum—such as Begrich's proposal that readers assume the presence of an oracle of salvation, delivered by

---

1. Patrick D. Miller Jr., *Interpreting the Psalms* (Philadelphia: Fortress, 1986), 3.
2. William P. Brown, *The Psalms* (IBT; Nashville: Abingdon, 2010), 41.

a priest.[3] As Frederico Villanueva commented, there has been "a stubborn bent … to impose a one-way linear movement lament-praise on every psalm where the two elements are present."[4] But this narrow construal of sudden changes in the psalms is restrictive. So this approach has been questioned at a number of levels, including by those who pointed out the rather obvious datum that these and other psalms also evidence other sudden shifts in mood—not only from lament to trust, but also shifts from trust back to lament, shifts from addressing God to suddenly addressing the community or enemies, shifts from complaint to instruction, and so on. Again, to quote Brown, "Any attempt to explain the surprising shift in these must be done on case-by-case basis"—or, as Brown quite earthily put it, "shift happens."[5]

CANONICAL CRITICISM

A second approach that will continue into at least the near future is the approach that is often called canonical criticism, or shape-and-shaping research—as represented by the late scholars Gerald Wilson and Erich Zenger as well as others. Canonical criticism of the Psalter has shown convincingly that there is an intentional canonical shape to the Psalter. This shape had been recognized long before in precritical biblical scholarship, of course. But in his landmark dissertation, published in the SBL Dissertation Series in 1985 as *The Editing of the Hebrew Psalter*, Wilson presented what I take as an incontrovertible historical argument for recognizing this canonical shape.[6] Based on a close examination of the Hebrew text of the

---

3. "When an individual, who had entered into a sanctuary with a lament for Yahweh, had exhausted his laments and prayers, then a priest came out. Perhaps on the basis of an offertory answer, he would turn to the pray-er with an oracle of Yahweh and, referring to his laments and prayers, he would assure him of God's hearing and help" (Joachim Begrich, "Das priestliche Heilsorakel," *ZAW* 52 [1934]: 81–92). For an excellent discussion of pertinent issues (including the form of the salvation oracle, extra-biblical salvation oracles, oracles in Old Testament prose texts, and oracles in the psalms, see Patrick D. Miller Jr., *They Cried to the Lord: The Form and Theology of Prayer* (Minneapolis: Augsburg, 1994), 135–77. But see Brown, *Psalms*, 168 n. 25.

4. Frederico Villanueva, *The "Uncertainty of Hearing": A Study of the Sudden Change of Mood in the Psalms of Lament* (VTSup 121; Leiden: Brill, 2008), 28.

5. Miller, *Psalms*, 51, 48.

6. Gerald Wilson, *The Editing of the Hebrew Psalter* (SBLDS 76; Chico, Calif.: Scholars Press, 1985).

Psalter and on analysis of comparative ancient Near Eastern texts, Wilson fashioned a historical-critical foundational argument upon which further research could build. In Europe and especially in Germany, the main direction canonical research has taken has been historical, investigating the *shaping of the Psalter*,[7] while in North America the main direction that canonical research has taken has been literary, investigating the *canonical shape* of the final form of the Psalter.[8]

Wilson and others have noted the presence of certain genres of psalms at the "seams" of the books of the Psalter.[9] Wilson argues that the presence of the instructional Ps 1 as the introduction to the Psalter meant that the Psalter is "to be *read* rather than to be *performed*; to be *meditated over* rather than to be *recited from*."[10] Similarly, the presence of the royal Pss 2, 72, and 89 at the seams of the Psalter seem to pose a theological question about the promises to David and "to express the exilic hope for the restoration of the Davidic kingship and nation."[11] In addition, canonical interpreters have isolated psalm groups—usually construed chiastically and identified by the formal genres of the constituent psalms—such as Pss 3–14; 15–24; 25–34, and so on.[12]

---

7. This is apparent already in the titles of the European contributions to the recent compilation, Erich Zenger, ed., *Die Composition des Psalters* (BETL 238; Leuven: Peeters, 2010), which includes Jean-Marie Auwers, "Le Psautier come livre biblique: Edition, redaction, fonction," 67–90; Klaus Seybold, "Dimensionen und Intentionen der Davidisierung der Psalmen: Die Rolle Davids nach den Psalmenüberschriften und nach dem Septuagintapsalm 151," 125–140; Frank-Lothar Hossfeld, "Der elohistische Psalter Ps 42–83: Entstehung und Programm," 199–214.

8. See, for example, Gerald H. Wilson, "Understanding the Purposeful Arrangement of Psalms in the Psalter: Pitfalls and Promise," in *The Shape and Shaping of the Psalter* (ed. J. Clinton McCann Jr.; Sheffield: JSOT, 1993), 42–51; Nancy deClaissé-Walford, *Reading from the Beginning: The Shaping of the Hebrew Psalter* (Macon, Ga.: Mercer University Press, 1997).

9. Gerald Wilson, "The Use of Royal Psalms at the Seams of the Hebrew Psalter," *JSOT* 35 (1986): 85–94; Wilson "Evidence of Editorial Divisions in the Hebrew Psalter," *VT* 3 (1984): 337–52; Wilson, "The Qumran Psalms Manuscripts and Consecutive Arrangement of Psalms in the Hebrew Psalter," *CBQ* 45 (1983): 377–88; Wilson "Understanding the Purposeful Arrangement," 42–51.

10. Wilson, *Editing of the Hebrew Psalter*, 206–7, emphasis original.

11. Wilson, "Use of Royal Psalms," 91.

12. See, for example, those interpreters such as Hossfeld and Zenger, Auffret, Miller, and Brown who investigate Pss 15–24 as a group. As one example, see William P. Brown, "'Here Comes the Sun!': The Metaphorical Theology of Psalms 15–24," in

One can imagine that canonical research that follows both the European and the North American models will continue. And, as with form-critical approaches, it will continue in a way that will deepen our understanding of the data that canonical researches have unearthed. As stated above, I am convinced that the existence of a canonical shape of the Psalter has been incontrovertibly established. The data unearthed by researchers is impressive. I believe that canonical research is ready to take such data deeper and (perhaps for the first time) genuinely to evaluate the conclusions of shape-and-shaping research. In her introductory essay in chapter 1, Nancy deClaissé-Walford states that in canonical psalms research, "the meta-narrative [of the Psalter] seems agreed upon." As soon as a group of scholars seems to arrive at a point of consensus, that usually is precisely the time when the consensus either falls under assault or the next big breakthrough occurs. One thing that may happen soon is that the consensus results of the shape-and-shaping approach will be reevaluated.

Two examples come to mind. The first has to do with interpreting the final "shape and shaping" of the Psalter as a whole. The second has to do with interpreting the shape and shaping of a smaller subcollection within the Psalter.

First, let us examine an example of those approaches the interpreting the "shape and shaping" of the Psalter as a whole. Wilson dates the final form of the Psalter rather late—toward the end of the first century C.E. or later.[13] Yet, as I noted earlier, he argued that the editorial shape of the Psalter was a response to the problems of the exile. To me it seems that there is a rather obvious question that needs to be asked: "If the Psalter's final form is dated to about 100 C.E., why should one construe the final form of the Psalter as an "answer" to the theological crisis of the fall of Jerusalem and the failure of the Davidic monarchy more than 650 years earlier?" I am quite skeptical. Based only the great temporal gap, this seems a problematic argument to me. If that is truly the date of the Psalter's final formation, why not search in the first century for some catalytic event that may have caused the Psalter to be shaped into its final form? Most scholars do not follow Wil-

---

Composition des Psalters (ed. Erich Zenger; Leuven: Peeters, 2010) and see the bibliography offered there on p. 259. See also Frank-Lothar Hossfeld and Erich Zenger, *Die Psalmen I* (DNEB; Würzburg: Echter, 1993), 12–16 and 103ff.

13. Gerald Wilson, "A First Century C.E. Date for the Closing of the Hebrew Psalter?" in *Haim M. I. Gevarjahu Memorial Volume* (ed. J. J. Adler; Jerusalem: World Jewish Bible Center, 1990), 136–43. Also, personal conversation with Wilson.

son's late dating of the Psalter. But even for those who might date the final redaction to sometime in the fourth or third century B.C.E., the temporal distance between the failure of the monarchy in 587 and the final shaping of the Psalter remains a problem. North American scholarship often seems to frame the problem that the Psalter is wrestling with as a failure of the monarchy. Does this framing of the problem square with the best theories about when and where and under whom the final form of the Psalter was shaped?

Furthermore, I am skeptical of this seeming consensus based on evidence of how the Psalter was read in antiquity. It seems to me that it is time to integrate and test what we know about how the communities were actually reading the psalms with theories about what the final form "means." Are there any congruencies or incongruences between how the New Testament, Qumran, and other first-century Jewish communities were actually interpreting the psalms and the canonical theories about what the Psalter's final form means? Were any of these readers who were approaching the Psalter as a "book" and interpreting in the psalms with anything like what we call "plot" or "characterization"? What theological questions did they seem to be bringing to the Psalter? Are these the same questions that canonical criticism has posited that narrative interpreters of the psalms should bring?[14]

The European approach to this question has focused more on the "shaping" than on the final "shape" of the Psalter—although attention is given to both. As an example of the more dominant approach in Europe, we shall consider the research of Erich Zenger and Frank-Lothar Hossfeld. Zenger and Hossfeld offer a reconstruction of the process by which the Psalter reached its final form. Using very broad brush strokes, I will briefly recreate the picture that the paint of the Psalter's development. They discern that "at the beginning of the fifth century a Psalter beginning with Ps 2 concluded with Ps 100 and the whole composition can be called the 'YHWH is king Psalter.'"[15] Then, Pss 101–106, offering "the

---

14. For what it is worth, it seems clear that both in the New Testament and in the Dead Sea Scrolls, the psalms were being read primarily as legal texts, as prophetic texts applicable to messianic interpretation, and that they were being reappropriated liturgically as part of the worship life of various communities. I do not see any evidence, for example, that people were reading "psalms groups" such as Pss 15–24, or 25–34, and thinking about the meaning of such purported groups as "sections."

15. Frank-Lothar Hossfeld and Erich Zenger, *Psalms 3: A Commentary on Psalms 100–150* (Hermeneia; Minneapolis: Fortress, 2011), 1.

perspective of Moses" were added, sometime "in the middle of the fifth century."[16] Psalms 107–136 as a sequence were then developed so that there came into existence a Psalter consisting of:

> Pss 2–136, within which a clear Zion horizon is constituted by Pss 113–118 and 120–134, 135–136, one may call the Psalter of Pss 2–136 'the Psalter of Zion.' It was created around 400 B.C.E. by (Levitical) Temple singers through the addition of Pss 107–136 (sometimes using existing individual psalms or groups of psalms).[17]

A "Davidic Psalter (138–145)" was added later, with theme of "wisdom and Priestly language and concepts, here appearing in a synthesis of wisdom and universal space and restricted time. The suggested dating is at the end of the Persian period, therefore near the close of the four century B.C.E."[18] Finally, Ps 1 was added as prologue to the whole Psalter and other internal changes occurred, such as inserting Ps 137 and Ps 86, and appending the last five psalms. "We can imagine this redaction taking place between 200 and 150 B.C.E., in the context of the struggle against the Seleucids, but it could have been completed as early as the third century."[19]

Once again, I think a rather obvious question exists with regards to the reconstruction offered by Hossfeld and Zenger. "How can we know, with anything approaching confidence, that this reconstruction is accurate? Why should we not regard the process as far more messy than this? And why should we not regard any accurate historical reconstruction of the process as impossible?" The great psalms scroll found in Qumran cave 11 (11QPs^a) seems to suggest either that, as late as the first century C.E., there were rival Psalters with differing orders, or that the order of the final books of the Psalter had not yet been set.[20] The evidence at Qumran seems especially to suggest that the order of psalms in the latter books of the Psalter remained fluid for longer than the order in the earlier books. Thus, based on the evidence at Qumran, Peter Flint has concluded that "the scrolls strongly suggest that during the entire Qumran period Pss 1–89

---

16. Ibid., 2.

17. Ibid., 2–3.

18. Ibid., 6.

19. Ibid, 7.

20. See James A. Sanders, *The Psalms Scroll of Qumran Cave 11* (DJD 4; Oxford: Oxford University Press, 1965).

were virtually finalized as a collection, while Pss 90 and beyond remained much more fluid."[21] In this regard, I find Zenger's interpretation of the Qumran data, in which he concludes that "the Psalms scroll, *11QPsa*, is not a witness to a second "canonical" form of the Psalter alongside that of the MT/LXX" to be unconvincing.[22]

Second, an example of how some of the smaller collections in the Psalter are being interpreted. Similar to the data about the canonical shape of the Psalter as a whole, I believe that the data about smaller collections within the collection is impressive. It is clear that the Psalter as we have it did not come into shape all at once. The Psalter grew in stages over a long period of time. Smaller collections existed independently, I believe—collections such as the "Psalms of David," the "Psalms of the Korahites," the "Psalms of Asaph," and the "Psalms of Ascents." I also believe that it has been clearly established that, within the Psalms of David, smaller collections of psalms are clearly evident. Book 1 of the psalms comprises Pss 1–41. It seems clearly established that Pss 1–2 are a two-part introduction to the Psalter. I am impressed with the data that suggests that Pss 3–14, 15–24, 25–34, and 35–41 are subcollections within book 1. But I am less impressed with what scholars have done in terms of interpreting those smaller collections.

In Europe, one impulse is to investigate the growth of these smaller collections.[23] For example, Hossfeld and Zenger postulate that in early postexilic times, a previously existing collection of prayers for help, lament psalms, and psalms of thanksgiving that included Pss 17–18 and 20–22 was expanded by the addition of psalms, including 15 and 24. As part of this redaction, the four subcollections 3–14, 15–24, 25–34, and 35–41 were created. In terms of this level of redaction, the second group now included Pss 15, 17–18, 20–22, and 24. A later postexilic redaction representing a "poor person's piety" (*Armenfrömmigkeit*; referring here no longer to just a social category now but primarily a religious category) integrated Pss 16, 19, and 23 into this collection. Finally, in a further Hellenistic redaction, the concept of the poor was further developed, affecting the collection at smaller point.

---

21. Peter Flint, *The Dead Sea Psalms Scrolls and the Book of Psalms* (Leiden: Brill, 1997), 148. For a discussion of the evidence and approaches to interpreting the data, see pp. 135–49.

22. See Hossfeld and Zenger, *Psalms 3*, 607.

23. See Hossfeld and Zenger, *Psalmen I*, 12–16.

In North America, one impulse is to investigate this sort of sub-collection from a literary perspective. Thus Patrick Miller and William Brown have explored the theological meaning of this collection, guided more by literary hermeneutical assumptions than historical assumptions. The key to this analysis is to recognize that the psalms are arranged chiastically, according to form-critical genres. This chart is adapted from Brown's analysis:

Psalm 19 (Torah Psalm)

Psalm 18   Psalms 20-21 (Royal Psalms)

Psalm 17   Psalm 22 (Laments/Prayers for Help)

Psalm 16   Psalm 23 (Trust Psalms)

Psalm 15   Psalm 24 (Entrance Liturgies)

Miller reads this collection of psalms "together as an act of theological imagination stimulated by their arrangement" while Brown attends "primarily to the poetic imagery, particularly metaphor."[24] We shall use Brown as the example. He writes, "The concentric arrangement give rise, not fortuitously, to a literary configuration shaped by ascent and descent.... Together, Pss 15–24 form a theological 'tell,' whose horizontal and vertical cross sections reveal an abundance of layered connections."[25] Brown reads the collection from the ends inward, climbing up from the "footills" of Pss 15 and 24 to the "summit" of Psalm 19:

"At the Foothills: Pss 15 and 24"
"From Trust to Torah: Pss 16 and 23"
"From Petition to Praise: Pss 17 and 22"
"The Ascent to Victory: Pss 18 and 20–21"
"The Cosmic Torah: Ps 19"[26]

Yet again, I think some obvious questions need to be asked.

---

24. Patrick Miller Jr., "Kingship, Torah Obedience, and Prayer: The Theology of Psalms 15-24," in *Neue Wege der Psalmenforschung* (ed. Klaus Seybold and Erich Zenger; Freiburg: Herder, 1993), 127–42; Brown, "'Here Comes the Sun!'" 259. See also a versions and sections of Brown's analysis in *Seeing the Psalms*, 55–79, and *Psalms*, 85–107.

25. Brown, *Psalms*, 98.

26. Ibid., 98–105.

- On what hermeneutical grounds shall the community of critical scholars read and interpret the subcollections in the Psalter?
- Shall we try to reconstruct the historical development of these collections?
- Shall we, as does Brown, read them chiastically from the outside edges in?
- Shall we read them in canonical order and impute to them narrative logic (with such categories as "plot" and "character"), as is more the approach in North America? Identification of subcollections within the Psalter rely mostly on analysis of the superscriptions of the psalms and on genre classification of the psalms using modern form-critical categories (see the concentric analysis of Pss 15–24 above). There are potentially problems of anachronism here.
- Did the ancients who arranged these collections according to genre classification understand the genres and the relationship between the genres in the same way we do? If not, how should we "read" these collections?
- Were the ancients reading these collections narratively? If not, should we?

I can imagine that in the near future psalms scholars will be ready to go deeper on such hermeneutical and methodological questions. Such hermeneutical and methodological conversations will in turn serve to help scholars drive more deeply into questions as to the Psalter's formation and as to what meanings we will attribute to its final shape.

So much for my first point, that in the near future of psalms research, I expect that recent fruitful approaches shall continue, but they shall also continue to evolve, to go deeper, to test recent developments. In addition, please remember that I have also asserted that *poetic approaches* and *theological approaches* shall continue and shall similarly yield increasingly fruitful results. But because of limitations of space, I am not able to address those here.

"If You Can't Imitate Him, Don't Copy Him."—Yogi Berra

To introduce point two, another quotation from the great Yogi Berra— "If you can't imitate him, don't copy him." That is to say, when I imagine the near of future psalms studies, I imagine that scholars will look over the fence from their own backyards and imitate the methods that they see scholars in other fields employing. In our era, methods of study are like soups du jour at restaurants—people employ a method for a while, but then the seek out new methods, because they ask new questions and approach topics from fresh angles. All of which is to say that psalms scholars will likely approach the vast array of interpretive methods in the same fashion that my brother-in-law Gahlord Dewald once advised people to approach the bewildering array of varieties of beer: "There are lots of them, try one."

When I imagine what the near future in psalms studies will look like, other than more of the same, two things seem obvious to me. First, methods that have proven fruitful for the interpretation of other parts of the scriptures will be applied to the psalms. And second, research will increasingly be more interdisciplinary. A comment about each of these in turn.

Borrowing Methods from Other Biblical Scholars

First, I imagine that methods that have proven fruitful for the interpretation of other parts of scripture will be applied to the psalms. In most cases, this research has already started. A short list of these methods would include the following:

- postcolonial and post-imperial approaches;
- approaches that take seriously gender- and ethnic-construction of identity;
- postmodern approaches, in all their disarray;
- iconographic approaches; and
- above all, reception history

To take the last of these as an example, one can already note how scholars interested in reception history are turning to the psalms. Some examples include Sam Janse's recent study on the reception history of Ps 2 in early Judaism and the early church, the collection of essays edited by Dirk Human and Gert Jacobus Steyn on the reception history of Psalms and Hebrews, John Choi's study that included sections illuminating how the psalms themselves received earlier legal and narrative traditions, and, perhaps most comprehensively, Susan Gillingham's monumental *Psalms through the Centuries*, which every psalms scholar should study and commit to memory.[27] It should be noted how quickly and broadly reception-history approaches open up the psalms to other areas of study—art, music, dogma, worship, and so on. This approach will doubtless flower, flourish, and scatter to the far corners.

Borrowing Methods from Other Disciplines

Second, I suspect that psalms research will become increasingly more interdisciplinary. The life of the mind—both more broadly conceived in light of the democratization and digitalization of knowledge, and more narrowly conceived as the scientific study of knowledge and ideas in academic settings—is going interdisciplinary. We now live in an interdisciplinary, increasingly postspecialized world. Interdisciplinarity—if such a word even exists—is the future. And it will impact psalms studies.

It already has, of course. Since Gunkel, each of the monumental moments in psalms studies has essentially been a breakthrough born of interdisciplinary discovery. Gunkel's and Mowinckel's insights were generated in basically interdisciplinary fashion. Erhard Gerstenberger employed the study of clan behaviors and ritual. Brueggemann's approach to the Psalter included object-relations theory and grief studies. And indeed, as Brueggemann has been kind enough to point out to me, the entire "historical" approach to interpreting the psalms was an interdisciplinary movement.[28] So-called "historical-critical approaches" to the psalms borrowed in an interdisciplinary fashion from the canons, methods, and categories of history.[29]

As an example of one field in which the sod has yet to be extensively broken, I would suggest the topic of embodiment. In many fields, from traditional academic fields such as sociology, psychology, and anthro-

---

27. Sam Janse, *"You Are My Son": The Reception History of Psalm 2 in Early Judaism and the Early Church* (Leuven: Peeters, 2009); Dirk Human and Gert Jacous Steyn, eds., *Psalms and Hebrews: Studies in Reception* (New York: T&T Clark, 2010); John Choi, *Traditions at Odds: The Reception of the Pentateuch in Biblical and Second Temple Period Literature* (New York: T&T Clark, 2010); Susan Gillingham, *Psalms through the Centuries*, vol. 1 (BBC; Oxford: Blackwell, 2008).

28. Personal communication.

29. This borrowing was, to be sure and as Brueggemann above all others would note, not a borrowing without cost. When biblical studies began to borrow the methods and canons of historical studies, certain hermeneutical and methodological contamination occurred.

pology, to more vocational fields such as medicine, to theological fields such as systematic theology, the insights from the field of embodiment are making a great impact. In the university, we tend to conceptualize what we are doing as the "life of the mind"—with one unfortunate result being that we ignore, minimize, or marginalize our bodies—which are, after all, the only place where ideas occur. As Bryan Turner notes, "We speak about having bodies or about how people carry their bodies, or about being bodies, but following the phenomenological tradition it would be equally sensible to speak about the ways in which we *do* our bodies, since we are embodied. We can speak about doing our bodies, but at a deeper level it also makes sense to talk about *being* a body." [30] In other words, we have abstracted the ideas that we have from the bodies in which we have them.

Without offering an introductory survey of the field of embodiment, I would like to suggest that the Psalms are perhaps the most natural part of the Old Testament for the application of embodiment studies. Although we have often abstracted our "selves" and our "minds" and our "ideas" from our bodies, it seems to me rather obvious that the psalms themselves refuse to do so. The psalms are replete with self-references or other-references that are explicitly bodily—starting with the bodily reference נפשׁ that is so unfortunately translated "my soul," and continuing with "my bones," "my flesh," "your hand," "your eyes," "your ears," "my body," "my tongue," "my heart," "my feet," "my head"—as well as countless more abstract references to the body, such as "my strength," "my life," "my days," or "my spirit." I would submit, in fact, that there is no corpus of scripture in which there is a more concentrated locus of terms and imagery drawn from the matrix of bodily referentiality than the Psalms. The Psalms may be the part of scripture with the most concentrated set of references to the human body. And for that reason alone, the Psalter seems an apt corpus for the insights of embodiment studies to be applied.

In addition to studies in embodiment, other fields that scholars of the Psalms might integrate into their research might include:

- studies in orality;
- studies in literacy;

---

30. Bryan Turner, "The Body in Western Society: Social Theory and Its Perspectives," in *Religion and the Body* (ed. Sarah Coakley; New York: Cambridge University Press, 1997), 15–41.

- insights from ritual theory; and
- studies in identity formation

As already noted, these musing are offered not as predictions. Rather, in the spirit of Gerald Wilson and of the way in which his fecund imagination helped open up new questions and create new spaces for conversations, I offer my thoughts here as an invitation to generative conversation about what questions psalms scholars should be asking in the future and what new spaces we should be clearing for conversation, so that a generation of scholars yet unborn can open the Psalter and join the conversation.

BIBLIOGRAPHY

Auwers, Jean-Marie. "Le Psautier come livre biblique: Edition, redaction, fonction." Pages 67–90 in *Die Composition des Psalters*. Edited by Erich Zenger. BETL 238. Leuven: Peeters, 2010.
Begrich, Joachim. "Das priestliche Heilsorakel." *ZAW* 52 (1934): 81–92.
Brown, William P. "'Here Comes the Sun!': The Metaphorical Theology of Psalms 15–24." Pages 259–77 in *Composition des Psalters*. Edited by Erich Zenger. Leuven: Peeters, 2010.
———. *The Psalms*. IBT. Nashville: Abingdon, 2010.
Choi, John. *Traditions at Odds: The Reception of the Pentateuch in Biblical and Second Temple Period Literature*. New York: T&T Clark, 2010.
deClaissé-Walford, Nancy L. *Reading from the Beginning: The Shaping of the Hebrew Psalter*. Macon, Ga.: Mercer University Press, 1997.
Flint, Peter. *The Dead Sea Psalms Scrolls and the Book of Psalms*. Leiden: Brill, 1997.
Gillingham, Susan. *Psalms through the Centuries*, vol. 1. BBC. Oxford: Blackwell, 2008.
Hossfeld, Frank-Lothar. "Der elohistische Psalter Ps 42–83: Entstehung und Programm." Pages 199–214 in *Die Composition des Psalters*. Edited by Erich Zenger. BETL 238. Leuven: Peeters, 2010.
Hossfeld Frank-Lothar, and Erich Zenger. *Die Psalmen I*. DNEB. Würzburg: Echter, 1993.
———. *Psalms 3: A Commentary on Psalms 100–150*. Hermeneia. Minneapolis: Fortress, 2011.
Human, Dirk, and Gert Jacous Steyn, eds. *Psalms and Hebrews: Studies in Reception*. New York: T&T Clark, 2010.

Janse, Sam. *"You Are My Son": The Reception History of Psalm 2 in Early Judaism and the Early Church.* Leuven: Peeters, 2009.

McCann, J. Clinton Jr., ed. *The Shape and Shaping of the Psalter.* Sheffield: JSOT, 1993.

Miller, Patrick D. Jr. *Interpreting the Psalms.* Philadelphia: Fortress, 1986.

———. "Kingship, Torah Obedience, and Prayer: The Theology of Psalms 15–24." Pages 127–42 in *Neue Wege der Psalmenforschung.* Edited by Klaus Seybold and Erich Zenger. Freiburg: Herder, 1993.

———. *They Cried to the Lord: The Form and Theology of Prayer.* Minneapolis: Augsburg, 1994.

Sanders, James A. *The Psalms Scroll of Qumran Cave 11.* DJD 4. Oxford: Oxford University Press, 1965.

Seybold, Klaus. "Dimensionen und Intentionen der Davidisierung der Psalmen: Die Rolle Davids nach den Psalmenüberschriften und nach dem Septuagintapsalm 151." Pages 125–40 in *Die Composition des Psalters.* Edited by Erich Zenger. BETL 238. Leuven: Peeters, 2010.

Turner, Bryan. "The Body in Western Society: Social Theory and Its Perspectives." Pages 15–41 in *Religion and the Body.* Edited by Sarah Coakley. New York: Cambridge University Press, 1997.

Villanueva, Frederico. *The "Uncertainty of Hearing": A Study of the Sudden Change of Mood in the Psalms of Lament.* VTSup 121. Leiden: Brill, 2008.

Wilson, Gerald. *The Editing of the Hebrew Psalter.* SBLDS 76. Chico, Calif.: Scholars Press, 1985.

———. "Evidence of Editorial Divisions in the Hebrew Psalter." *VT* 3 (1984): 337–52.

———. "A First Century C.E. Date for the Closing of the Hebrew Psalter?" Pages 136–43 in *Haim M. I. Gevarjahu Memorial Volume.* Edited by J. J. Adler. Jerusalem: World Jewish Bible Center, 1990.

———. "The Qumran Psalms Manuscripts and Consecutive Arrangement of Psalms in the Hebrew Psalter." *CBQ* 45 (1983): 377–88.

———. "Understanding the Purposeful Arrangement of Psalms in the Psalter: Pitfalls and Promise." Pages 42–51 in *The Shape and Shaping of the Psalter.* Edited by J. Clinton McCann Jr. Sheffield: JSOT, 1993.

———. "The Use of Royal Psalms at the Seams of the Hebrew Psalter." *JSOT* 35 (1986): 85–94.

Zenger, Erich, ed. *Die Composition des Psalters.* Leuven: Peeters, 2010.

CONTRIBUTORS

Phil J. Botha
Professor
Department of Ancient Languages
University of Pretoria
Pretoria, South Africa

Nancy L. deClaissé-Walford
Carolyn Ward Professor of Old Testament and Biblical Languages
McAfee School of Theology
Atlanta, Georgia

Peter W. Flint
Professor of Religious Studies
Trininy Western University
Langley, British Columbia, Canada

Jaco Gericke
Associate Researcher Professor
North-West University (Vaal Triangle Campus)
Vanderbijlpark, South Africa

Erhard S. Gerstenberger
Professor Emeritus of Old Testament
Philipps-Universität
Marburg, Germany

Karl N. Jacobson
Teaching Pastor
Lutheran Church of the Good Shepherd
Minneapolis, Minnesota

Rolf A. Jacobson
Associate Professor of Old Testament
Luther Seminary
St. Paul, Minnesota

Christine Brown Jones
Associate Professor of Religion
Carson-Newman University
Jefferson City, Tennessee

Jonathan Magonet
Emeritus Professor of Bible
Leo Baeck College
London, United Kingdom

J. Clinton McCann Jr.
Evangelical Professor of Biblical Interpretation
Eden Theological Seminary
Webster Groves, Missouri

Harry P. Nasuti
Professor of Theology
Fordham University
Bronx, New York

Sampson S. Ndoga
Research Fellow
University of Pretoria
Pretoria, South Africa

Catherine Petrany
Assistant Professor of Theology
St. Vincent College
Latrobe, Pennsylvania

W. Dennis Tucker Jr.
Associate Professor of Christian Scriptures
George W. Truett Theological Seminary
Waco, Texas

Robert E. Wallace
Associate Professor of Biblical Studies
Judson University
Elgin, Illinois

Derek E. Wittman
Covenant Presbyterian Church
Marshall, Missouri

Index of Ancient Sources

INDEX OF MODERN AUTHORS

CPSIA information can be obtained
at www.ICGtesting.com
Printed in the USA
FFOW02n1548060215
10875FF